F.V.

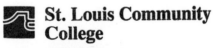

From the beginnings of our republic the concept of a citizen soldiery, organized through militias, has undergirded American military philosophy. This
nation fought the Revolution, the War of 1812, and the Mexican War, and began the Civil War, relying on volunteer militias and only a skeletal professional military force. The Civil War demonstrated the need to adapt state militias
to the requirements of modern war, yet the United States retained its original
philosophy in what became the National Guard.

The Rise of the National Guard describes in thorough detail the evolution
of the state militia system to a more federally controlled National Guard during the crucial years of development. The subject is important because the
"citizen soldier" and "militia–national guard" tradition is one of the two pil-
lars on which American military policy is built; a professional, regular military force is the other. Jerry Cooper's detailed research, unique examination
of the experience of individual states, and careful analysis will make this the
standard treatment of the subject.

Jerry Cooper is a professor of history at the University of Missouri–St.
Louis. He is the author of *The Army and Civil Disorder: Federal Military In-
tervention in Labor Disputes, 1877–1900* and *The Militia and the National
Guard in America since Colonial Times: A Research Guide*.

The Rise of the National Guard

The Evolution of the
American Militia,
1865–1920

Jerry Cooper

University of Nebraska Press
Lincoln and London

♾ The paper in this book
meets the minimum requirements of
American National Standard for
Information Sciences—Permanence
of Paper for Printed
Library Materials, ANSI Z39.48-1984.

Library of Congress
Cataloging-in-Publication Data

Cooper, Jerry M.
The rise of the National Guard:
the evolution of the American
militia, 1865–1920 / Jerry Cooper.
p.   cm.—(Studies in war, society,
and the military v. 1)
Includes bibliographical references
(p. 229) and index.
ISBN 0-8032-1486-3 (alk. paper)
1. United States—National Guard—
History.   2. United States—Militia—
Finance—History.   I. Title.   II. Series.
UA42.C73   1997
355.3′7′0973—dc21
97-7630   CIP

For Christine

Contents

Tables

Acknowledgments

It has taken me far longer to research and write this book than I ever imagined, let alone intended. Many good people have assisted and encouraged me over the past two decades, and I fear that without their support and advice the effort surely would have come to naught. Thanks to them I no longer need to avoid eye contact when colleagues ask the eternal academic question, "What are you working on, Jerry?"

Jack Lane and Richard Kohn read and criticized my initial efforts to write this complicated story. Their early advice set me in the right direction. Edward M. Coffman, Peter Maslowski, Allan Millett, and Timothy Nenninger read the final manuscript version. They not only provided suggestions for improving the manuscript, but each has materially assisted me over the years either by providing research leads and work done by their graduate students or, in the case of Tim Nenninger, by helping me to use the National Archives wisely. Eleanor Hannah, University of Chicago, shared information on the Illinois National Guard by allowing me to read draft chapters of her doctoral dissertation. Major General Bruce Jacobs, National Guard of the United States (Ret.), offered encouragement and advice on how to use the library at the National Guard Association of the United States headquarters in Washington DC. My colleague Gerda Ray at the University of Missouri, St. Louis, provided a sounding board for ideas and also shared research items and her knowledge on how state police came to replace the National Guard as a keeper of the civil peace. For all of those mentioned above, and to those whom I inadvertently neglect, many, many thanks. Your support has proven to me once again that scholarship at its best is always a collegial effort. Errors of fact or unsupported generalizations found herein are my responsibility alone.

Institutional support has been vital to my work as well. The University of Missouri, St. Louis, provided several grants over the years that allowed research to continue, and a grant from the University of Missouri Research Board relieved me from my academic responsibilities for a year so that I could write. An Advanced Research Grant, and later a visiting professorship, allowed me to work at the finest library and manuscript collection devoted to American military affairs, the U.S. Army Military History Institute. A grant from the Penrose Fund of the American Philosophical Society came early in the project. I particularly want to thank the staff of the Interlibrary Loan office, Thomas Jefferson Library, University of Missouri, St. Louis, for tracking down obscure sources dealing with the National Guard. They never quit trying. At the Military History Institute, Dr. Richard Somers and David Keough in the archives and John Slonaker and Dennis Vetock in the reference branch were just as accommodating.

In ways that cannot be enumerated, Ellie Cooper gave support that kept me working on a project that sometimes seemed to be going nowhere. DDJ listened, advised, researched, and read every version of the manuscript. Surely that was service above and beyond the call of duty.

Introduction

From the end of the Civil War through American intervention in World War I, the National Guard evolved from a self-supporting, independent, localized volunteer militia to a centralized state/national military force largely funded by the federal government. In its formative years, the late 1860s through 1898, the Guard first developed through the initiative of local supporters but then came under greater state control. The decision of state governments to provide the Guard with permanent financial support marked a major break from past militia practice. Long-term funding also led states to create small military bureaucracies to regulate and supervise local units that accepted state support. Money and regulation in turn created militia units that demonstrated a stability and military effectiveness rarely seen in the years before the Civil War. The states, of course, appropriated funds with the expectation that the state soldiery would serve certain public ends. In this period the Guard's main service was to quell civil disorder, notably, but not exclusively, upheavals connected to labor-employer disputes.

Although state financial support and the Guard's publicly identified civil disorder function marked it off from antebellum militia practices, the National Guard nonetheless represented an evolutionary development rather than a new state institution created to meet the circumstances of late-nineteenth-century America. The post–Civil War Guard retained the antebellum volunteer, uniformed militia's predilection for local control, especially the election of its officers and its enthusiasm for nonmilitary activities. Deeply enmeshed in local communities, National Guard units long resisted outside efforts to regulate them, as had their forebears.

Guardsmen's desire for local control conflicted with their quest for increased national financial aid. The National Guard Association (NGA), founded in 1879, articulated Guardsmen's desire for more money, arguing that because the National Guard represented the traditional American volunteer in organized form, it deserved greater federal aid to increase its military efficiency in case of war. The plea fell on deaf ears. Congress saw no need to alter military policy or open the national treasury to part-time citizen soldiers in an era of profound security.

Another reason the National Guard's appeal for increased financial support failed was their resistance to legislative demands that they accept more stringent supervision in return for money. Guardsmen believed that they had contributed more to the revival of the volunteer militia through their own hard work and personal expense than had either state or federal governments. Many resented efforts to impose state control over their burgeoning units. State soldiers took even greater offense to suggestions that War Department bureaucrats establish partial federal regulation over their organizations in return for federal money.

Congressional indifference and the Guard's reluctance to accept outside supervision left the service underfunded and unconnected to national military policy. War in 1898 offered the National Guard the opportunity to fulfill the role of reserve force that it maintained was its historical right; however, the state soldiers failed to provide the nation with an adequately trained and equipped volunteer reserve. The chaos of the 1898 mobilization and the changing demands of modern war spurred efforts to adopt a public policy that would govern how state volunteers became national soldiers. From 1899 through 1916, Guardsmen, the War Department, and Congress struggled to develop a policy that was mutually acceptable to Guardsmen and the Army General Staff. All parties agreed to an increase in federal financial support to the states, beginning in 1900, but sharply disagreed over the extent of regulation the War Department might impose on the state soldiery. Guardsmen particularly resisted substantive regulation because they saw their companies and regiments as peculiarly their own, the products of their time, money, and hard work.

Inevitably, the lure of federal dollars and an assured place in military policy eroded Guardsmen's efforts to remain semi-independent of the War Department. State soldiers largely embraced the National Defense Act of 1916, which greatly increased federal aid to the states but also granted the War Department extensive regulatory authority over the National Guard. Mobilization for duty along the Mexican border in 1916 and for World War I a year later demonstrated that the War Department controlled the Guard completely when it reported for federal duty. Today, the federal government provides 95 percent of the National Guard's funding and exerts such control over state military forces that some scholars contend, with only slight exaggeration, that the Army and Air National Guards are federal forces on loan to the states.

The years 1865 through 1920 form a distinct period in the history of the state soldiery. Scholarly treatments of the militia and National Guard rarely discuss how the state soldiery was, or was not, funded. This study contends that the lack of adequate funding is a central issue in understanding the history of the state soldiery. Money, or the lack of it, and not states' rights, determined the National Guard's military value as a reserve force and its willingness to accept federal regulation.

From its revival in the early 1870s through 1916, the state soldiery existed as a volunteer military force largely controlled by National Guardsmen. The essential nature of the Guard in this era can only be grasped by an examination of its operations in the armory, at summer camp, and in the offices of the state adjutants general. National Guard units often functioned as athletic, social, or fraternal clubs as well as military organizations. Thus, Guardsmen and their friends ensured the financial and organizational survival of their units far more than did the money states spent on their military; they also resisted outside control vigorously.

The National Guard of this era represented a diverse force that varied greatly from region to region; there was no truly "national" Guard. Significant regional differences that existed when the modern Guard began to evolve in the 1870s persisted to the turn of the century. Federal funding after 1900 did not eliminate these differences; the level of state support continued to determine the overall quality of each force until 1920. Greatly expanded federal aid and regulation largely eliminated most disparities in the interwar years.

Guardsmen persistently clung to the idea that the National Guard represented the institutional embodiment of the volunteer soldier until they endorsed the bill that became the National Defense Act of 1916. Volunteer soldiers recruited and organized by the states had provided the nation's war armies from the Revolution through the Spanish-American War. Ardent Guardsmen believed that the reinvigorated state soldiery appearing after the Civil War offered volunteers who were already trained, equipped, and organized for war. As long as the nation continued to rely on volunteers to fight its wars, Guardsmen could justifiably maintain that tradition supported their claim to the reserve role. The adoption of conscription following American intervention in World War I destroyed the volunteer practice and fundamentally altered the character of the National Guard.

Abbreviations

AGR   Adjutant General Report. Refers to annual or biennial reports of state adjutants general. The appropriate year or years and state are included in the citation, as in, for example, AGR Massachusetts, 1876.

ARU   American Railway Union

AWC   Army War College

DMA   Division of Militia Affairs. Annual reports from the division are cited as, for example, DMA 1912.

JMSI   *Journal of the Military Service Institution of the United States*

MBR   *Militia Bureau Report*, with appropriate year cited.

MID   Military Information Division, with appropriate year cited. Refers to the division's annual report, *The Organized Militia of the United States*, published 1893 through 1898.

NARA   National Archives and Records Administration

NDA   National Defense Act

NGA   National Guard Association

NRA   National Rifle Association

RG 94   Record Group 94, entry 25, Adjutant General's Office Document File, 1890–1917, NARA, Washington DC.

RG 165   Record Group 165, Records of the War Department General and Special Staffs, in NARA.

RG 168   Record Group 168, Records of the National Guard Bureau, 1822–1954, in NARA.

SWR   *Secretary of War Report*, with appropriate year cited. Refers to the
          annual report of the Secretary of War, which included reports of
          the Army chief of staff and various War Department bureau
          chiefs.

UMW   United Mine Workers

WCD   War College Division, an agency of the Army General Staff.

The Rise of the National Guard

I

The Militia in American Military Practice and Policy, 1607–1865

THE MILITIA, 1607–1815

Patterns of thought and behavior that long shaped American military practice and policy took root in the seventeenth century. When Englishmen settled permanently in North America, they relied on the militia for defense. The English militia, with a heritage extending back to the Middle Ages, required all militiamen to arm and train themselves and to be available to serve the king upon call. On the eve of the establishment of permanent English settlements on the Atlantic seaboard, the English militia had abandoned universal service for a more select system of trainbands composed of property owners. Colonists, however, revived the universal militia to meet the challenges of settlement, for they were responsible for their own self-defense. In America, as in England, the militia proved a remarkably adaptable institution.[1]

Colonists rejected Elizabethan practice, which centered on a select militia controlled by the Crown, and reinstituted the obligation that all qualified able-bodied men serve under local authority. The militia became ubiquitous throughout British North America, with all colonies except Quaker-dominated Pennsylvania embracing the institution. In theory, the militia imposed a universal obligation, but in practice it often excluded African Americans, Native Americans, and indentured servants. Colonies exempted some individuals whose occupational specialties and civic or religious responsibilities were vital to colonial life. Militia laws required obligated males to arm and equip themselves, enroll in local units, and report for periodic training. Militiamen were expected to serve only in defense of their settlements and towns for a limited time.

Ubiquity masked the diversity of the militia from region to region and also hid changes adopted by the colonies as they matured. This diversity belies easy generalizations, but certain common patterns prevailed. Initially, the militia was organized as an inclusive system for the immediate defense of new settlements. Once colonies established local security, they developed more differentiated organizations for colonywide protection. Some created small permanent forces to patrol and defend the frontier. When conflicts with Native Americans or the demands of imperial warfare required offensive operations, colonies raised temporary expeditionary units, enticing volunteers to serve for pay and bounties, rather than mobilize the obligated militia. In pressing circumstances, a selective militia draft proved necessary. Generally, however, colonial officials preferred to use volunteers in extended campaigns and, from the late seventeenth century on, increasingly recruited men who were excluded from compulsory military by race, condition of servitude, or poverty.

Colonies nonetheless retained the compulsory militia.[2] Although New England settlements enforced enrollment and training practices more effectively than did their Southern counterparts, no colony abandoned the system altogether. Musters and training days provided rudimentary instruction as well as a means for taking a census of the military-age population and selecting officers. Musters served social and political functions as well. Along with religious institutions, the militia affected a broader segment of the population than did other aspects of colonial life. More significantly, colonies maintained their militia organizations to serve as mobilization systems: to recruit frontier garrisons and ranger forces, to organize and sustain temporary field forces to fight Native Americans, and to raise provincial units that served Great Britain in the imperial wars.

The colonial response to war was inefficient and inevitably reactive. Limited financial resources, the absence of substantive military administrative agencies, and the lack of an imperial military policy for North America left the colonies with no option but to respond to each emergency as it arose. The onset of conflict led to hurried efforts to select officers; call for volunteers from the obligated militia or recruit nonobligated men; and initiate the cumbersome process of collecting arms, equipment, and foodstuffs to supply temporary armies. This pattern for responding to war prevailed virtually everywhere, but the kinds of forces fielded by individual colonies varied markedly. During the Yamasee War (1715–16), for example, fully half the forces South Carolina raised were conscripted African American slaves. Massachusetts, on the other hand, recruited white volunteers from depressed farming regions to make up the force that captured Fort Louisbourg during King George's War (1744–48).[3]

In the process of defending themselves, colonial Americans gained experience organizing, financing, and directing military forces that helped them expand their original settlements. Because the Crown rarely interfered in militia matters, local officials and colonial legislators became accustomed to shaping military practice according to their own interests. Local militiamen gained and retained the privilege of electing their own officers despite the efforts of colonial legislators and royal governors to end the practice. Colonial officials also discovered that they had to defer to the demands of the marginal men they had enlisted to serve in expeditionary forces. Enlistment bounties, decent pay, and land grants proved essential to winning the service of men from the periphery of colonial life.

By the middle of the eighteenth century, the militia had proved its worth. However, the very conditions that led to its adoption contributed to the militia's most egregious weaknesses. For example, it assured local defense from within each community, but the citizen soldiery proved less effective when military threats were distant and required colonywide or regional cooperation. All too often, myopic localism thwarted coordinated efforts. Despite their lengthy military experience between 1607 and the 1750s, the British settlements failed to institutionalize military practice. Since militia training became largely ceremonial in function and the colonies readily demobilized their expeditionary forces as soon as conflict abated, no institutional means existed to standardize procedure or preserve the experience of the latest war. Each new crisis brought an improvised response that was based only on past general practice and the immediate memory of the experienced men available.

During the French and Indian War (1756–63), the British encountered fully the fragmented and inefficient American military practice. As the first conflict in which the Crown assumed the major burden of prosecuting a colonial war, the French and Indian War brought colonial soldiers and their legislatures into constant contact with the British army for the first time. It tested the colonial militia system's capacity to provide effective, well-led troops for a prolonged war effort centrally controlled by a professional military force. A century and a half of colonial practice thwarted cooperation between the colonies and the Crown. The colonial view of military affairs demonstrated a suspicion of central authority, a preference for local control of military forces, a strong predilection for voluntary over compulsory service, and an open distaste for military professionalism.

The retention of ten thousand British troops in North America following the defeat of the French in 1763 and Parliament's decision to regulate and tax the colonies, of course, precipitated the political conflict leading to the American Revolution. In identifying the British army as the symbol of imperial oppression, colonial agitators appropriated the anti-standing-army rhetoric of seventeenth-century English Radical Whig thinkers. American opponents of Crown policy found radical ideas appealing because they emphasized that only citizen soldiers, that is, the militia, were fit to defend a republic. Whig ideology maintained that an aroused citizenry organized in an effective militia could save republicanism by restoring constitutional balance, protecting property rights, and preserving civil liberty. Virtuous citizen soldiers would rise in righteous anger to remove the king's armed mercenaries and reassert republican rule.

Radical Whig ideas on the evils of a standing army and the virtues of a citizen militia well suited both the colonial military experience and the ongoing political contest between the colonies and Great Britain. As Americans viewed their military history, they saw an armed people creating their own destiny while combating a harsh geography and savage native peoples. Left alone to defend themselves until 1756, according to this version, doughty colonial soldiers then experienced the command of haughty, contemptuous British officers and the dissolute behavior of the redcoat rank and file during the French and Indian War. After the French withdrew from North America, ruthless British troops remained behind to wrest political and economic freedom from honest, republican-minded Englishmen.[4]

During the first year of the Revolution the American militia matched its Whig idealization. Throughout 1775, patriot militia restored constitutional balance by ousting royal governors, arresting Crown tax officers, and seizing control of local and colonial governments. Other citizen soldiers cowed fellow Americans who questioned rebellion or remained loyal to the Crown. On the battlefield, New England militiamen nearly took the measure of General Sir William Howe's professionals near Boston, seized Fort Ticonderoga on Lake Champlain, and lay siege to Quebec City and Montreal. The vaunted prowess of an aroused citizenry in arms, which had been extolled in English

Radical Whig literature, became a reality in 1775 and made the rebellion possible.

Unfortunately, what Charles Royster calls the *rage militaire* evaporated in December 1775 as rapidly as it had appeared in April.[5] The army in front of Boston, now commanded by General George Washington, dwindled to fewer than five thousand early in 1776. Benedict Arnold's assault on Quebec ended ignominiously when more than half his force abruptly departed in December as their enlistments expired. Like colonial militiamen of yore, these citizen soldiers abandoned their comrades in the snow and marched home. Throughout the year contentious state militia officers squabbled with each other over relative rank and the right of command.

Following the collapse of the *rage militaire*, the new nation struggled to field an effective army. Even before the initial militia enthusiasm faded, General Washington sought congressional approval for a permanent national force independent of the states. Efforts to create a regular-style army equal to that of the British fell well short of Washington's aspirations. In the end, the Continental Army more closely resembled the provincial forces the colonies organized to assist Great Britain during the French and Indian War than it did an eighteenth-century European standing army. Washington's quest for an American professional army faltered because the new nation he fought for lacked the essential elements that underwrote European military professionalism: money, bureaucracy, and central political authority.

The absence of these elements weakened American manpower policy. Congress relied largely on the states to recruit men. The states in turn mobilized the Continental regiments through their militia systems and followed established colonial practice when commissioning regimental officers and permitting enlisted men to elect company officers. They offered cash and land bounties, permitted drafted men to hire substitutes, and as the war endured turned more and more to economically marginal men. They made every effort to recruit volunteers and thus avoid having to draft men for Continental service. Attempts to recruit men to serve for more than one year failed miserably, and calls for national conscription fell on deaf ears. During the dark days of 1780–81, Congress slashed the authorized strength of the Army and placed upon the states not only the responsibility to recruit that slender force but to equip and subsist it as well. The nearly bankrupt states in turn passed the recruiting effort to local government, a devolution of authority that nearly lost the Revolution.[6]

A gap clearly existed between Whig theory regarding the role of militia-men in a republic and the problem states faced in recruiting soldiers. When they adapted the theory for their own purposes, American Whigs ignored the way colonial militia had actually functioned. A close reading of their own history would have revealed that civic virtue was a scarce commodity in the colonial militia. The imperative for civic duty that was required of a republi-can citizen soldier too often fell prey to human frailty. Militiamen too often failed to train, arm, or equip themselves. Many refused to respond when called to serve. Those who reported for duty served grudgingly and often de-camped in the face of the enemy when their enlistments expired. Revolution-ary militiamen, that is, generally behaved like their English and colonial fore-bears.

Given the task of providing the Continental Congress with men and money, the states also behaved like their colonial predecessors. They jeal-ously guarded their rights and privileges, resisting congressional dictates on military and fiscal matters, much as they had resisted the Crown. Pervasive localism, a preference for raising short-term troops almost exclusively through volunteering, and the preservation of the right to select officers for the Continental regiments—all highlights of colonial militia practice—per-sisted through the Revolution. Wartime nationalists, and later many histo-rians, damned Radical Whig ideology for its corrosive effects on the conduct of the war.

Axiomatically, to condemn the ideology was to condemn the militia. To lament the failure of the state militia systems, however, was to ignore the ad-ministrative shortcomings of state governments and the difficulties state and local militia officials faced in mobilizing a male population reluctant in the extreme to render military service. The harsh reality of the war years was that too few men were willing to fight. Moreover, for all the purported negative effect of Radical Whig ideology during the Revolution, it often bore only in-cidentally on the conduct of the war. The problems revolutionary leaders faced in creating an effective fighting force stemmed from more prosaic con-ditions. Geography and topography—the sheer expanse of the rebellious col-onies' territory—bedeviled American military commanders as much as they did the British. Furthermore, practicality dictated that Congress rely on the states to provide men and money. The new nation lacked the central govern-mental administrative agencies and executive authority essential for fighting a war. Reliance on the states to recruit manpower meant that colonial practice, not an articulated national policy, would shape the way the newly born United States fought the Revolutionary War.

For all its failings, however, the militia played a crucial role in the Revolution. First and foremost, patriot militia ensured that rebellious Americans gained control of local and state governments early in the war. The British failed to devise a counterrevolutionary strategy that would have allowed them to restore the Crown's authority in even one colony. Local patriot control ensured use of the militia system to mobilize troops. The states managed to provide enough soldiers to sustain the Continental army, organize their own forces, and turn out temporary militia units. Patriot control of the state militia systems gave the Americans the only institutional means available for mobilization.[7]

The major challenge the United States faced during the Revolutionary War was to create the effective institutions essential to the conduct of war in the eighteenth century. To do so in the midst of war is extraordinarily difficult, and it was made all the more formidable in America because of the disagreements over the essential political nature of the emerging new nation. This was the real dilemma of the war years—*not* the apparently simple question of whether to rely on the militia, as Radical Whigs argued, or to create a European-style army, as the nationalists surrounding George Washington contended. Despite the claims of Radical Whig supporters in the postwar years, the militia served a vital function not because it was militarily superior to a regular army, a silly assertion, but because it already existed. As Congress possessed neither the political legitimacy nor the administrative means to organize a large army, colonial militia practice as executed by the states served in lieu of national policy.

Problems that dominated the revolutionary years persisted after 1783. Notably, questions continued regarding the extent of power held by the central government and the kinds of organizations required to meet national military needs. Wartime nationalists, who would form the core of the Federalist Party, articulated a military policy immediately after the war. They wanted a centrally controlled system to replace the ad hoc decentralized colonial practices that so bedeviled revolutionary leaders. General Washington's "Sentiments on a Military Establishment," submitted to the Confederation Congress in 1783, outlined nationalist thinking. The "Sentiments" called for a permanent policy to provide a small regular army and navy, a coastal fortification system, the means to educate the officer corps, and a well-organized militia under national control. Three decades would pass before the nation embraced a policy that resembled Federalist proposals.

The new nation faced many challenges between 1783 and 1787 that the Confederation Congress, working with the states, could not solve. Congress's inability to stem incipient conflicts with Indians in the Ohio Valley or to protect an arsenal in Massachusetts during a debtor's rebellion of former Continental soldiers in 1786 led the nationalists to organize the Constitutional Convention of 1787. Opponents of increased national military authority, soon known as Antifederalists, disagreed sharply with Federalist proposals for enhancing national power. At the Constitutional Convention and in the debates preceding adoption of the Constitution, Antifederalists defended the military system inherited from the colonies. In terms often more strident than those of the early 1770s, supporters of Radical Whig ideas opposed a strong central government and standing army. For them, the best means to defend both republican rights and the nation was to adopt a decentralized political system that assigned the states substantial political power and control of the militia.[8]

The Constitution gave the federal government potentially great military authority by permitting Congress to collect revenues directly, raise and support an army, and maintain a navy. By making the president the commander in chief of the armed services, including the militia when in service to the United States, the Constitution established a single agent to conduct war. It also allowed Congress to call the militia to federal service (to repel invasion, suppress insurrection, or enforce federal law) and to provide the means to arm, organize, and discipline state forces. However, the fundamental document reserved for the states the right to appoint militia officers and to train the militia according to the system Congress provided. Because the Constitution did not specifically guarantee the existence of the militia, Antifederalists, who feared the national government might kill the state soldiery by neglect, won approval for the Second Amendment to assure constitutional protection of the militia.

Creation of an army stood high on President Washington's agenda under the new government. Although freed from the necessity of relying on the states to field a fighting force, Washington's administration and those succeeding it through 1815 never found it easy to maintain a stable army. The history of the U.S. Army during the years of the early republic was marked by sharp fluctuations in force structure and institutional stability. Nonetheless, by the end of the era even the purportedly antiarmy Jeffersonian Republicans accepted the necessity of a regular army. When Thomas Jefferson left the presidency in 1809, the army issue centered only on its strength and function, not on its existence.[9]

The Federalists, however, failed to establish a national militia system. Devising an acceptable and effective militia policy was the most intractable military issue of the era. Secretary of War Henry Knox presented a bill to Congress in 1790 calling for a national compulsory militia organized, trained, and equipped by the federal government. However, even Federalist congressmen believed the Knox plan was too centralized to fit the American idea of militia service. Following two years of indifferent debate, Congress approved the Militia Act of 1792, which for all intents and purposes perpetuated colonial practice. The law continued a universal militia obligation for able-bodied men between the ages of eighteen and forty-five. Although it prescribed tactical organization in detail and specifically listed how each militiaman was to equip himself, it provided neither measures for forcing states to comply with the law nor financial support. With the failure of the Knox plan, the Federalists abandoned efforts to make the militia an effective national institution. After he assumed the presidency, Jefferson asked Congress more than once to create a classified militia under partial federal control, but to no avail. The best he could obtain was an 1803 law requiring state adjutants general to report their militia enrollments to the War Department and an 1808 statute that provided for the annual distribution of $200,000 in arms to the states, apportioned according to the number of enrolled soldiers each had.

Throughout the 1790s, the Washington and Adams administrations sought ways to avoid using the ineffective militia. The most obvious alternative was to enlarge the Army. Congress approved increases twice in the 1790s, first to defeat the Ohio Indian coalition, then for the Quasi-War with France, but it reduced the Army once the crises ended. Federalist administrations also experimented with recruiting levies, that is, volunteer forces raised directly by the federal government. Congress authorized volunteers for the Ohio campaigns and the Quasi-War episode. Federalist leaders preferred the volunteer levies because they were raised outside the militia system, and the president commissioned their officers. For all that, the levies resembled provincial colonial forces not only in their military inefficiency but in the way they were recruited. Moreover, presidents could not always avoid using militia. Washington called state forces to federal service to quell the Whiskey Rebellion of 1794 because national law required the use of only militia and no other forces to enforce federal statutes. John Adams faced the same reality during the

Fries Rebellion of 1799. Jefferson secured federal authority in 1807 to use the Army to enforce federal law, but he too often turned to state forces in his failed efforts to compel obedience to the Embargo Act.[10]

Jeffersonians ignored the Federalist experiment with federal levies but adopted a complex and confusing array of manpower policies between 1803 and 1814. In sum, both Presidents Jefferson and James Madison pursued a mixed policy that increased the Army, authorized volunteer forces raised by the states but serving as federal forces, and relied on the standing militia to augment regulars and volunteers. The militia's woeful performance during the War of 1812 is the best illustration not only of the failure of the Militia Act of 1792 but of the demise of the regular militia in American military affairs. However, as Emory Upton pointed out over a century ago, the Jeffersonian Republicans established a precedent by winning congressional authority to take state volunteers into federal service while permitting the states to organize the units and appoint their officers. In "confusing volunteers with militia," Upton lamented, the Jeffersonians committed the nation to waging its wars "on the theory that we are a confederacy instead of a Nation." The practice endured to the end of the nineteenth century.[11]

State retention of the militia obligation directly affected the central military problem of the era. By 1800 Americans came to accept a standing army, but financial problems and lingering Whiggish suspicions left the United States Army too small to handle serious crises. The essential policy question concerned how to augment the Army when necessary. Federalists failed in their proposals to develop a national militia sufficiently trained and equipped to reinforce the Army in times of war. The political culture of 1775 prevailed, and militia reform drowned in a sea of local particularities and indifference to the development of national institutions.

Federalist attempts to establish a national militia also foundered because the nation lacked the funds and bureaucratic agencies to implement even a modest national system, had one been politically acceptable. In any event, neither Federalists nor Republicans made serious efforts to improve the citizen soldiery, including the District of Columbia system, which fell directly under congressional control.[12] Finally, as John Shy suggests, the nation faced only limited probabilities of internal dissolution and even less likelihood of external destruction, for the nation's geographic expanse and wealth assured its security. Fundamental security, coupled with an enduring provincialism, a distaste for armies and strong central governments, and administrative underdevelopment explain the failure of militia reform. Although Americans accepted the need for a constabulary army, they did not see the need to rationalize and centralize the state citizen soldiery. As a consequence, the Militia Act of 1792 became a part of American military policy by perpetuating the colonial practice through which the states mobilized the citizen soldiers necessary to bolster the Army in a national emergency.[13]

THE STATE MILITIA SYSTEMS, 1816–1865

In the half century following the War of 1812, the United States pursued the military policy that had taken shape between 1783 and 1815. The acceptance of an enduring policy and essential security from threats outside the continent gave a consistency to military and naval affairs that was decidedly missing during the years of the early republic. The Army entered an extended period of gradual growth and institutional maturation. Reforms instituted by Secretary of War John C. Calhoun gave the Army a commanding general and effective administrative and logistical bureaus. Calhoun also provided the regular service with a central institutional sense of purpose through the idea of the expansible army. He explicitly rejected the militia as the mainstay of national defense through a plan that called for the expansion of a skeletonized peacetime army led by well-trained regular officers prepared to fight a European power.

William Skelton concludes that although American politicians continued to praise citizen soldiers as the nation's chief defenders, after Calhoun's reforms "the regular army effectively replaced the militia at the center of the land defense system."[14] Although the Army dominated wartime command throughout the nineteenth century, its institutional maturation did not eliminate, as Skelton implies, the nation's need to call on state soldiers in time of war. Although Congress occasionally expanded the Army in these years, it refused to support a peacetime regular force large enough to absorb new men to fight a war. Calhoun's reforms failed to solve the major military problem left over from the early republic era: how to augment the Army with trained soldiers in a crisis. State-recruited volunteer soldiers, whose only qualification for military duty was their willingness to serve, remained the mainstay of wartime forces.

Unfortunately, no institutional mechanism existed to train, mobilize, and deploy state volunteers. Calhoun's reforms dramatically improved Army operations in peace but did not provide institutional means to prepare for war. The Army suffered from administrative bifurcation between line and staff and, given the nature of transportation and communication, necessarily relied on a decentralized command system. Nothing in the Army's short history or its prevailing institutional arrangement encouraged centralized long-range planning. Victims of professional parochialism, Army officers continued to embrace the expansible army concept as the best means to fight a war despite the evident fact that the service remained reliant on untrained state volunteers. Regulars damned the chaotic manner in which their country raised a war army and the amateurism of the volunteers, which demeaned an otherwise great nation. Few, however, offered ideas on how to prepare the state soldiery for wartime service.[15]

The failure to plan for wartime mobilization was more a reflection of the nation than a failing of the Army. Although the United States experienced significant economic, geographic, and population growth in the five decades following the War of 1812, its government remained limited in function and purview. Robert Wiebe argues that Alexander Hamilton's vision of a dynamic capitalist nation directed from the center collapsed, leaving the United States without an institutional core. Philip S. Paludan reminds us that on the eve of the Civil War, the United States "was a federal union of states with a national government singularly inactive." Americans firmly believed, he continues, that local government was "an administrative necessity," performing functions "Washington could not, and should not, supply."[16]

Although a state role in mobilizing wartime troops was an "administrative necessity," it was a part the states played badly. From the Black Hawk War of 1832 through the Second Seminole War in the 1830s up to the Mexican War call-up in 1846, federal requests for troops demonstrated the lack of a substantive state administrative capacity. Successive mobilizations became extemporized events as states reactivated their moribund militia systems to recruit volunteers and, in methods reminiscent of colonial practice, called on local officials to organize units.

At no time during the first half of the nineteenth century did the federal government or the states seriously attempt to alter prevailing practice. Inertia—buttressed by essential security and military success in spite of the vagaries of the state soldiery—stymied reform. Proposals to classify the militia appeared regularly after 1815, some stressing compulsory service, others a voluntary system. Secretary of War Joel R. Poinsett's failure to win congressional support for such a plan in 1840 ended national reform efforts. In contrast to the years 1775 through 1815, the militia question no longer attracted attention, and after 1815 calls for substantive change spoke to an even more indifferent audience then had been the case during the period of the early republic.[17]

The difficulties states faced in mobilizing troops together with federal failure to reform the institution have led historians to conclude erroneously that the militia had disappeared by the 1830s. If the term *militia* is defined to mean compulsory military training and service rendered to the state then indeed it had ceased to function. It is more instructive analytically, however, to think of the states as maintaining *militia systems*, rather than militias. Militia systems in the period 1816 to 1860 varied enormously from region to region and state to state, but general patterns are discernible that indicate why state systems persisted. They endured in part because states and territories complied with the Constitution and the Militia Act of 1792. Mary Ellen Rowe discerns a "militia tradition" that migrants took with them wherever they went.[18] Moreover, the militia remained a vehicle for political advancement at the local level until compulsory musters disappeared. More importantly, state militia systems supported the volunteer uniformed militia and administered mobilizations. Through these functions, the states preserved their traditional role of providing wartime soldiers and kept alive the idea of the citizen soldier.[19]

The compulsory militia played no part in meeting that role, for it ultimately died. It was a lingering demise, however, because despite its obvious failings during the War of 1812, the most striking feature for the next thirty years was a widespread effort to keep the compulsory militia functioning. Newly organized territories and states invariably included an obligated militia in their constitutions and laws, while older states amended or rewrote their militia laws well into the 1840s. South Carolina exerted greater energy than most to animate its militia, largely to sustain slave patrols, but its efforts finally went for naught. To greater or lesser degrees, states east of the Mississippi River attempted to keep the compulsory militia active into the mid-1840s before abandoning it. On the frontier, the universal militia never took root. Although exposed to Indian attacks into the 1840s, neither Texas nor Arkansas, for example, established viable militias because the presence of the Army on the frontier vitiated the need for beleaguered settlers to establish their own military forces.[20]

States relied on fines to enforce participation in the compulsory militia. The system collapsed, however, even when fines were increased, and officials made diligent efforts to collect them. Increased fines led to political protest that by the mid-1830s had convinced most state legislatures to abolish compulsory training and the fine system. Thereafter, states either levied a modest commutation tax in lieu of training or simply required county assessors to take an annual census of obligated men. In any event, the militia collapsed of its own weight well before state legislatures abolished it.[21]

The problems that plagued the militia after 1815 differed little from the difficulties that hindered the institution in the colonial and early republic years. States and territories faced a daunting challenge in enrolling a growing male population that was constantly on the move and extremely reluctant to render militia duty. The onus for enforcing militia laws fell on local militia officers who were largely ill-informed citizen soldiers with little financial or political support from local or state governments. When militia courts martial levied fines, civil officials rarely exhibited much enthusiasm for collecting them. Once states replaced musters and training with mere enrollment, town and county assessors neglected to enroll men and seldom collected the commutation tax. Kenneth McCreedy finds state administrative capacity for enforcing militia laws "remarkably thin, weak, and powerless."[22] Legislatures approved innumerable laws affecting the militia but rarely appropriated funds to enforce them. Although state adjutants general carried the main burden of supervising the militia, few were full-time executives or received salaries, and most lacked a clerical staff. Without administrative or financial support, the militia was doomed to collapse.

After 1815, the United States experienced dynamic demographic, economic, geographic, and social change. The vestiges of a society of deference and hierarchy rapidly eroded as the corporate, communal nature of colonial life evolved into what Steven Watts describes as a "liberal political culture." The new culture saw increasing economic specialization, expanded ethnic diversity, and a greater emphasis on private activity. Change, Watts argues, and especially the exaltation of the market and individual effort, destroyed republican deference and the traditional sense of an organic society. These changes contributed substantially to the collapse of the compulsory militia because the new emphasis on individualism broke the bonds of the older sense of communal obligations.[23]

In 1826, Secretary of War James Barbour created a board of Army and militia officers to consider militia reform. Barbour's survey of governors and militia officers revealed a preference for volunteer militiamen. No response better represented this opinion, and the changing nature of society, than that of Major General Asa Howland of Massachusetts. Howland favored volunteers, especially men between the ages of eighteen and twenty-five, and urged that they be paid. "*A young man's 'time is money,'*" he argued, "*and*

when called to spend it for his country, his country should compensate him"
(emphasis in original).[24] Howland's views represented the antithesis of Radical Whig thinking on a republican soldiery wherein *all* virtuous citizens rendered military service freely to defend the community.

The volunteer uniformed militia was not a new phenomenon.[25] It too had
roots in the English militia and American colonial experience. The Militia
Act of 1792 recognized existing "independent" military companies with a
colonial lineage and provided for uniformed volunteers to serve as light infantry, artillery, and cavalry. Prior to 1820, however, the few companies in
existence were socially elite units confined to the older urban centers. From
the late 1830s to the eve of the Civil War, the uniformed militia blossomed.
New companies appeared alongside established older organizations in Massachusetts, New York, and New Orleans. In more recently settled areas,
towns like Milwaukee and San Francisco developed a lively uniformed militia even as they became cities. By the mid-1850s, volunteer participation in
militia units was national in scope, touching all regions from New England to
California.[26]

As the responses to Secretary of War Barbour's 1826 survey revealed,
state officials viewed the uniformed militia as a viable alternative to the moribund compulsory system. During the next two decades, most states repealed
compulsory service and recognized the volunteers as the only functional segment of their militia systems. States that required a commutation tax from obligated militiamen used the funds to assist uniformed organizations. They
also aided the volunteers by giving them arms from the annual federal distribution. The greater emphasis on volunteers represented a concession to reality, rather than a deliberate decision to replace militiamen with volunteers.
The social and economic forces that eroded the remnants of a communal
sense of obligatory service underwrote the impulses that led men to join uniformed companies. In an increasingly specialized and diverse society, people
sought new institutions to replace older social practices destroyed by dramatic change. Rowland Berthoff sees "the voluntary association" as one
such response, for here was "an institution which existed because its members chose to create and sustain it."[27]

Berthoff's observation describes well the uniformed militia. Although the
traditional militia was compulsory and inclusive, uniformed organizations
were explicitly voluntary and exclusive. Uniformed militia companies in the
antebellum era encompassed a broad social spectrum drawing largely from
urban-based middle and skilled working classes, rather than from the

wealthy. Volunteer companies flourished where men with the leisure and money could afford the luxury of part-time military activity. From the mid-1840s on, a large number of ethnic companies appeared, most of them German or Irish. Native-born Americans found this development disturbing and organized their own organizations to meet this "foreign" threat.

Antebellum uniformed companies functioned like other fraternal societies, such as the Masons, which appeared at the same time. A civil association adopted a constitution and set of bylaws to govern membership and group behavior. Enlistment came only by invitation. The civil rules governing uniformed militia units reveal the underlying social and fraternal nature of these military clubs. Uniformed companies hosted balls, dinners, and theatricals with members sporting self-designed uniforms worthy of Hungarian hussars or any number of European grenadier guards. As the steamboat and railroad improved transportation, companies exchanged visits with other cities to take part in demonstration drills and marching competitions.

It is tempting to make fun of the uniformed militia. Their outlandish uniforms, wholly unfit for field service; their intricate drill tactics, more appropriate to a marching band than a military unit; and their hyperbolic assertions about the fighting prowess of the American citizen soldier—all mocked the serious content of Whig ideology and the realities of nineteenth-century battlefields. The social activities and pretensions of uniformed militiamen undercut the potential value of part-time military training. All too often, their club features disrupted units as yearly officer elections led to endless electioneering and factionalism. More disturbing was the ephemeral nature of a majority of the organizations. Far too many succumbed to financial failure, declining membership, or internal dissension. As voluntary organizations, uniformed companies held no legal authority over their members and lost them all too easily.

Although essentially private fraternal associations, the uniformed volunteers carried a public imprimatur. A company originated when a group of like-minded men recruited others, wrote a set of bylaws, and elected officers. The unit became active when the state issued it a charter and the governor commissioned its officers. Governors held the power to revoke the charter or remove the officers when they saw fit. Uniformed companies were part of the state militia systems. They were subject to the call of municipal and state officials in times of civil disorder and, theoretically, subject as well to gubernatorial and presidential calls in times of war or insurrection.

Uniformed soldiers provided states and localities with an organized, partially trained armed force better able to cope with civil disorder than the old militia. In the two decades before the Civil War, infrequent labor disputes and civil disorders involving rival ethnic and religious groups struck urban areas. Slave insurrections in the South, real or imagined, threatened racial warfare. From the mid-1850s on, enforcement of the Fugitive Slave Act provoked violent resistance in Northern cities, particularly in the Mid-Atlantic region. Municipal and state leaders turned to the uniformed militia to quell the uprisings. Some scholars contend that middle- and upper-class property holders fostered the uniformed volunteers to ensure the availability of a reliable riot police firmly under their control to maintain order. Although this was true in some localities, little evidence exists to demonstrate that class fears of rampant social conflict underlay the broader development of the uniformed militia.[28]

The volunteer companies were of limited value as riot police in any event because they were militarily ineffective. Although *uniformed* militiamen, the volunteers could not be described as a *uniform* militia. Besides granting official recognition and providing the arms and equipment distributed by the federal government, states took little interest in the units. Possessing no financial hold over local companies, states lacked the power to impose control on them. In any case, few attempted to create an active, centrally controlled militia. To have done so would have meant overcoming the institutional vacuum so evident in antebellum America, a vacuum that pervaded not only militia affairs but society as a whole. No social imperative existed to make the uniformed volunteers militarily efficient by providing financial support and establishing statewide standards through which volunteer companies could qualify for the aid. Volunteers thus governed their affairs as they saw fit. With self-support the *sine qua non* of unit survival, militiamen naturally devoted themselves to activities that would simultaneously earn money and attract dues-paying members. Some companies fared well in fund-raising and attained stability. Others failed and either collapsed or struggled along ineffectively.[29]

Beginning in the mid-1840s, some militia officers, particularly those from Connecticut, Massachusetts, and New York, called for reform of the uniformed militia. Within a decade, the three states had reformed their systems along similar lines, providing financial support to the volunteers and requiring companies to hold a set number of drills per year and attend annual regimental training camps to qualify for state aid. The requirements for state support gave adjutants general authority to disband companies not meeting state standards, while the need to administer the systems created permanent, although small, militia bureaucracies.

Unwisely, New York did not limit the number of companies receiving state aid and therefore lacked funds to assist all units adequately. The state relied on the commutation tax to support the volunteers, but local officials did not collect the tax effectively. Although it supported units with armory rent and equipment, New York found it difficult to disband understrength units or compel them to wear the state-prescribed uniform. Connecticut and Massachusetts created more centrally controlled systems. By the late 1850s, Massachusetts set a national standard. It organized its companies into regiments, applied statewide standards to all units, and paid its volunteers a small stipend to attend drills and training camp. By the close of the decade, the entire Massachusetts Volunteer Militia, limited to five thousand men, met annually for summer training. Although far from perfect, the Massachusetts approach stood in marked contrast to militia systems in the rest of the nation.[30]

Under normal circumstances, how states managed their militia systems was incidental to national affairs. When war came, however, the effectiveness of state systems mattered a great deal. Mobilization exposed national and state institutional weaknesses, notably the dearth of any policy for coordinating federal and state military efforts and the inadequacy of administrative means at both governmental levels. For the Mexican War, Congress and President James K. Polk called on the states to provide some twenty-five thousand volunteers in May 1846. An ad hoc mobilization ensued in which decentralization reigned supreme, with each state organizing troops as it saw fit. Some governors simply issued a statewide call for companies to tender their services on a first-come, first-accepted basis. Existing uniformed companies were free to volunteer although they were not given precedence over scores of hastily recruited new companies. Many peacetime uniformed organizations refused to volunteer. The open call permitted ambitious men filled with entrepreneurial spirit to use their political connections or their own money to raise units. Some states, on the other hand, mustered compulsory militia regiments, then solicited volunteers who elected their company officers. Regimental officers were either elected when local companies rendezvoused at state camps or were appointed by governors.

The mobilization generated a chaotic, unseemly scramble for local unit recognition and, above all, commissions. Reliance on the volunteer principle epitomized the political culture of the era. At best, state governments played a benign role, offering to accept for military service those who were willing to serve and were most adept at winning the governor's attention. Governors granted commissions to men who won election, the guiding principle being that one man's claim to the rank of captain or colonel was as good as another's as long as he could convince his comrades to grant him the privilege. For all the flaws in the mobilization, however, it is difficult to see how the federal government could have raised the same number of regiments as readily as the states had organized theirs.[31]

Most states faced little difficulty raising men in 1846. The war was most popular in Western and Southern states, and in these areas volunteers came forth in far greater numbers than were needed to fill quotas. Arming, equipping, and clothing these men posed a daunting challenge, however. States used their own finances to recruit, organize, and equip their soldiers, severely testing their limited capacity to raise money. After their volunteers entered national service, states submitted requests for federal reimbursement. It was an inefficient system prone to mismanagement, unnecessary expense, and fraud yet unavoidable given federal dependence on the inadequate logistical and administrative agencies of state militias. In most respects, then, the 1846 mobilization differed little from those in the early years of the American Revolution or the War of 1812.[32]

Despite the problems exposed during the Mexican War mobilization, neither the Army nor Congress attempted to alter public policy so the growing uniformed militia of the 1850s might more easily be incorporated into the next war army. The militia systems of the Union and Confederacy confronted problems in 1861 similar to those faced by the states in 1846. However, in both regions individual states demonstrated the flexibility of their militia systems. The great failing from the colonial years to 1860 had been the reluctance of colonies and states to spend money on their citizen soldiers. From Abraham Lincoln's election in November 1860 through April 1861, however, governors and legislatures in the North and South animated their militia systems in unprecedented ways, most notably by appropriating funds to prepare for war. With money in hand, Northern and Southern governors organized, armed, and equipped volunteer companies. The latter activity led governors to seek effective adjutants and quartermasters general to supervise the volunteers. State military bureaucracies grew rapidly after the firing on Fort Sumter as the Union and Confederacy each turned to the states for volunteers. Throughout 1861, the states remained not only the recruiting agencies for their central governments but the providers of arms and equipment as well.

The development of the uniformed militia during the preceding two decades contributed only minimally to the Civil War mobilization. Most of the troops organized by Northern and Southern states were raised by calling for volunteers from the body politic at large. The more effective response of 1861 is better explained by the improvements in communication and transportation that had occurred after 1846 as well as by the willingness of state governments, particularly when led by dynamic governors, to improve their militia systems in the months before hostilities broke out. Although the Northern and Southern mobilizations of early 1861 were hardly models of efficiency, they stood in marked contrast to the chaos and confusion of 1846. State recruiting efforts in the early months of the war revealed the militia's inherent capacity to organize a military force of substance when state leaders were intent on doing so.[33]

After 1861, the dynamics of the war diminished the importance of state recruiting. The ever expanding logistical and manpower needs of the field armies led the administrations of Lincoln and Jefferson Davis to centralize management of the war, particularly manpower policy. The Confederacy moved first in March 1862 when it adopted conscription. Its draft successfully stimulated volunteering and ensured central allocation of manpower whether soldiers entered as volunteers or conscripts. President Lincoln found it more difficult to break state dominance of manpower policy. When state efforts to recruit volunteers faltered, Congress amended the Militia Act of 1792 in July 1862 by giving Lincoln the authority to set rules for state militia drafts where none existed. The law left recruiting in state hands but forced governors to either intensify their efforts to recruit volunteers or draft militiamen. Yet Northern governors clung to the volunteer approach, winning their plea for increased federal bounties to encourage volunteering. Gubernatorial resistance to increasing federal control of manpower policy failed. The Enrollment Act of March 1863 asserted a national military obligation for the traditional militia. If the Northern draft proved less effective than Southern conscription, it did stimulate volunteering and greatly diminished gubernatorial control of manpower policy.[34]

The adoption of conscription and the greater control of manpower policy exerted by the Union and Confederacy asserted a national military obligation. Although the assertion failed to endure after the war, it temporarily made the states the minority partners in manpower mobilization. The Lincoln and Davis administrations gained control of recruiting as part of a broad wartime centralization of national power through expanded administrative agencies.

Only the demands of a mass war requiring large armies overcame the inherently decentralized nature of America. Seen in the light of these developments, the inability of reformers to create a uniform national militia between 1783 and the early 1840s becomes more understandable.

The vicissitudes of war spurred some state governments to adopt unprecedented militia policies. Southern states fared poorly in their efforts because of national conscription, a shortage of men, and lack of funds. Some Northern states reactivated their compulsory militias, with Missouri approving the most wide-ranging system.[35] The reanimated compulsory militia disappeared rapidly in 1865, never to appear again, but many Northern states also established active units that set precedents for the postwar years. Legislatures approved funds to provide arms, uniforms, and equipment, with the federal government often providing additional support. Following draft riots in Milwaukee in 1862, for example, Wisconsin approved legislation to establish a state-supported home front force of three thousand men in three regiments. Ohio's 1864 militia law named its part-time soldiers the National Guard and provided an allowance to buy uniforms and aid to rent armories from a military fund of $500,000. California appropriated several hundred thousand dollars to equip an active militia that totaled eight thousand in 1865 and renamed its state troops the California National Guard a year later. New York maintained a National Guard of New York, with nearly forty-five thousand troops—the largest state force in the North. In all, Robert Chamberlain estimates, the Northern states maintained active forces totaling at least 150,000 in the last two years of the war.[36]

The Northern active militia failed to achieve military efficiency. Continued demands for volunteers and conscripts stripped units of able men. Many men came to resent militia duty. For all its foibles, however, the active militia served to keep public order, turn out when invasion threatened, provide units for short-term federal service, and give a modicum of training to men who volunteered for the field regiments. Perhaps the Northern militia's greatest liability lay in its particularity. Each state did as it saw fit and according to its financial resources. The federal government offered no advice and only limited funds. Nonetheless, state efforts to maintain an organized militia with financial assistance and administrative supervision set an example for transforming the uniformed militia into a viable state institution.

In his 1865 annual report, Adjutant General Augustus Gaylord found Wisconsin's current militia law an "utter failure." Based on his wartime experience, Gaylord concluded that "no time can be more propitious" to reorganize the Wisconsin militia. "Give it a new name, the 'National Guard,' or any other distinctive name, and a new law," he advised, and sufficient state money to make the citizen soldiery effective.[37] In 1865, no state was interested in embracing General Gaylord's suggestions. Within a decade of the war's end, however, Wisconsin and other Northern states were following a state military policy similar to the one Gaylord outlined in 1865.

2

The Rise of the
National Guard, 1866–1898

The active militia systems Northern states created during the Civil War disappeared rapidly with the end of hostilities. Wartime Southern militias collapsed even as the Confederate Army fought its last battles. A review of the state military scene in 1868 led the *Army and Navy Journal* to conclude that "no country in Christendom is so careless of its volunteer militia" as is the United States.[1] In the ensuing thirty years, the state soldiery underwent an alteration unlike any in militia history. The rise of the National Guard in these years was marked by standing military budgets, organization of local companies into higher echelon organizations, and centrally controlled state inspection and supervision. Long-term state funding and centralized regulation of local units set off the National Guard from the antebellum militia. Although there was no overnight transformation, by the outbreak of the Spanish-American War the National Guard represented the most efficient and best trained, armed, and equipped soldiery the states had ever fielded.

A perfunctory survey of the historical literature for the decade following the Civil War would suggest that the state soldiery offered little prospect for future development. Besides the Northeast and parts of the Midwest, states ignored their organized militia well into the mid-1870s. Minnesota's mandatory annual militia return to the War Department merely listed men liable for military duty and in 1875 stated that "owing to the lack of efficient legislation there is no fully organized state militia."[2] In the Trans-Mississippi West, where Kansas and the Colorado Territory had fielded federal volunteer units to fight Indians during the Civil War, interest in part-time military service lapsed as well. West Virginia abolished its adjutant generalcy and consigned his duties first to the state superintendent of schools, then to the state librarian.[3]

Economic exhaustion and the rancor that accompanied Reconstruction rendered the militia systems of the former Confederacy ineffective from the end of the war into the 1880s. From the end of the war to early 1867, Southern states organized forces composed largely of Confederate veterans to restore white control and enforce the notorious Black Codes. Congress abolished the militia in all the former Confederate states except Tennessee in March 1867, then restored it once those states returned to the Union under Republican control. In the bitter racial-political conflicts that afflicted the South from 1869 through 1875, Reconstruction militia, widely referred to as "Negro" militia because it was integrated and used to defend freedmen, took to the field to support Republican administrations and thwart white terrorism. In the end, these soldiers were not sufficient to retain a Republican hold on the South.

White Democrats abolished the Reconstruction militias when they regained control of Southern governments in the 1870s. Democratic governors abandoned the policy of their Reconstruction predecessors of actively organizing militia units and returned to the traditional policy of recognizing volunteer companies organized through local private initiative. Nine post-Reconstruction Southern militia systems retained segregated black volunteers (Arkansas and Mississippi were the exceptions) but provided them with little financial support.[4]

In many respects, the early National Guard resembled the antebellum uniformed soldiery. Joseph Holmes describes the Pennsylvania National Guard of these years as "a happy-go-lucky organization" that indulged in fun, games, and fancy uniforms.[5] New York suffered as well from a soldiery committed to street parades, dinners, concerts, and balls. George Wingate, longtime member and historian of New York City's Twenty-second Regiment, recalled that "altogether too much time and money . . . were spent on these."[6] Both Pennsylvania and New York maintained elaborate divisional organizations with a plethora of major and brigadier generals and their supporting staffs.[7]

At this point, the state soldiery stood between the self-contained uniformed militia of the 1850s and what the National Guard would become by the end of the century. The volunteers lacked cohesion and centralized control, with less than half the states and territories supporting their soldiery monetarily. Reconstruction policies in the South and the persistence else-

Table 1 Organized Militia Strength, by Region, 1873

Region	Aggregate
Northeast	50,775
South	94,400
Midwest	5,269
Plains	0
West	2,876
Total:	153,320

Source: U.S. Congress, Senate, *Militia Force of the United States*, 43d Cong., 1st sess., 1873, S. Exec. Doc. 41.

where of older militia traditions sanctioned the formation of volunteer units out of all proportion to public need. Consequently, the states collectively maintained far more Guardsmen than they could support or supervise properly, as table 1 shows.[8]

An analysis of the 1873 aggregate strength demonstrates the hollowness of the state forces. Fifteen of the thirty-seven states reported no organized force. New York alone accounted for nearly half the troops in the Northeast, with over twenty-four thousand, while Delaware and New Hampshire maintained no soldiery at all. Reconstruction forces in Arkansas, South Carolina, and Texas totaled over eighty-nine thousand, yet six states in the region neglected their militia entirely. The Texas claim fell far short of reality. It neither armed nor equipped the majority of its Reconstruction militia, and in any event it disbanded it in 1873. Four states in the Midwest ignored their soldiery completely, with Missouri's nineteen hundred men constituting the largest force in the region. Of the five states in both the Plains and West regions in 1873, only California and Oregon supported an organized soldiery.[9]

Despite the apparent moribund condition of the state soldiery, however, closer examination identifies the elements from which the National Guard would evolve. The evidence is incomplete, but the rapid growth of the National Guard from 1875 on makes it clear that the Civil War did not entirely destroy the state military systems. As is the case for all militia history, broad generalizations must be tempered by examining the state soldiery from a regional perspective and sometimes state by state within regions.

In the Northeast, states that financially supported home front volunteers in the antebellum and Civil War years continued to do so after 1865. In 1871, both Massachusetts and New York appropriated nearly $200,000 annually for their soldiery and Connecticut over $60,000. Pennsylvania increased its modest aid in 1873 by allocating $400 a year to each company. In the West, California amended its wartime law in 1866 by renaming its militia the National Guard and providing $600 a year to each of its thirty-two companies. In the early 1870s, some Midwestern states resumed military spending that had been cut off in 1865. For example, Milwaukee militiamen lobbied the Wisconsin legislature to compel Milwaukee County to pay them armory rent as required by an 1863 law. Milwaukee politicians convinced the legislature to have the state assume the burden. Wisconsin first offered aid to its volunteer companies in 1873 by providing an annual $100 allotment to each unit.[10]

Some states revised wartime laws to meet peacetime needs. Vermont, for example, reduced its Civil War force of thirteen regiments to three in 1866, then further reduced the state force to only one infantry regiment in 1872. Pennsylvania limited its National Guard to ten thousand men when it increased its annual allotment in 1873. A year later, it eliminated ten divisional organizations and directed independent companies to form regiments. Wisconsin's decision to offer aid to its companies in 1873 did not create an effective militia. The $100 yearly allotment tempted many to organize units but was insufficient to support permanent organizations. In 1875, the state raised yearly company support to $300 but limited its force to only twenty-four units.[11]

The evolving National Guard of the late nineteenth century was national in name only, with federal influence limited to the annual arms distribution. Forces varied widely from state to state. No two organized their Guardsmen in exactly the same manner, nor were all armed with the same weapons. Training standards and requirements for commissioning officers differed widely. Not all state soldiery carried the name National Guard. Proud of their heritage and not ashamed of the term *militia*, Bay Staters marched under the name of the Massachusetts Volunteer Militia. Until 1895, when it became the National Guard, Indiana's soldiery was legally known by its Civil War nomenclature, the Indiana Legion. All states from the former Confederacy except Mississippi used either the term *State Guards* or *Volunteers*, although Louisiana confused matters by calling its troops the State National Guard. Although the state soldiery lacked uniformity, it nonetheless evolved along the same lines after 1875. Each state attempted to establish a permanent military force supported to a greater or lesser degree by state funding and subject to some form of command above local unit authority.

Table 2 Population, by Region (in thousands), for 1880, 1890, 1900

Region	Population (percentage of national total)		
	1880	1890	1900
Northeast	15,590 (31.0%)	18,617 (30.0%)	2,420 (29.5%)
South	15,259 (30.0%)	17,329 (28.0%)	22,083 (29.0%)
Midwest	15,780 (31.5%)	19,378 (31.3%)	23,076 (30.4%)
Plains	1,837 (4.0%)	3,909 (6.0%)	4,923 (6.5%)
West	1,514 (3.0%)	2,483 (4.0%)	3,216 (4.2%)
District of Columbia	178 (.04%)	230 (.04%)	279 (.04%)

Source: U.S. Department of Commerce, Bureau of the Census, *Historical Statistics of the United States: Colonial Times to 1970*, Part 1 (Washington DC: Government Printing Office, 1975).

Table 3 Newly Admitted States, 1876–1896

1876	1889	1890	1896
Colorado	Montana	Idaho	Utah
	North Dakota	Wyoming	
	South Dakota		
	Washington		

Note: There were thirty-seven states in 1875; forty-five in 1897. Arizona, New Mexico, and Oklahoma remained territories through 1898.
Source: U.S. Department of Commerce, Bureau of the Census, *Historical Statistics of the United States: Colonial Times to 1970*, Part 1 (Washington DC: Government Printing Office, 1975).

Tradition, regional wealth, and the extent of urbanization substantially affected the Guard's evolution, as did population growth and distribution and the addition of new states (see tables 2 and 3). Some territories created modest forces prior to statehood but lacked sufficient budgetary authority to develop efficient soldiers until they joined the Union.[12]

The growth of the National Guard occurred erratically, with two periods of contraction each followed by a spurt of growth (see table 4).[13] From 1885 on, however, the service demonstrated increasing stability and steady expansion. The fluctuating strength of the Guard from 1873 through 1885 reflected national political and social turbulence as well as uncertainty about the kind

Table 4 National Guard Strength, Selected Years

Year	Aggregate	States/Territories Not Reporting
1873	153,320	Fifteen states
1875	90,865	Ten states
1880	127,231	Three states
1885	84,739	Seven states, five territories
1890	106,269	Two states, three territories
1895	115,699	One territory

Note: The annual returns did not include data on territorial organizations until 1885.

Sources: Data for 1873, 1875, 1880, 1885, and 1890 are taken from *Militia Force of the United States*, Senate, 43d Cong., 1st sess., 1873, S. Exec. Doc. 41; Senate, 44th Cong., 1st sess., 1875, S. Exec. Doc. 45; House, 46th Cong., 3d sess., 1880, H. Exec. Doc. 74; Senate, 49th Cong., 1st sess., 1885, S. Exec. Doc. 52; and Senate, 52d Cong., 2d sess., 1890, S. Exec. Doc. 48. For 1895, see MID 1895.

of military force the states needed. In 1875, Texas accounted for most of the drop in the Guard's aggregate strength over the previous two years through its disbanding of its Reconstruction militia. The state reported a purported 74,600 militiamen in 1873 and a mere 1,276 Volunteer Guardsmen two years later. The broader development of the Guard continued in the mid-1870s, however, as several Midwestern states revived their forces, as did Kansas and Nebraska. Even so, in 1875 ten states failed to report an organized force.

The 1880 return shows a major expansion during the preceding five years—an addition of 36,366 men. Growth occurred in several ways. Seven states reporting no organized militia in 1875 submitted returns in 1880, adding over 6,500 troops to the new total. Thirty-five states claimed an organized force in the latter year. More dramatically, Arkansas and South Carolina accounted for over 28,000 new militiamen in 1880, despite the return of white Democrats to political control in both states. Contrary to general historical opinion, the 1877 railroad strikes did not engender a major expansion of the National Guard of the Northeast. The region saw little increase in strength from the railroad strikes to 1880 despite the fact that nearly all available forces in Maryland, New York, and Pennsylvania mobilized to meet the disorder. Total strengths in the three states remained little changed in 1880. However,

Table 5 National Guard Strength, Midwest, 1875 and 1880

State	1875	1880	Gain
Illinois	3,271	7,919	+ 4,648
Indiana	0	1,814	+ 1,814
Iowa	2,619	4,581	+ 1,962
Michigan	1,084	1,816	+ 732
Minnesota	160	388	+ 228
Missouri	228	1,909	+ 1,681
Ohio	4,630	8,374	+ 3,744
Wisconsin	1,737	2,130	+ 393
Aggregate:	13,729	28,931	+15,202

Sources: Militia Force of the United States, Senate, 44th Cong., 1st sess., 1875, S. Exec. Doc. 45; and House, 46th Cong., 3d sess., 1880, H. Exec. Doc. 74.

the 1877 disorders affected the Midwest profoundly. States in the region that experienced the worst disorder—Illinois, Indiana, Iowa, Missouri, and Ohio—added nearly fourteen thousand Guardsmen between 1875 and 1880 (see table 5).[14]

Returns for 1885 show a second significant reduction in the strength of the National Guard, although not as large as the one between 1873 and 1875 (see table 4). Most of the losses occurred in the South as Reconstruction militia forces collapsed in Arkansas, Florida, and South Carolina. All told, Southern states reported nearly thirty-three thousand fewer state soldiers than five years earlier (see table 6).[15]

Significant reorganizations in key states account for the remaining losses. As so often in the history of the state soldiery, Massachusetts set the precedent nearly a decade earlier. The Bay State reformed and reduced its Volunteer Militia in 1876, disbanding its divisional organization and cutting the number of companies eligible for state aid from one hundred to sixty-six. It subjected companies to a strict inspection, disbanded the thirty lowest-rated units and also reduced four regiments to battalion strength. Although the state increased its authorized force somewhat in 1887, the Massachusetts Volunteer Militia kept from 4,800 to 5,500 men to the end of the century.[16]

Several Northeastern and Midwestern states emulated Massachusetts in the early 1880s. Reorganizations in New York and Pennsylvania stemmed from the inefficient mobilization and lack of discipline their forces exhibited

Table 6 Regional Distribution, National Guard, Selected Years

Region	Number of Guardsmen (percentage of national total)				
	1875	1880	1885	1890	1895
Northeast	48,967	46,098	37,536	41,921	40,213
	(54.0%)	(36.0%)	(44.0%)	(39.0%)	(35.0%)
South	22,857	46,191	12,559	25,535	29,938
	(25.0%)	(36.0%)	(15.0%)	(24.0%)	(26.2%)
Midwest	13,729	28,931	23,894	22,737	27,801
	(15.0%)	(23.0%)	(28.0%)	(21.5%)	(24.3%)
Plains	2,774	1,262	4,925	5,909	6,221
	(3.0%)	(1.0%)	(6.0%)	(6.0%)	(5.4%)
West	2,538	4,749	5,654	9,207	10,025
	(3.0%)	(4.0%)	(7.0%)	(9.0%)	(9.0%)
District of Columbia*				1,590	1,471
				(.5%)	(.1%)
Aggregate:	90,865	127,231	84,739	106,269	115,699

*The annual militia returns did not report strengths of the District of Columbia until 1887.

Source: Militia Force of the United States, Senate, 49th Cong., 1st sess., 1885, S. Exec. Doc. 52.

during the 1877 disorders. Both states learned that large numbers of poorly financed, inadequately trained and undermanned Guard units were a liability in times of trouble. They determined, as had Massachusetts, that a smaller, better supported Guard subject to more direct state supervision provided a more effective force. In 1876, Pennsylvania carried ten major generals on its table of organization and supported 194 companies only nominally organized as regiments. After major reorganizations in 1879 and 1881, the Keystone Guard supported no more than 160 companies organized in a three-brigade division and commanded by the state's only major general. As a consequence, the state's reported strength fell by nearly thirteen hundred in the five years following 1880.[17]

New York made more drastic cuts. As late as 1880, the state maintained an unwieldy force of over twenty thousand. It reduced the authorized strength to twelve thousand two years later. The New York Guard, however, refrained from adopting a divisional organization that would have provided tighter tac-

tical and administrative control. In the Midwest, states that expanded their
soldiery in the aftermath of 1877 reduced their forces in the early to
mid-1880s; they also discovered that too large an authorized force generated
unit instability and inefficiency. Taken together, reorganizations in the East
and Midwest eliminated nearly fourteen thousand Guardsmen between 1880
and 1885.[18]

Newer states sometimes erred on the side of excess before absorbing the
lesson discovered farther east. After gaining statehood, Colorado's legislature approved a National Guard of 118 companies organized in two divisions.
Failing to sustain even four infantry battalions, the state reduced its force to a
four-regiment brigade in 1883. When that collapsed, the legislature provided
for twelve infantry companies in two battalions in 1889. In the West, Washington repeated Colorado's errors and was forced to cut its initial two-regi-
ment authorization of 1890 to one regiment five years later.[19]

The reorganizations of the early 1880s represented the final stage of state
military development following the Civil War. From the middle of the decade
to the end of the century, the National Guard in all regions grew steadily, as
table 6 shows. Stable growth was evident by 1887. In militia returns for that
year, all states except Arkansas and Tennessee reported organized forces.
Overall, the aggregate totaled 97,267. By 1892, all forty-four states and three
of the four territories, Utah excepted, maintained a National Guard of just
over 112,000 men.[20]

It took twenty years following the end of the Civil War for the citizen soldiery to establish itself as a permanent state-supported institution. The rise of
the National Guard in those two decades proceeded irregularly, hindered by
Reconstruction in the South, lingering militia practices and exaggerated ex-
pectations in the Northeast and Midwest, and low population in the Plains and
West regions. By the mid to late 1880s, however, the Guard had taken root everywhere and had assumed the institutional form that would govern it into the
twentieth century.

A regional overview illustrates this conclusion.[21] From 1876 to the end of
the century, the Northeast consistently maintained the largest number of
troops of any of the regions, even though its percentage of the total population
differed little from that of the South and Midwest (see table 2). From 1885 on,
strength in the region remained stable, with no dramatic expansions or reductions (see tables 6 and 7). The Northeast's numerical predominance, although
slowly declining in percentage terms into the 1890s, stemmed from the number of Guardsmen maintained by New York and Pennsylvania, the two largest

Table 7 National Guard Strength, Northeast, Selected Years

	1885	1890	1895
Connecticut	2,324	2,627	2,740
Delaware	302	564	427
Maine	1,225	1,094	1,337
Maryland	1,723	2,036	1,885
Massachusetts	4,145	5,289	5,344
New Hampshire	1,333	1,110	1,380
New Jersey	3,535	4,301	3,938
New York	12,509	13,710	12,901
Pennsylvania	8,477	8,444	8,482
Rhode Island	1,270	1,332	979
Vermont	693	784	800
Aggregate:	37,536	41,291	40,213
Percentage of Population	31	30	29.5
Percentage of National Guard	44	39	35

Sources: Militia Force of the United States, Senate, 49th Cong., 1st sess., 1885, Exec. Doc. 52, and 52d Cong., 2d sess., 1890, Exec. Doc. 48; and MID 1895.

states in the nation. They accounted for 20 to 25 percent of the entire National Guard in any given year. Except for Delaware, other states in the region remained stable or experienced modest growth.

The varying troop levels in the Northeast reflected not only state population but traditional militia practices. New York and Massachusetts had maintained the largest volunteer militia forces in the antebellum years. Conversely, Delaware had demonstrated indifference toward its soldiery since it abolished the obligatory militia in 1816. New England's strong militia tradition was evident in Connecticut, for example, where the state supported 3.7 soldiers per one thousand population, the highest ratio in the region. Pennsylvania broke with its antebellum tradition by maintaining a substantial National Guard after 1870. Overall, the Northeast, Delaware excepted, gave its soldiery stronger financial support than any other region.

National Guard development in the South contrasted sharply with that of the Northeast. Although the population of the thirteen states in the South nearly matched that of the eleven states of the Northeast, Northeasterners supported 2.2 soldiers per thousand population, Southerners only 1.5. The Guard grew slowly in the South as the region struggled to recover from the

Table 8 National Guard Strength, South, Selected Years

	1885	1890	1895
Alabama	1,747	2,954	3,120
Arkansas	0	0	974
Florida	0	996	1,088
Georgia	0	4,041	4,355
Kentucky	1,171	1,316	1,469
Louisiana	1,657	1,665	1,883
Mississippi	0	1,525	1,695
North Carolina	1,107	1,478	1,403
South Carolina	4,561	5,213	5,711
Tennessee	0	0	1,389
Texas	1,851	2,691	3,000
Virginia*	0	2,808	3,006
West Virginia	465	848	845
Aggregate:	12,559	25,535	29,938
Percentage of Population	30	28	29.1
Percentage of National Guard	15	25	26.2

*Virginia failed to send returns to the War Department in 1885 but reported strengths of 2,635 in 1880 and 2,961 in 1887.

Sources: Militia Force of the United States, Senate, 49th Cong., 1st sess., 1885, S. Exec. Doc. 52, and 52d Cong., 2d sess., 1890, S. Exec. Doc. 48; and MID 1895.

Civil War. Its largely rural population and agricultural economy stymied growth as well, for National Guard companies fared best in urban areas. As table 8 indicates, however, the Southern Guard grew steadily after the mid-1880s, more than doubling its strength between 1885 and 1895. Growth came more from states reactivating their military forces following Reconstruction than from an increase in the size of those already established in 1880 or 1885.

Unlike the Northeast, state population was no predictor of the size of a state's force. Kentucky, for example, was the most populous state in the region in 1880 and second only to Texas in 1890, yet it never led the region in organized strength. Divided loyalties during the Civil War dampened postwar interest in military matters. Texas, first in population in 1890, failed to support its soldiers. The Texas Volunteer Guard waxed and waned in strength from the late 1870s well into the next decade. In 1889, the legislature set the

Table 9 National Guard Strength, Midwest, Selected Years

	1885	1890	1895
Illinois	3,839	3,722	6,226
Indiana	3,512	2,166	3,026
Iowa	2,555	2,521	2,398
Michigan	2,335	2,491	2,875
Minnesota	1,426	1,907	2,027
Missouri	1,791	2,161	2,107
Ohio	5,843	5,110	6,493
Wisconsin	2,593	2,659	2,649
Aggregate:	23,894	22,737	27,801
Percentage of Population	32	31	30.4
Percentage of National Guard	28	22	24.3

Sources: Militia Force of the United States, Senate, 49th Cong., 1st sess., 1885, S. Exec. Doc. 52, and 52d Cong., 2d sess., 1890, S. Exec. Doc. 48; and MID 1895.

maximum strength for the Guard at three thousand, a level maintained to the end of the century. Arkansas, Mississippi, Tennessee, and West Virginia, in particular, lagged behind the nation because of a lack of financial support. As will be noted later in this chapter, all maintained modest forces by the mid-1890s only by virtue of an increase in federal assistance to state military forces approved by Congress in 1887.[22]

As mentioned earlier, nine former Confederate states tolerated black Guard units. African-American organizations in the South reflected the lingering power of the Republican party and the desire of Southern politicians to deflect federal attention from the treatment of former slaves. Georgia and South Carolina maintained the largest forces in the South largely because they accepted more black volunteers than others in the region. South Carolina's total strength fell by 40 percent between 1895 and 1896, following the disbandment of most of its black organizations. Georgia also eliminated over one thousand of its African-American Guardsmen in 1895. Both states treated black troops differently than white organizations, segregating African Americans and excluding them from training activities involving white forces.[23]

Ohio and Illinois, the two most populous states in the Midwest, fielded the largest forces in the region. By the early 1890s, they also represented, respectively, the third- and fourth-largest organizations in the nation. Taken together,

Table 10 National Guard Strength, Plains, Selected Years

	1885	1890	1895
Colorado	1,032	780	833
Kansas	1,942	1,859	1,815
Montana	0	677	510
Nebraska	548	1,344	1,137
North Dakota*	1,133	513	525
Oklahoma	0	0	153
South Dakota*	0	493	798
Wyoming	0	243	450
Aggregate:	4,925	5,909	6,221
Percentage of Population	4	6	6.5
Percentage of National Guard	3	6	5.4

*The total for 1885 represents Dakota Territory.

Sources: Militia Force of the United States, Senate, 49th Cong., 1st sess., 1885, S. Exec. Doc. 52, and 52d Cong., 2d sess., 1890, S. Exec. Doc. 48; and MID 1895.

the two regularly accounted for 40 to 45 percent of Guardsmen in the region (see table 9).

Overall, the Midwest exhibited steady growth from 1885 to 1895, adding 3,900 troops during the decade. The region matched the South in organizing between 1.2 and 1.5 Guardsmen per thousand of population. Other than the two dominant states, Guard organizations in the region shared similarities by supporting a soldiery of from 2,000 to 3,000 men. When efforts to re-create an antebellum-style militia in the early to mid-1870s faltered, volunteer soldiers in Iowa, Minnesota, and Wisconsin successfully lobbied their legislatures for funds to support their medium-sized forces. Institutional stability was well under way in the region by the mid-1880s, except in Missouri.[24]

The Plains and West regions may be described together, for they shared common features and problems. At first glance, these two regions appeared to fare well from 1885 to 1895, as tables 10 and 11 show. Over that period, they exhibited a 50 percent increase. Additionally, the regions virtually matched the Northeast in the proportion of soldiers fielded in relation to their population—2.4 per thousand in 1890 and 2.0 per thousand near the end of the decade. Given the general conditions prevailing from the Dakotas and Oklahoma west to the Pacific coast, the growth of the state and territorial soldiery of the regions seems impressive.

Table 11 National Guard Strength, West, Selected Years

	1885	1890	1895
Arizona	0	313	500
California	3,271	4,340	4,364
Idaho	0	308	535
Nevada	487	565	439
New Mexico	1,468	835	470
Oregon	0	1,701	1,530
Utah	0	0	1,003
Washington	428	1,145	1,184
Aggregate:	5,654	9,207	10,025
Percentage of Population	3	4	4.2
Percentage of National Guard	7	9	9

Sources: Militia Force of the United States, Senate, 49th Cong., 1st sess., 1885, S. Exec. Doc. 52, and 52d Cong., 2d sess., 1890, S. Exec. Doc. 48; and MID 1895.

A perusal of tables 10 and 11 shows that the three most populous states in the Plains and West, Kansas, Nebraska, and California, accounted for 50 percent or more of the Guard in 1885 and 1890 and 45 percent in 1895. Exclude Kansas, Nebraska, and California from regional totals and the condition of the National Guard in the Plains and West appears far less successful. Low population, few urban centers, and a faltering economy from the early 1890s on limited National Guard development in these regions. Few states and territories in the Plains and Western regions possessed the population and funds to support an effective soldiery.

Seven states from these regions joined the Union between 1889 and 1896, and the remaining three territories lay within the broader area. All faced grave difficulties in establishing and maintaining effective National Guards. To an extent, they fell victim to the temptation to emulate the older states by creating at least regimental-sized organizations. Few could meet the challenge. For example, Dakota Territory fielded two regiments, with an aggregate of over a thousand in the mid-1880s. The regiments were already floundering when the territory became North and South Dakota. Neither state could sustain the effort. As the 1890 figures in table 10 show, the two states failed to equal the territorial total of five years earlier. Similar troubles prevailed in the new state of Washington and in Utah Territory.[25]

Among the territories, only New Mexico fared well for a time, as the figures for 1885 in table 11 indicate. However, the territory's impressive strength of nearly fifteen hundred in that year dropped to less than five hundred a decade later after territorial governors ceased supporting the organized militia as a *posse comitatus* to suppress banditry. Among the established states, Colorado struggled to keep even a thousand men in effective units, Oregon achieved stability only after 1890, and a historian of the Kansas National Guard remains unimpressed with that state's military efforts throughout the 1890s. Indeed, California was the only state in the two regions to field a soldiery equal in state support and efficiency with the better organizations in the Northeast or Midwest.[26]

For all the vicissitudes and weaknesses of individual systems within the regions and across the nation, the most important aspect of the state soldiery by the mid-1890s was its ubiquity. The War Department's 1895 report on the organized militia indicated that of all the states and territories, only Alaska Territory did not keep up troops. As the region-by-region overview indicates, National Guard strength varied enormously. Nonetheless, the effort begun in the early to mid-1870s to institute a permanent volunteer soldiery backed by state funding eventually succeeded. At the end of the century, the National Guard was firmly established across the nation.

The willingness of states to spend money on their soldiery in the late nineteenth century proved crucial to the rise of the National Guard. Except for Massachusetts, Connecticut, and New York, few had done so prior to 1861. The demands of civil war temporarily broke the state fiscal parsimony that had governed militia affairs since 1783, at least in the North, but many states abandoned the practice for a time after 1865, leaving volunteers to fend for themselves. As long as local units supported themselves, they would remain unstable, conducting their affairs largely as they saw fit and ignoring larger state needs. Twenty years after the war, all but a few states allotted money to their soldiers. Consistent state financial support not only assured unit stability but gave state executives a means for imposing control over the historically independent volunteer companies. Inevitably, as New York Guardsman and reformer George Wingate later commented, "as the states gave more aid to their troops, they felt justified in demanding more and stricter discipline."[27]

State aid contributed to company and regimental continuity largely in the form of armory support. Antebellum volunteer units almost invariably collapsed due to financial insolvency brought on by their inability to pay armory rent or construction costs. No company, battery, or troop could last long without a place to meet, drill, and store equipment. In the years after 1865, state assistance for armories consistently figured large in their total military budgets and continued to do so well into the twentieth century. As had been the case in the antebellum years, units initially rented armory facilities. As the Guard grew, however, Guardsmen sought to acquire their own buildings. Some units raised sufficient funds through private efforts, but most turned to the states for aid.

As Robert Fogelson has shown, the campaign for state assistance in armory support and construction gained its greatest success in New York. Between 1886 and 1900, the state legislature funded the construction of twenty-five armories outside New York City and authorized municipalities within the metropolitan area to pay for twelve regimental armories. Only Massachusetts approached the Empire State in armory support, while some other Northeastern states, Connecticut and Pennsylvania, for example, granted lesser amounts. Most states made modest efforts to house Guard units by providing armory rent support. Some required that cities or counties provide armory facilities. Municipalities often found it cheaper and more convenient to build an armory than to give local units rental funds. Since armories built by cities and counties could serve as general meeting facilities as well as drill halls, municipalities were more willing to fund them. Although it is nearly impossible to determine the combined dollar amount of state and municipal funds provided in the late nineteenth century to rent, build, and equip National Guard armories, state and local armory support was nonetheless the single greatest public aid given to the Guard.[28]

For many Guard leaders, the most essential need for state support, beyond armory assistance, was money to send Guardsmen to summer camp. An annual encampment met a number of needs. The opportunity for a week in camp provided a recruiting tool and a ready escape from the often dull armory routine of the manual of arms and close order drill. Above all, camps offered the only opportunity to bring otherwise isolated local units under direct state supervision. Annual training gave regimental and brigade officers a chance to exercise command and put their men through tactical exercises. More important, camps tested company efficiency and its ability to muster the required number of men. State inspectors reviewed the military knowledge of unit officers, inspected arms and equipment, and oversaw the company's facility at drill, guard duty, and the manual of arms.

Only Massachusetts and Connecticut regularly mustered their volunteers for annual training and inspection in the antebellum years. Until the early

1880s, few states provided the funds to bring the Guard into camp each year. Efforts to hold camps without state assistance nearly always foundered. From the early 1880s, however, states increasingly sponsored yearly encampments, paying the larger part of the costs, especially transportation and subsistence, and in some instances giving the men a modest stipend. Camp expenses accounted for an equal or greater portion of total yearly spending than armory assistance.

Finally, state money assisted companies in providing Guardsmen with a basic uniform and other personal equipment, such as haversacks, overcoats, web belts, and other small items. Wealthier states made special appropriations to equip their soldiers. As one example, in 1893 New York allotted $100,000 beyond the usual Guard appropriation for this purpose. Aid to units varied considerably from state to state, according to their annual spending. Some gave each company a yearly uniform maintenance allotment and a small sum to cover administrative expenses of company commanders and regimental adjutants. In other cases, state support to companies fell well short of being adequate. Delaware tendered a mere $197 a year to each of its six companies in the mid-1880s to cover all unit expenses. In poorer states, Guardsmen continued to purchase their own uniforms into the 1890s.[29]

As had been the case during the antebellum years, states acquired rifles, artillery, and weapons accoutrements from the annual federal distribution of arms originally approved in 1808. Through the lobbying efforts of the National Guard Association (NGA), founded in 1879, Congress doubled the dollar amount of the distribution to $400,000 in 1887 and permitted states to draw their allotments in the form of clothing and camp equipment as well as arms. Other than the annual arms distribution, the federal government gave little attention to state military affairs. Some agencies in the War Department, especially the Army's office of the adjutant general, established informal relations with the Guard. Neither federal law nor War Department practice, however, attempted to coordinate state military efforts with national needs.

For many forces, the federal allotment merely supplemented state assistance, but for others the annual distribution proved fundamental to their existence. By the late 1880s, nearly all states assisted their soldiery, although a House of Representatives report in 1891 indicated that five of the forty-four states had no military budgets (Arkansas, Idaho, Mississippi, Missouri, and Wyoming). The regional distribution of state spending illustrates yet again the difficulties of making generalizations about the National Guard (see table 12).[30] Population and wealth, of course, greatly determined how much a

Table 12 Aggregate State Spending, by Region, Selected Years

Region	Spending (percentage of national total)		
	1891	1895	1897
Northeast	$1,358,046	$1,479,766	$1,524,401
	(58.0%)	(55.0%)	(56.0%)
South	145,300	116,013	253,400
	(6.0%)	(4.0%)	(9.4%)
Midwest	474,617	735,201	617,364
	(20.0%)	(27.0%)	(23.0%)
Plains	96,350	116,808	89,050
	(4.0%)	(4.0%)	(3.3%)
West	264,773	233,475*	218,174
	(11.0%)	(9.0%)	(8.0%)
Aggregate:	2,339,086	2,681,263	2,702,389

Sources: U.S. House, Committee on the Militia, 52d Cong., 1st sess., 1891, H. Rept. 754; MID 1895, 4–5; MID 1897, 4–5.

given state appropriated for military affairs. So too did historical practice, however. Antebellum Connecticut, Massachusetts, and New York led the nation in supporting their uniformed militia, and the same states stood out after 1865. Moreover, the Northeasterners who settled in Wisconsin, California, and other frontier states carried that tradition with them. On the other hand, with their history of curtailing state governmental activity, Southern states were much more reluctant to assist their soldiers.

Although aggregate spending in any given year suggests that states supported their soldiery adequately, closer scrutiny belies such a conclusion. The Northeast led military spending throughout the postwar years. In 1884, New York appropriated $825,000, which exceeded the federal allotment (then only $200,000 annually) by a factor of four. Citing 1895 as a sample year, five of the eleven states in the Northeast (Connecticut, Massachusetts, New York, Pennsylvania, and Rhode Island) accounted for 50 percent of all state funding. For 1895, nine states appropriated over $100,000 and represented 75 percent of total state spending. Appropriations for the year ranged from no money allocated in Arkansas to New York's $430,000. Similar patterns prevailed throughout the 1890s.[31]

State spending often reflected not only the number of troops each entity fielded but also state population and total wealth. There were exceptions, however: states with smaller populations and Guard strength, such as Connecticut and Wisconsin, still broke the $100,000 level in 1895. Missouri, on the other hand, ranked as the fifth most populous state yet gave its Guardsmen only $10,000 yearly throughout the 1890s.

Regional disparities stand out starkly. Using 1895 again as an example, eight of the nine states allocating over $100,000 in the year exceeded the amount the Southern states expended collectively. In 1895, Northeastern states provided an average of $36.79 per soldier and Midwestern states $26.45 in 1895. The South stood second in the total number of Guardsmen yet appropriated only $3.87 per soldier. Guardsmen fared somewhat better on average in the Plains and West, the regions allocating $18.77 and $21.76 per man, respectively. West of the Rocky Mountains, California accounted for 75 percent of the region's military expenditures, with $40.39 per Guardsman. With California's budget excluded, however, the regional average fell to $10.10 a man.[32]

Compared to the antebellum and immediate post–Civil War years, combined state support during the last two decades of the nineteenth century remained significant despite the many disparities. Yet for all that effort, state military spending fell short in supporting a viable volunteer soldiery. In lamenting his commonwealth's failure to assist its volunteers adequately, Virginia's adjutant general estimated in 1892 that it would cost $48.35 a year per man to equip and sustain an infantry soldier. Cavalry and artillery men required even more money. Virginia allotted only $3.35 each year for its soldiers, and few states approached the $48.00 figure.[33] In 1895, state appropriations collectively allotted only $23.17 per Guardsman, but, as noted earlier, these funds were not distributed equally across the nation or within regions. Among the nine states providing more than $100,000, only Connecticut exceeded the $48.00 ideal.[34]

Given the inadequacy of support in some states, Guard forces often depended upon the annual federal distribution to sustain their organizations. Modest as it was, the $400,000 in arms, clothing, and equipment the War Department sent to the states after 1887 allowed systems on the verge of collapse, especially in the South, to establish a Guard for the first time. Laps D. McCord, adjutant general of Tennessee, reported in

1888 that during his first two years in office "there has not been a cent
. . . available for any purpose."[35] After Congress increased federal aid
in 1887, the legislature approved a law organizing the Tennessee National Guard, but McCord's men depended wholly on the federal distribution. Ten years later, ten states—eight from the South, and one each
from the Plains and West regions—received military equipment from
the War Department that exceeded in value their total state allocations.

Federal aid might have assisted the most destitute states and territories more adequately, but federal law distributed the allotments according to the size of each state's congressional delegation. By this method,
states receiving the largest amounts of federal aid, with some exceptions such as Missouri, needed it the least. In 1895, for example, New
York led the list with $33,171 while states with the lowest population—
and hence the smallest congressional delegations—together with all
the territories, collected only $2,764 each.[36]

Pleas from adjutants general and National Guard officers failed to
move state legislatures for additional funding. Colorado law, for example, levied a poll tax on all militarily obligated men: fifty cents a year to
1881, one dollar annually thereafter. The tax constituted the military
fund for the state. Unfortunately, as Colorado's adjutant general complained, the law was "feebly enforced."[37] At best, the tax produced
$30,000 a year, a sum insufficient to lift the Colorado Guard out of in-
efficiency. Throughout the remaining years of the century, requests to
change how the Guard was funded failed to move the legislature. In
many instances, state legislators left military budgets unchanged for
years, regardless of National Guard needs. North Dakota appropriated
$11,000 per year from 1891 through the end of the Spanish-American
War. Alabama's adjutant general complained in 1894 that despite great
efforts to control costs, his soldiers had exceeded their allotment for
state camps four years in a row. Private subscriptions and the contributions of Alabama Guardsmen made up the difference, which in 1894
alone amounted to $4,000. Requests for more camp money, and a sal-
ary for the adjutant general, went unanswered.[38]

The advent of state support broke precedent and engendered a permanent state soldiery in the two decades after the Civil War. With few
exceptions, however, the growth of state and local support, and the
twofold increase in federal assistance, was inadequate for underwriting
an efficient National Guard. Morton Keller's study of late-nineteenth-

century governmental practice concludes that "state spending did not keep pace with economic or population growth." When compared with federal and local government fiscal policy, Keller observes, "the states were a relatively minor source of expenditure."[39] As a result, the Guard suffered from government's reluctance to expend substantial sums on any state institution, not just the organized militia.

3

The National Guard and

Civil Disorder, 1866–1899

Historical opinion identifies the 1877 railroad disorders as the crucial event that led state legislatures to aid the National Guard. Although the upheavals of that year influenced many states to enact reform, the impact of the railroad riots did not revolutionize the militia across the nation. Their most lasting impact was to give adjutants general and other Guard supporters a pretext for requesting state funding by presenting the organized militia as a defense against future social disorder. Some state legislatures responded to the appeal, but others waited until their own commonwealths actually confronted a major civil disturbance. Throughout its history, the National Guard's role as a constabulary force and the advent of state financial aid have been closely connected. The connection between the 1877 disorders and the state soldiery's improved fiscal position two decades later is an indirect one, however, not a demonstrable one of cause and effect.

William H. Riker was the first to argue that the National Guard garnered state aid by serving as industrial policemen from 1877 on. Riker, however, ignores the use of antebellum uniformed militia to control civil disorder. For example, New York City's Seventh Regiment, the most publicized National Guard organization in the late nineteenth century, served in thirteen civic upheavals between 1825 and 1863, but only three times from 1871 to 1898. Antebellum volunteers from Massachusetts and Pennsylvania to Wisconsin and California turned out to suppress urban mobs. Moreover, state troops intervened in labor troubles prior to the 1877 railroad strikes. Pennsylvania's National Guard, the centerpiece of the thesis of state soldiery as "industrial policeman," intervened in coal strikes four times between 1871 and 1875. The only instance in which the Massachusetts Volunteer Militia intervened in a labor dispute for the entire post–Civil War period occurred in 1875.[1]

Although quelling civil disorder played an important part in the rise of the National Guard, it is erroneous to treat the post–Civil War state soldiery as a single entity. To do so distorts both the mixed history of the Guard and the part it played in suppressing a variety of civil upheavals. How the National Guard dealt with riots, strikes, lynchings, political turmoil, and social disorder varied from state to state and region to region. Significantly, the amount of financial support a state force received did not directly reflect the services it rendered to civil authorities whether in strikebreaking or in other domestic disturbances. The importance of civil disorder service to the development of the National Guard is best understood by reviewing constabulary duty generally, then examining regional experiences more specifically.

It is difficult to determine the frequency and type of Guard interventions in civil disorders in the late nineteenth century. A few sources contain collected data sufficient to form a qualified overview, however. Adjutants general reports and secondary works add substance and detail to the broad picture. The general sources refer only to incidents state governments reported, many of which were described in vague terms or were incomplete. Just as problematical are the terms the general sources use to describe the causes of Guard intervention. More often they use vague phrases such as "to quell a riot" or "to preserve order." As a result, the categories are defined broadly and require analysis and commentary.[2]

Scrutiny of the general sources reveals, first, that a significant minority of state forces performed little or no civil disorder service after 1877. Twelve never served in any kind of civil disorder, and another seven did not take part in labor-related troubles. Nineteen of the forty-four states thus had no strikebreaking record. In addition, another five fielded their troops to confront strikers only once in the years following the great railroad upheaval. Many states escaped industrial policing because there were few workers to police, particularly in the Plains region and in much of the West. Southern states only infrequently used their troops in labor disorders. In any case, the assertion that *the* National Guard served primarily to break strikes cannot be sustained. Neither can it be argued that large state budgets purchased an industrial constabulary. In 1891, for example, ten states supported their troops with budgets of one hundred thousand dollars or more. Three of them—Connecticut, Massachusetts, and New Jersey—did not perform strike duty after 1877, and one, California, turned out only once.[3]

States relied on their soldiers for a variety of constabulary functions. One of the best known uses of the modern National Guard is to aid civil authorities during and after natural or man-made disasters. State soldiers served infrequently in this capacity in the late nineteenth century, only twenty-five times between 1886 and 1895, for example. States with well-identified strikebreaking records provided disaster relief occasionally. Pennsylvania's Fourteenth Infantry Regiment served throughout June 1889 after the disastrous Johnstown Flood, and elements of four New York City regiments enforced a cholera quarantine on Fire Island during September 1892.[4]

Guardsmen served in other ways to help civil officials maintain order. Throughout the 1880s, for example, detachments of the Kentucky State Guard mobilized to quell vigilantism and factionalism in the state's eastern counties. Governors Lew Wallace and Lionel Sheldon of New Mexico Territory organized and deployed volunteer companies in the early 1880s to break up organized bands of cattle rustlers and robbers closely allied with local law enforcement officers. In the Pacific Northwest, Oregon and Washington officials faced a unique problem in 1896 when fishermen working the Columbia River from both states engaged in a dispute over fishing rights and prices, which led armed men from both sides to cross state lines to compel their opponents to stop fishing. Guardsmen from Oregon mobilized for six days to keep Washington fishermen out of their state; Washington kept a forty-five-man detachment on duty for nearly three months before the dispute ended.[5]

From the mid-1870s to the late 1890s, Southern states used their troops to aid civil authority more frequently than all other regions combined. Virginia, with at least seventy-four instances, and Texas, with over fifty cases, led the nation in mobilizing volunteers. The majority of interventions involved racial conflicts. All told, the following categories in table 13, "Aiding civil authorities," "Protecting prisoners," "Quelling riots," and clearly identified "Policing racial incidents" total two hundred fifty-eight. Bruce Olson estimates that at least one-third of all interventions by the Texas Volunteer Guard involved racial affairs, largely white assaults against blacks. Other Southern states joined Texas and Virginia in their frequent use of soldiers to quell race-related disorders. Some of these instances were political in nature, but the vast majority involved efforts to prevent white mobs from lynching African-American men.[6]

Table 13 National Guard Interventions in Civil Disorders, by Category, 1868–1899

Suppressing election disorders	20
Aiding civil authorities	80
Protecting prisoners	106
Policing racial incidents	31
Quelling riots, cause unlisted	41
Suppressing labor-related incidents	118
Handling Indian difficulties	15
Total:	411

Sources: U.S. House, Committee on the Militia, 52d Cong., 1st sess., 1891, H. Rept. 754, 16–20, for 1868 through 1885; Major Winthrop Alexander, District of Columbia National Guard, "Ten Years of Riot Duty," *JMSI* 19 (July 1896), 1–26, for 1886 through 1895; Report AWC 9744-C, "Duty Performed by the Organized Militia in Connection with Domestic Disturbances from 1894 to 1908, Inclusive," RG165, for 1896 through 1899.

Although not exclusively confined to the South, racial lynchings were nonetheless largely a Southern phenomenon. From 1889 through 1918, over thirty-two hundred men were hanged by mob rule. Nearly 90 percent of the lynchings took place in the South, and almost 80 percent of those lynched were African American. Control of mob violence belonged to local law officials, and if they made little effort to halt lynchings, state leaders often acted hesitantly as well. Leaders at both levels could respond quickly when white prisoners were threatened, as an 1882 incident in Kentucky suggests. Studies of Georgia, Kentucky, Texas, and Virginia make clear that concerted gubernatorial efforts could control, if not stop, illegal hangings of black men. Leaders from the last three states feared that if they tolerated lynchings then law and order generally would decline rapidly. That Texas and Virginia governors made the most serious efforts to prevent black prisoners from being lynched largely explains why those two states led the nation in using troops to aid civil authorities.[7]

State intervention to prevent lynchings usually required that a company only be on duty for a day or two. The service performed by the First Battalion, Florida State Troops, in Jacksonville on 1 March 1890, was typical. Fearing the lynching of a black man charged with shooting a white policeman, the mayor called out the battalion. The unit commander assembled his men in their armories, held them until midnight, and then posted men to guard armory arsenals, sending the rest home when the crisis passed. Two Texas companies, totaling sixty men, served for three days at Sherman, Texas, in April 1892 to prevent the lynching of an alleged black rapist. Virginia's adjutant general reported in 1890 that individual companies served five times during that year to protect black prisoners. "In none of these cases," he reported, "was there an actual attempt made to carry into execution the suspected or rumored purpose."[8] Much too often, however, troops arrived too late to prevent mob action, either because local officials delayed in requesting troops or because the deed was done before units arrived at the scene.[9]

Occasionally, the defense of a black prisoner became ugly and bloody. Company G, Second Regiment, Virginia Volunteers (the Roanoke Light Infantry), reported to protect an alleged black murderer of a white woman at the Roanoke jail in September 1893. The company confronted "a large assemblage of infuriated men," according to Virginia's adjutant general. The mob refused to disperse, attacked the jail, and forced militiamen to fire, killing eight men and wounding twenty others. Tragically, while the Light Infantry's initial efforts saved the accused murderer, a mob caught and hanged the man the next day, the bloody battle at the jail having left the company too demoralized to stop the second attempt.[10]

Given that lynching was largely confined to the South and openly identified with racial suppression, it is ironic that the most destructive lynch riot occurred north of the Ohio River, in Cincinnati in March 1884. Resenting entrenched political corruption and its own exclusion from the political process, an incensed crowd of laboring men assaulted the county jail and courthouse to lynch a murderer given a moderate sentence. When the city's First Regiment failed to prevent the destruction of the jail and courthouse, Governor George Hoadly belatedly sent other units to Cincinnati. The first to arrive, the Fourth Regiment from Dayton, failed to relieve besieged police and Guardsmen at the ruined courthouse. Only after units from Columbus and other cities reached Cincinnati did the Guard rescue the weary courthouse defenders. With three thousand troops in town, city officials and the Guard restored order. Nearly fifty lay dead, including two soldiers, and some two hundred wounded, among whom were forty Guardsmen.[11]

The Cincinnati riot was extraordinary. Only industrial disorders caused as much property destruction and loss of life and demanded so much of the state soldiery. Unlike the Cincinnati affair, the majority of interventions listed in

table 13 and summarized in the preceding paragraphs involved a small number of troops, little loss of life, and at most a few days of active duty. In these
forays Guardsmen experienced more discomfort, perplexity, and fatigue than
mob violence. To say so, however, is not to demean the service Guardsmen
rendered. The tragedy in the South was that states too seldom used their military forces to stop lynchings. When troops were committed it became evident
that even a single company willing to do its duty could stem racially moti-
vated lynchings.[12]

Although less frequent than lynching episodes, National Guard interventions in labor-related disturbances were of a different magnitude altogether.
The states with the highest number of strike interventions were in the indus-
trialized Northeast and Midwest. Illinois led the list with fifteen interventions
between 1877 and 1899, nine in its always tumultuous coal mining region.
Ohio with eight and New York with six came next. For all the attention historians have given to Pennsylvania, Keystone State soldiers carried out only
five strike interventions during the 1870s and mobilized only four times for
similar duty after 1877. Outside these four states, strike duty was an uncom-
mon experience for the state soldiery. Moreover, as seen clearly in Illinois
and Ohio, frequent service in labor disorders did not automatically bring generous legislative support. Neither of these states fared well financially, particularly when contrasted with such well-funded states as Connecticut and Massachusetts, which performed no strike duty after 1877.[13]

State soldiers had intervened in strikes prior to 1877, but the great railroad
disorders rattled the nation more than any event since the firing on Fort Sumter. One commentator explicitly compared the two, noting that the "Southern
cyclone of '61 and the tornado of '77" each found the nation without "an anchor with which to outride the storm."[14] Most observers identified the state
soldiery as the anchor that failed insofar as Guardsmen nearly everywhere
proved ineffective in suppressing disorder. Fifteen states mobilized or organized forces to quell disorder in 1877. Eleven states maintained units sufficiently organized to answer the call, although Maryland's volunteer units collapsed, forcing the state to organize two emergency regiments composed of
Civil War veterans. The few existing volunteer companies in Iowa, Indiana,
Missouri, and West Virginia also collapsed in the face of disorder. New York
and California mobilized large numbers of Guardsmen that in the end did not
confront strikers. The failure in West Virginia led to the commitment of federal troops there. Regulars also eventually served in Pennsylvania, Maryland, Indiana, Illinois, and Missouri. The Guard lacked the basic attributes of

military effectiveness to quell disorder in 1877. Mobilization plans, centralized command and control, logistical support, tactical training, and discipline were all absent. Political and military leaders found it particularly disturbing that some Guardsmen openly sympathized with strikers and either
refused to use force or simply left the scene, especially in West Virginia and
Pennsylvania. A few even joined the railroad workers.[15]

The legacy of 1877 moved many state legislatures to do something they
had refused to do in the past, namely, provide substantive monetary support
to place their soldiers on a permanent footing. Pennsylvania led the way. In
1878, the legislature completely reorganized the National Guard, increased
its annual budget to $200,000, reduced its strength, and eliminated nine of its
ten divisions. Ineffective regiments were disbanded or reorganized and new
ones formed. Two years later, another major law established a tactical division and reduced the number of brigades from five to three.[16]

Increased appropriations came in 1887 when the legislature allotted
$300,000 annually and added another $20,000 in 1892. From the early 1880s
to the end of the century, aggregate strength averaged eighty-five hundred to
nine thousand men as increases in state aid went to improve the existing
force, not to enlarge it. By the late 1880s, 55 percent of the Guard's 136 companies were located in the five counties that encompassed the major industrial
facilities around Pittsburgh, the eastern coalfields, and the city of Philadelphia. The Pennsylvania Guard became known throughout the nation as a
no-nonsense outfit trained and equipped for field service. Lieutenant A. R.
Paxton, Fifteenth Infantry, U.S. Army inspector, was impressed by the Keystone Guard's ability "to mobilize and concentrate with rapidity and ease
when unexpectedly called out," adding that "regular troops might well be
proud of it."[17] The Pennsylvania Guard was more firmly under tactical and
administrative control and better prepared for mobilization than any other
state force.[18]

No other commonwealth reformed its militia to cope with civil upheaval
in the aftermath of 1877 as thoroughly as Pennsylvania. The Pennsylvania
Guard fared better at the hands of its legislative appropriations committees
and shared closer ties with the corporate elite than most other forces. Businessmen, lawyers, editors, corporate leaders, and prominent Republicans
dominated the Keystone State officer corps more thoroughly than in any other
state, as demonstrated by Scranton's Thirteenth Infantry. Organized by busi-
nessman Henry M. Boies in the fall of 1877, the regiment contained the "elite
of the community," its historian boasted.[19] Within a year of its founding, the

Thirteenth owned an armory paid for largely by Boies and other Scranton businessmen and industrialists.[20]

Elsewhere, the Illinois National Guard probably benefitted the most from the railroad disorders. The state's volunteers were undergoing reorganization after years of neglect when the strike hit Chicago. Although poorly organized and equipped, the Chicago regiments performed creditably in 1877. In the next two years, administrative changes and a new militia law that for the first time provided substantive state support solidified the Illinois Guard. As in Pennsylvania, businessmen and industrialists provided funds through the Chicago Citizen's Association to support the city's First and Second Regiments as well as a full cavalry battalion. The association claimed it gave $100,000 to Guard units in Chicago between 1874 and 1883.[21]

New York fielded nearly twenty thousand soldiers in 1877. Although its militia did not encounter the violence Pennsylvania Guardsmen faced, its unwieldy soldiery proved highly inefficient. The Empire State revamped its Guard substantially in the ensuing three years, reducing the force from twenty thousand to twelve thousand, increasing state appropriations, and imposing stricter standards on the remaining units. For all the changes, and despite the state's large military budget, the New York Guard never achieved the efficiency or centralized command established by Pennsylvania. The state's antebellum militia tradition, with its emphasis on fancy dress uniforms and socially elite units, worked against the establishment of a tightly controlled military organization. Despite its size, the New York Guard did not adopt a divisional command system and maintained some infantry companies that were not even attached to a battalion, hindering effective mobilization.[22]

Militia reform proceeded less dramatically elsewhere. Although Kentucky escaped disorder during the strike, a short-lived walk off of railroad workers in Louisville provoked a new militia law in 1878. The reform was a limited one, however, establishing a force of 1,280 men that remained inadequately funded into the 1890s. Iowa also reanimated its military system in response to the upheaval, but both the Guard and its budget failed to match those maintained in nearby Illinois and Wisconsin. In states where the militia did little more than report to armories and stand in readiness, changes appeared unnecessary. The success of California troops in suppressing disorder in San Francisco negated major reform there.[23]

Some states needed either to improve demonstrably weak units or create a force for the first time. Efforts in Maryland to revive an ineffective militia and in Indiana to establish a new force bore moderate results at best. Ohio's volunteers in 1877 had no organization higher than the company. Although increased state support and the creation of regiments led to some immediate improvement, the Guard's performance at Cincinnati in 1884 indicated Buckeye State volunteers remained ill prepared for riot duty. Finally, although legislatures in Missouri and West Virginia quickly authorized enlarged state forces in 1878, neither provided sufficient funds to sustain them.[24]

Other forces underwent reorganization and expanded funding following strike interventions that occurred after 1877. Nebraska's Guard gained new life in the aftermath of strikes in 1879 and 1880. An 1881 law placed the force on a modest permanent footing, providing $5,000 a year to support two thousand men. Ronald Gephart concludes that the Guard's officer corps, composed largely of "important figures" from small towns, had little interest in protecting "the property of the vested interest groups in Omaha."[25] Calamity in Cincinnati at last compelled the Ohio legislature to reorganize the Buckeye State Guard and increase its support. Success in suppressing the riots surrounding a strike in Milwaukee in 1886 solidified the future of the Wisconsin National Guard. Before the intervention, Badger State soldiers had struggled to win full support from the legislature and Governor Jeremiah Rusk. Its sound performance in Milwaukee gained their favor, however, and by the mid-1890s the Wisconsin Guard claimed an annual budget of over $100,000.[26]

Guard leaders sought to capitalize on the fears provoked by the railroad disturbances even when civil peace reigned in their own jurisdictions. The adjutant general of Massachusetts cited "the troubles of last summer" in his 1877 report, suggesting that the Bay State avoided difficulty because of the well-known efficiency of its militia.[27] Noting several labor conflicts in 1886, the adjutant general of Delaware argued that "it would seem that the logic of recent events in some of our sister states" required an improvement of his force "to meet any temporary emergency that might arise."[28] In 1892 the adjutant general of Virginia stressed that the citizen soldiery "signally demonstrated" what a "necessary adjunct they are to the civil power, notably in Pennsylvania, New York, and Tennessee."[29]

Guard leaders recognized that legislators were unlikely to fund the state soldiery for other purposes and invariably emphasized constabulary service when requesting increased financial support. Major Samuel C. Mower of the Wisconsin National Guard underscored the need for a "well-organized military force" to "prevent or circumvent the mob" in a speech entitled "A Plea for the Proper Support of State Troops."[30] Following extensive service during a coal strike in 1894, Alabama's adjutant general took care to note that "state troops are not as some are pleased to term them an 'ornament,' but an absolute necessity."[31] As mentioned earlier, however, appeals for larger military budgets in the name of preserving civil peace failed more often than not. The railroad upheaval of 1877 highlighted the need for state constabulary forces. It led most states to revise their militia laws and encouraged many to increase their military spending. With the exception of California and a few states in the Northeast and Midwest, however, most Guard forces remained woefully underfunded and militarily inefficient until the end of the nineteenth century. This was particularly true in the South. Although Southern soldiers turned out for peacekeeping duty more frequently than anywhere else, the region lagged in annual per-soldier spending.

If a majority of states refused to finance their troops in the name of constabulary duty, a greater number neglected to train them specifically for riot service. Guard and Army officers produced a plethora of riot duty tactical manuals, especially during the 1880s, that were aimed at instructing Guardsmen on the intricacies of urban riot suppression. The manuals outlined tactics so detailed and intricate in execution that they were of limited value to part-time Guardsmen. Indeed, the Guard seldom trained for riot duty. Comments from state inspectors general and Regular Army officers make clear that the limited instruction given to Guardsmen involved ordinary drill in armories and simple field exercises at camp. The annual surveys of the Army's Military Information Division (MID) on the organized militia included general observations and specific commentary on state training under the category "Drills and Ceremonies." General remarks in 1893, for example, noted that close order drill and the manual of arms constituted armory work. In camp, "most commands devote all possible time to military duties," including company close order drill, regimental skirmish drill, and sometimes brigade or divisional maneuvers.[32]

There were exceptions to the general neglect. Lecturers occasionally discussed riot tactics at state and national NGA meetings, and state leaders sometimes dealt with the topic at training sessions. Adjutant general Charles R. Boardman required his officers to write plans "supposing a riot in progress" in their home cities during the 1897 Wisconsin Guard officer's school. Boardman set the problem because an Army inspector named Lieutenant William L. Buck had criticized Wisconsin officers for their lack of knowledge about leaving an armory under riot conditions.[33] The efforts of the Texas Volunteer Guard to learn riot tactics under the tutelage of Army Captain J. T. Haskell at its 1891 summer camp earned scorn from the San Antonio *Daily Light*. Mocking the exercise, the *Daily Light* reported that "Austin had her riot quelling circus yesterday, to the delight of the street arabs."[34]

Only a few states prepared "well-developed plans for concentrating and supplying troops in case of emergency," according to an 1893 MID report. Although Pennsylvania had no set plan, the report noted that "staff officers and railroads thoroughly understand what is needed."[35] The 1895 MID report observed that New York had "no plans for emergency," but Ohio designated certain cities as concentration points because they were "in the center of districts with great manufacturing and commercial interests." Buckeye State officers also developed plans to notify their men in emergencies and maintained equipment at their armories "in a constant state of preparation for hasty movement."[36] Given that the Guard's first function was the suppression of civil disorder, the fact that few states prepared even rudimentary mobilization plans appears remarkable.

Although the business community supported the Guard's work as a constabulary, many employers found it difficult to take their eyes off their ledger books when dealing with individual Guardsmen. In 1877, the *National Guardsman*, a short-lived New York City weekly, damned employers "who were base enough to discharge their employees for attending to the call of military duty during the strikes."[37] Labor journals highlighted similar incidents in 1894 when employers fired workers who served with the Guard during the Pullman and coal mine strikes. In Ohio, the *Railroad Trainmen's Journal* reported that Guardsmen "were notified in advance by their employers" not to report for duty "under penalty of discharge."[38] Oregon Guardsmen faced the same difficulty during the fishing dispute along the Columbia River in 1896. Captain A. J. Coffee, Company I, First Regiment, complained that some employers punished their Guard employees monetarily. Coffee wrote angrily to his regimental commander that "if possible shame should be brought to these *unpatriotic citizens* of the U.S. who unrightfully call themselves '*Americans*' " (emphasis in original).[39]

Employers were even more reluctant to release employees for summer training, either refusing to grant time off to Guardsmen entirely or demanding that workers provide a substitute while at camp. According to an Army inspection report on the poor turnout for camp of the Emmett Light Artillery of the Minnesota National Guard in the summer of 1883, "many of them were threatened with discharge by their employers in case they persisted in going to camp."[40] The Army officer inspecting the Wisconsin National Guard in 189 reported that Milwaukee's Fourth Battalion brought less than 60 percent of its members to camp due to "the greed and selfishness of the employer[s]."[41] States did little to assist the Guard in the matter, and Guardsmen came to resent the Scrooge-like attitude of employers, as expressed by Wisconsin Guardsman Joseph B. Doe: "let the fire bell ring, let the riot alarm be sounded, let the necessity for soldiers develop itself, and who is the first man that calls upon the government for aid? Why it is the gentleman down there on Water Street who would not allow his employee to go to camp . . . last summer."[42]

Guardsmen lacked the means to alter employer behavior other than by persuasion. They had even less control over when, where, or why they were committed to quelling civil disorder. Laws varied from state to state. Many permitted municipal and county officials to order out local units when their law enforcement agencies failed to end civil disorder. Massachusetts, New York, and Ohio, for example, gave this power to local officials, but it was most common in the South. Mayors and sheriffs frequently called for the Guard when facing disasters or lynch mobs. State laws intended that local officials call for militia only when their normal forces could not quell disorder. Too often, city and county leaders turned to the Guard immediately to avoid the monetary or political costs of suppressing their disorderly constituents.[43]

Serious difficulties arose when a sheriff or mayor called the Guard to intervene in strike disorders. In labor difficulties, local leaders were likely to be aligned with either employers or strikers and eager to involve state power in the conflict. Washington territorial law, for example, left unclear whether it referred to the traditional *posse comitatus* or the organized militia when it authorized sheriffs to call for armed assistance in quelling violence. In 1889 and 1891, county sheriffs and coal mine operators collaborated with Colonel John C. Haines, commander of the First Regiment, but also attorney for a mining firm, to break strikes at Newcastle and throughout King County. Both Governors Eugene Semple and Elisha P. Ferry found it difficult to end Haines's blatant use of the Guard to break the strikes. A ruling by Washington's attorney general in July 1891 confirmed that state law did not intend the Guard to serve as a *posse comitatus* and could be used for civil disorder only upon the governor's orders. Despite their protests, Illinois Guardsmen were regularly sent to assist sheriffs and mayors clearly allied with coal mine operators.[44]

In most states, in their function as commanders in chief of the militia, governors faced the decision to use troops to quell strike disorders. They were not necessarily the compliant tools of industry. Many learned after 1877 that automatically sending in the Guard provoked protest from either offended constituents at the strike scene or budget-minded legislators. Governor Ferry of Washington, for example, was condemned by strikers and their political allies for failing to rein in Colonel Haines in 1891. Guardsmen damned Ferry as well when he refused to approve state pay for the strike intervention. Ferry argued that King County bore the responsibility. County officials refused to appropriate the funds. Guardsmen sued the state and won their case before the state supreme court late in 1891.[45]

Governors politically wiser than Ferry took care to ascertain the necessity of armed intervention or to supervise the actions of the Guard. Ohio's governor, Thomas Young, and his adjutant general went to the railroad center of Newark during the 1877 disorders, first to determine the necessity of sending in troops, then to oversee directly how soldiers were used. Increasingly, cautious governors sought independent information on strike conditions before committing troops. Many dispatched trusted Guard officers to survey the situation because local officials and employers facing strikes often exaggerated violence or even called for troops before violence broke out. At the order of Governor William Lord, in 1896 Brigadier General Charles E. Beebe of the Oregon National Guard sent two majors to investigate the fishing conflict along the Columbia River. The two men reported that the sheriff "has made no attempt whatever to preserve the peace" because Columbia County was deeply in debt and did not want to incur the expenses of raising a *posse comitatus*. They recommended to General Beebe that troops not be sent.[46]

General political conditions affected gubernatorial decisions to commit troops as much as the special pleading of business leaders. In states where neither major political party dominated, chief executives moved cautiously. In New York, Republican as well as Democratic governors hesitated to call out the Guard for strike duty because party power was so closely balanced. Democratic Governor Robert E. Pattison faced a dilemma when asked to send troops to Homestead, Pennsylvania, in 1892. Elected with strong labor support, especially from Allegheny County, Pattison resisted the pleas of County Sheriff William H. McCleary and pressure from Carnegie Steel Company executives and state Republican leaders for four days before sending the Guard to Homestead.[47]

Local sympathies and pressures also affected Guardsmen. John F. Hartranft, governor of Pennsylvania, observed of his soldiers' frequent fraternization with strikers in 1877 that "a citizen soldiery must always be more or less affected by the sympathies of the community in which they live."[48] Guardsmen, Hartranft argued, could hardly be expected to remain unaffected by citizens' values. Displays of sympathy for strikers by Guardsmen occurred most frequently in 1877 but always remained a possibility, especially in the enlisted ranks. The issue reappeared during the 1894 Pullman Strike, particularly in California when units from San Francisco and Sacramento refused to use force to push strikers out of rail yards at Sacramento and Oakland. At the same time, some Guardsmen of Washington's Second Infantry Regiment refused to ride trains manned by strikebreakers when the unit left summer camp to return to home station. The state disbanded Company G of the Second and discharged other officers and men from the regiment for "mutiny." Even the socially prestigious Twenty-second Regiment of the National Guard of New York questioned mobilization of the Guard for a trolley strike in Brooklyn in 1895 and expressed sympathy for the strikers. According to Colonel George Wingate, "the general feeling of the National Guardsmen who served in the Brooklyn strike was not kindly toward the trolley companies."[49]

Regardless of the complexities governors faced in committing state troops to quell labor upheavals or the ambivalent feelings Guardsmen carried with them to the strike scene, the state soldiery came to be seen above all as an industrial constabulary. The Guard gained this reputation in part because its more ardent advocates focused almost exclusively on organized labor and its immigrant members as the sole fomenters of disorder. The *National Guardsman* detected a "volcano of Communism" emerging in 1877.[50] In the mid-1880s, Major General Thomas Carroll, Kansas National Guard, feared that disorder "caused largely by the imported customs and usages of foreign despotism" brought to America by "anarchists, nihilists, and communists" might well threaten "even the liberty-loving state of Kansas."[51] Denouncing the turmoil that accompanied strikes in 1892, Guardsman Harry P. Mawson concluded that "organized labor within the past six weeks has shown itself to be synonymous with organized lawlessness."[52] Outspoken defenders of law and order in the Guard called for draconian measures. General Albert Ordway of the District of Columbia National Guard found the nation "overrun by hundreds of thousands of the most criminal and ignorant classes of Europe . . . men who know no law but force and can appreciate no punishment less than death."[53]

Public pronouncements by National Guardsmen identified the suppression of the civil disorder caused by organized labor as the Guard's major function. Largely a ploy to win public support and greater financial aid, the anti-labor rhetoric of Guard leaders also reflected fears common to many native-born Americans of the late nineteenth century. The advent of mass industrial production, the influx of hundreds of thousands of immigrants, and burgeoning urban centers created an uneasy sense that disorder, violence, and chaos threatened the entire nation. Guardsmen eager to garner public support depicted the state soldiery as a bastion of public order.[54]

Inevitably, organized labor came to see the Guard as an ally of employers. From the early 1890s on, labor spokesmen and journals consistently attacked the Guard. The role of the Pennsylvania National Guard in breaking a strike at the Carnegie Steel plant at Homestead in 1892 initiated a vigorous organized labor assault that persisted into the twentieth century. Union journals depicted the National Guard as a force "whose duty it is to overawe, and under threat of being shot, crush the workingmen into submission."[55] The widespread mobilization of state troops in 1894 to disperse the so-called industrial armies of unemployed men, to police coal mine strikes, and to suppress the Pullman railroad strike spurred labor journal editors to greater rhetorical anger. The *American Federationist* damned the Guard as "the staff and pride of the monopolistic and Capitalistic class—the class which would enforce any species of extortion and exaction at the point of the bayonet."[56]

Labor leaders admonished union members not to join the National Guard. The *Cleveland Citizen* editorialized in 1892 that "as the militia in Pennsylvania, New York, and Tennessee are used as tools to defeat workingmen on strike. Don't join the militia."[57] Two years later, the *United Mine Workers' Journal* hoped that use of state forces in the coal and Pullman strikes "has opened the eyes of workingmen, particularly organized workingmen, to the fact that their place is not in the militia."[58] By the close of the century, some unions refused to accept men serving in the National Guard. Workingmen, however, ignored the pleas of union leaders and continued to enlist. And if, as some scholars maintain, Guard commanders attempted to keep union men and labor sympathizers out of the state forces that effort also failed. The social composition of the late-nineteenth-century National Guard will be examined in chapter 4. Suffice to say at this point that workingmen regularly joined the National Guard, and state recruiters made little effort to keep them out.[59]

Ultimately, the Guard earned the image of strikebreaker because it broke enough strikes to attract national attention. Historians depicting the state soldiery as an armed adjunct of corporate America emphasize, sometimes exaggerate, the number of strike interventions.[60] The crucial question in evaluating the National Guard's role in strike intervention is not an arithmetical one. Rather, it is a matter of which strikes state troops broke and the impact intervention had on the unions leading strike efforts. Only a small number of the thousands of strikes involving hundreds of thousands of strikers occurring in the 1880s and 1890s degenerated into violence. Local law enforcement agencies handled the great majority of those that threatened disorder. In medium and large cities, urban police forces became the major means of controlling strike disorders, according to Sidney L. Harring.[61] As noted earlier, many state forces never performed strike duty and others only occasionally. The remainder of the National Guard served in only a few violent strikes. Overall, the state soldiery did not assume a major role in suppressing striking American workers in the late nineteenth century.

Still, the state soldiery could not avoid involvement in the disorder and violence that the labor-management conflict of the period generated. Public officials faced the necessity of finding an agency to quell upheaval when local law enforcement agencies failed. States were unwilling to create permanent statewide police agencies, and, except in the most dire of circumstances, the American people rejected a federal role in suppressing civil disorder. In consequence, the task fell to the National Guard. In some instances—at Pittsburgh and Chicago in 1877; at the Milwaukee riots of 1886; in Chicago, San Francisco, and Los Angeles during the 1894 Pullman Strike; and in the Brooklyn trolley strike of 1895—Guardsmen assisted police in the cities.

More frequently, however, Guardsmen were called to quell disorder in isolated mining areas or small railroad towns scattered across the countryside. Beleaguered constables and sheriffs too often either lacked the manpower to meet the challenge or faced a divided community when raising a *posse comitatus*. In sparsely populated regions, mine owners and railroad employers hired guards supplied by private agencies—the infamous Pinkerton Detective Agency, for example, or the Baldwin-Felts firm. In many instances, employers inveigled town constables and county sheriffs to deputize private guards to protect property and strikebreakers or to harass strikers and union organizers. The use of private guards almost always provoked violence, at which point local officials turned to the state and its soldiery to end labor disorders.[62]

Any strike intervention invariably assumed an antiunion bias, as much the consequence of the evolving nature of industrial relations as of an inherent antiunion attitude permeating the National Guard. As David Montgomery notes, although the strikes and riots of 1877 had insurrectionary overtones, from the early 1880s on unions developed a greater sense of purpose, more effective organizations, and a more direct role in leading worker protests. As the frequency of strikes increased from the early 1880s to the end of the century, unions assumed the leadership role in 60 percent of them.[63]

Unavoidably, the National Guard threatened the existence of organized labor when it intervened to quell violence in union-led strikes. The most virulent conflicts arose when employers deliberately sought to weaken or destroy unions. These contests in particular led organized labor to brand the Guard a tool of corporate capitalists. In the two decades after 1877, three years stand out as demonstrating the extent to which Guard mobilizations threatened the right of unions not only to bargain for their members but maintain their very existence. In 1886, the Knights of Labor represented the nation's largest and most effective labor organization. The Knights directed strikes against railroads in the Southwest controlled by Jay Gould and organized the eight-hour-day protest in Milwaukee. In Illinois, Kansas, Missouri, and Texas, Guardsmen broke the strike against the Gould lines while Wisconsin Guardsmen shattered the general strike in Milwaukee. The failure of the railroad strike and the eight-hour-day protest when coupled with the disastrous effects of the Haymarket bombing in Chicago left the Knights of Labor in disarray after 1886. Few workers could ignore the fact that over six thousand Guardsmen answered the call to duty that year.[64]

Many historians see 1892 as the key year in late-nineteenth-century labor relations. Almost fifteen thousand state soldiers mobilized to control industrial disorders. In Idaho, strikers in the Coeur d'Alene initiated a decade and a half of violence in the Rocky Mountain mining region where officials of Idaho and Colorado sought to break the power of the Western Federation of Miners (WFM). Farther east, over seven thousand New York Guardsmen served in Buffalo to crush a railroad switchmen's strike. More than any other state military intervention, however, the appearance of the Pennsylvania Guard at Homestead earned it, and the National Guard at large, the reputation as a union buster. After a fierce gun battle, three hundred Pinkerton Detective Agency guards failed to wrest control of the Carnegie Steel plant at Homestead from strikers occupying the site. Reluctantly, Governor Pattison sent in the Guard. The state's entire division, eight thousand soldiers, quickly occupied Homestead. Military occupation allowed the Carnegie Steel Company, with the help of the judiciary of Allegheny County and the state of Pennsylvania, to destroy the Amalgamated Association of Iron and Steel Workers.[65]

Both the strikers and Carnegie officials fully realized that the arrival of the Guard meant the defeat of the Amalgamated Association. Strike leaders cautioned their followers not to resist the soldiers. To assure Guardsmen that steelworkers would not fight, strikers welcomed the Guard with a peaceful demonstration that prominently displayed the American flag. Nonetheless, as a strike leader said when asked what the Guard's arrival meant, "It means just this—that the entire National Guard of Pennsylvania has been called out to enable the Carnegie Company to employ scab labor."[66] The role of the Pennsylvania National Guard at Homestead brought fierce denunciations of the state soldiery from organized labor and its friends across the nation.[67]

Finally, 1894 saw the largest mobilization of state forces since the rise of the National Guard, with just over thirty-two thousand called out. Nineteen states fielded troops during the year, some more than once, to meet real or potential disorder directly related to industrial conditions. In April and May, in addition to federal troops, Guardsmen from several states mobilized to observe and control the movement of so-called industrial armies of unemployed men on their march to Washington DC. A strike of coal miners directed by the United Mine Workers (UMW) affected eight states and overlapped with the industrial army problem. Soldiers from Ohio and Virginia, for example, saw service during both the industrial army march and the coal strike. Even before the miners' strike ended, Guardsmen and federal troops confronted the Pullman Strike directed by Eugene Debs and his American Railway Union (ARU). During the latter upheaval, soldiers from twelve states, several of whom had also been on duty during one of the two earlier disturbances, reported for duty. Iowa Guardsmen served in all three instances.[68]

Although the federal government and the Army took the lead role during the Pullman Strike, the combined use of state and federal forces destroyed the ARU and either gravely weakened or eliminated the UMW in many states. The ways in which a state force could not only control labor violence and break a strike but destroy a union are best seen in the activities of the Alabama State Troops. At the direction of Governor Thomas G. Jones, Lieutenant James B. Erwin of the U.S. Army, the inspector on duty with the Alabama troops, acted as de facto adjutant general to prevent violence during the coal strike, which lasted from mid-May to 15 August. Even as that strike dragged on, ARU members shut down rail traffic in Birmingham from July 8 through July 11. The energetic Erwin interrupted his oversight of the coal campaign to direct troops in the breaking of the railway stoppage. Erwin relied on Pinkerton detectives to spy on the UMW. He called Alabama State Troops to summer training at a camp in the coal region situated on land provided by the coal companies. To keep costs low and mitigate the unpleasantness of strike duty, Erwin rotated Alabama's three infantry regiments through the so-called training camp a unit at a time. The lengthy coal strike and the unexpected ARU walkout forced Erwin to call deactivated state troops back to duty several times, which the soldiers resented. In the end, however, the fledgling Alabama UMW collapsed, as did the recently organized ARU.[69]

A review of major National Guard strike interventions demonstrates the necessity of assessing the state soldiery's role as strikebreaker qualitatively rather than quantitatively. The consequences of major strikebreaking efforts like those of the New York National Guard in 1895—when nearly six thousand state soldiers quashed a trolley workers' strike in Brooklyn—or the Pennsylvania Guard's intervention during the UMW strike at Hazelton in 1897 should not be minimized. Nonetheless, the long-term results of these incidents were less profound than those at Milwaukee in 1886, Homestead in 1892, or Alabama in 1894, where state military power shattered key organizations formed by workingmen to assert control over their working conditions.[70]

State military interventions in labor conflicts were not simply "riot duty," although the state officials commonly used this phrase to explain the commitment of state forces. It is accurate to call Guard interventions strikebreaking, even when riot conditions did not prevail or when strikers refrained from resisting Guardsmen, which was usually the case. Laws governing property rights barred strikers from preventing either employers or nonstrikers from entering a struck plant or mine. Freedom-of-contract laws gave any person who desired to work the right to do so without hindrance. Since employers generally preferred to ignore unions and adamantly refused to take part in collective bargaining, organized labor had few choices other than to withhold their labor. The introduction of private guards to protect property and strikebreakers merely increased the tension and frustration so often present at the strike scene.

Under these conditions, neither governors nor Guardsmen could avoid the strikebreaking role, although few would admit it and many publicly refuted such a characterization. Wisconsin Guard officer Joseph Doe put the case succinctly by asserting "that there is no possibility of any hostile position being taken by the National Guard against any labor organization; that is an absurdity upon its face." Doe's fellow officer, Major Charles Boardman, explained further: "The National Guard is above all this. It simply represents the law and nothing else."[71] Guardsmen and their supporters everywhere echoed the Badger State soldiers, all the while failing to see that enforcing the law ipso facto made the National Guard a strikebreaker.[72]

Committed legally and personally to enforcing the law and generally fearing the breakdown of social order, few National Guard officers comprehended the labor point of view. Strikers and union men were not insurrectionaries intent on overthrowing the existing order. Instead, according to David Montgomery, workers accepted and even "celebrated . . . the legitimacy of the state."[73] Fears of urban class warfare and uncontrolled uprisings of an immigrant-dominated proletariat, which beset so many middle- and upper-class Americans—and not a few National Guard leaders—were widely misplaced. Instead of revolution, workers sought legal means through collective organization to counter the inordinate power corporations created in the late nineteenth century through mergers and finance capitalism. Consigned to the role of one more commodity like coal or iron ore available at the lowest market price, workers sought, according to Paul Krause, to assert and defend, "the idea of a laborer as a citizen versus that of laborer as a factor of production."[74]

Although only slightly less than 10 percent of industrial workers belonged to unions, organized labor led the majority of worker protests. Union tactics thus shaped industrial relations, and the strike was the primary weapon in labor's arsenal. Strikes, however, brought laboring men into conflict with the American legal system by violating the freedom of contract and the legal sanctity of private property. Employers used a variety of techniques to uphold both concepts, for the former assured them the right to employ strikebreakers and the latter to operate their firms as they saw fit. Violence came when factory and mine owners used private guards and local law enforcement agencies to keep their factories, mines, and railroads operating during strikes and to allow nonstrikers to work.[75]

Governors sometimes made efforts to be neutral in a strike and use troops to prevent violence while not affecting the outcome of the walkoff. On occasion they succeeded. During the Cripple Creek coal strike of 1894, Colorado Governor Davis Waite, a Populist, ordered his troops to the scene to prevent an armed clash between angry miners and a posse of deputized private guards. Colorado soldiers disarmed and dispersed the posse. Under the watchful eye of Governor Waite, strikers and mine owners peacefully agreed to a contract. Prior to Waite's tenure in office, at Leadville in 1880 and 1896, and indeed into the twentieth century, Colorado governors readily committed the National Guard to mining upheavals, not only to end strikes but to eliminate miner unions, especially the Western Federation of Miners.[76]

More commonly, National Guardsmen entered strike duty only with orders to preserve order and quell violence. Prior to their arrival, conflict between private guards, local law enforcement, and strikebreakers, on the one hand, and strikers, on the other, had already occurred. Strike violence was rarely a simple matter of law and order under these circumstances, for suppression of strike activity unavoidably became strikebreaking. Some Guardsmen understood this. The three-month occupation of Homestead by elements of Pennsylvania's Sixteenth Infantry Regiment ended in disillusionment and resentment, according to John Marsh, because the men were "reduced in their own eyes to little more than borough constables."[77] Others in the Keystone Guard agreed with this sentiment. In the aftermath of the Homestead strike, one brigade commander suggested that Pennsylvania should organize a state police for riot duty, and Guard officers raised the idea again following strike duty at Hazelton in 1897.[78]

Perhaps Colonel E. B. Hamilton, inspector general of the Illinois National Guard, expressed doubts about the Guard's police function with the most skepticism. In 1885, he disabused his readers of the idea that state service "is all fun and a parade day for the military." More bitterly, Hamilton urged the public to abandon any idea that Guardsmen "ought to be ready at all times to do the bidding of some worthless and cowardly mayor, sheriff, or other officer of the law" while nevertheless being expected to "pay their own way, buy their own uniforms, get shot, and thank God and the State for the use of a rusty old musket."[79] Hamilton's bitter observation suggests that many Guardsmen realized that policing their fellow citizens reaped little glory for them and rarely produced generous public financial support afterward.

4

The National Guard Paradox:

Volunteers in State Service,

1866–1898

In the late nineteenth century, the state soldiery remained essentially a locally based, provincially oriented institution despite the commitment of state financial aid. As voluntary part-time soldiers, Guardsmen clung to the well-established militia traditions of fraternal association and social activity. Regimental and company officers continued to oversee the weekly and monthly management of local units with little state supervision. Guard organizations came under central control only during annual inspections and summer training camps or when called out for civil disorder service.

State governments relied on the voluntary initiative of private citizens to organize the companies that were the basic element of Guard organization. Following the volunteer militia tradition, National Guard companies began as civil organizations. Men interested in military affairs formed an association with a constitution and bylaws, chose civil officers, and established membership rules. They then elected military officers and noncommissioned officers (NCOs) and petitioned the governor for recognition. The governor or his adjutant general informally investigated the men involved by seeking the opinions of local politicians or businessmen. If the petitioners seemed reliable and a slot within Guard tables of organization existed, the adjutant general mustered them in. States seldom established stringent military criteria for accepting companies. Wisconsin's adjutant general, Edwin Bryant, reported in 1878 that he sought organizations "composed of members of fixed residence, and good repute, and officered by men of force and dignity of character."[1]

Tradition and voluntarism shaped the state soldiery far more than state statutes. Older states included companies and regiments that had existed well before the Civil War. In 1900, the Massachusetts Volunteer Militia carried on its rolls one company and two battalions organized before the adoption of the U.S. Constitution and twelve other units founded before 1861. The nation's most lauded organization, New York's Seventh Regiment, first saw life in 1806. Forty-three companies and regiments actively serving in the National Guard in 1908 began before 1860. Socially prestigious units such as Boston's First Corps of Cadets, Philadelphia's First City Troop, Richmond's Light Infantry Blues Battalion, and New York's Seventh Regiment jealously guarded their traditional militia privileges and practices.[2]

Diverse groups of men formed new companies for a variety of reasons. Some, such as Pennsylvania's Thirteenth Infantry Regiment of Scranton, organized units in response to the railroad disorders of 1877. Company K, First Regiment, of the Oregon National Guard was formed in early 1886 following threatened disorders against Chinese laborers in Portland. Elsewhere, very different impulses underlay unit formation. In Wisconsin, the Garfield Guards and Racine Light Infantry, both of Racine, originated as Republican marching clubs during the 1880 presidential campaign. Company A, Second Minnesota Infantry Regiment, claimed modest beginnings when in 1871 a group of young men met in a grocery store in New Ulm to organize the unit for no other apparent reason than to have something to do. Some units sought to protect property and preserve order. Others followed different motives, usually a combined pursuit of fraternal, recreational, and social interests. A minority were formed to pursue an avocational interest in military affairs.[3]

Once they entered state service, companies retained the civil organizations that gave them life. Following antebellum volunteer tradition, the civil organizations theoretically controlled nonmilitary activities while captains and lieutenants bore responsibility for military matters. However, company bylaws intruded on command prerogatives by establishing membership requirements, controlling fines for disciplinary infractions, and governing the election of officers. As Wisconsin's Colonel Charles King noted acidly, the end result was to give a company "virtually two heads" because enlisted men often served in executive positions in the civil association and so held authority over the unit's commissioned officers.[4] Another Army officer, John H. Nankivell, bemoaned the fact that many companies in the Colorado National Guard were "apparently run on the principle of a Soviet or political club."[5]

Civil organizations met before or after weekly drills to consider the acceptance of new members when active Guardsmen presented candidates, usually friends or relatives. In some instances, the unit immediately accepted or rejected new recruits; in others, the chair appointed a committee to gather information on proposed members. Company G of Valley City, North Dakota, accepted new men provisionally, allowing them to attend drills for three months before the unit approved their enlistment. Emmons Clark, the historian of New York's haughty Seventh Regiment, justified the way his outfit recruited soldiers by observing that "comradeship can only exist where comrades are chosen; citizen soldiers will not allow any one to select for them their military associates."[6]

Citizen soldiers of the late nineteenth century also stoutly defended the election of officers. Clark put the view succinctly: "The election of officers and noncommissioned officers in the National Guard, *a right enjoyed by citizen soldiers since the formation of the republic*, is essential to the welfare of a regiment or company" (emphasis added).[7] The election of company officers was universal in the late-nineteenth-century National Guard and persisted well into the twentieth century. Only Wisconsin, in the early 1890s, modified this hoary militia tradition. The Badger State permitted companies to elect their second lieutenants from serving NCOs, but seniority governed other promotions through the rank of regimental colonel.[8]

Army officers condemned election as a corrosive influence on discipline because it established a sense of equality between officers and enlisted men. Guardsmen, however, defended the elective process by echoing the republican citizen soldier tradition. Others saw it as a reward for joining the state soldiery. "Be it remembered," one commentator noted, that Guardsmen were "volunteers without bounty" and that the opportunity to win a commission through election "is probably the keenest inducement that you can give them."[9] A Massachusetts Guardsman proudly boasted that the most recently recruited private immediately appeared "in the line of promotion, and may aspire to any elective or appointive position."[10]

Nearly all states permitted the election of battalion and regimental line officers. In most instances, only company officers could vote for field grade positions, but Ohio allowed enlisted men as well as officers to use the ballot. States that maintained brigades and divisions most commonly provided that brigadier and major generals be appointed by the governor. This was not always the case, however. In Rhode Island, the general assembly elected the brigade commander after field officers nominated candidates. The governor of New York had the power to appoint general officers but could ask the field officers of each brigade to nominate a candidate for the brigadier's position. Most governors accepted the nominee.[11]

Inevitably, the election of officers and NCOs fostered political opportunism and personality conflicts. Few units escaped at least some disruption from the politics that inevitably accompanied the quest for commissions and promotions. Instances of this are innumerable and need not be recounted here. In retrospect, they appear petty and involve specific instances or personalities of long ago that bear little on the broader history of the Guard. That these quarrels occurred frequently and affected the efficiency of companies and regiments is important, however, for they tell us much about the post–Civil War National Guard. As states invested more money in the service, they came to expect value in exchange. Although the state soldiery of the late nineteenth century demonstrated a stability and effectiveness not seen in the antebellum militia, the Guard nonetheless failed to make substantive progress toward military effectiveness. The state soldiery faltered because its fundamental element of organization, the company, remained largely self-governing and immune from state regulation.

"I think it is safe to say," wrote Colonel William Cary Sanger of the New York National Guard in 1893, "that but few men join the militia simply for the purpose of doing military work."[12] Indeed, few men did enlist purely for the military activities of Guard membership. In 1879, for example, on the founding of the Winona Guards of the Minnesota National Guard the Winona *Daily Republican* observed that the new company would attract "enterprising, capable young men" who would find "not only an agreeable pastime, but a healthful exercise."[13] To attract recruits, Guardsmen regularly deemphasized military duties. Some extolled the virtues that training would instill in the nation's youth. The Guard, Virginia's adjutant general stressed, provided a young man with officers "of a class who usually inculcate, by example and teaching, habits of sobriety, obedience and personal respect."[14] Personal discipline, physical fitness, and respect for authority would be dispensed to America's young men at the local armory. A New York Guardsman asserted that in the state soldiery "the young citizen can acquire that erect, manly, self-reliant bearing, which is so distinguishing a mark of the model soldier."[15]

Lieutenant George B. Duncan of the U.S. Army noted that the average National Guard company "is not unlike a local athletic club."[16] The very process by which companies came to life—incorporation through a civil organization—resembled the ways in which social clubs and fraternal organizations functioned. Colonel Allen F. Caldwell of Wisconsin's First Regiment urged companies to establish "a club-room comfortably furnished" at their armories. The room would aid recruiting, maintain interest in a company, and provide "a *good* place for the boys to spend their evenings" (emphasis in original).[17] In larger cities, where regimental armories housed several companies, the facilities often included a gymnasium, small-bore shooting gallery, library, and perhaps a swimming pool. In small towns as well as cities, Guard companies sponsored dances, dinners, theatricals, and concerts. These events served chiefly as fund-raisers but also played a significant role in community social life by demonstrating that the unit included members of leading local families and contributed to the annual social calendar. Just as important, they were essential to recruiting and retaining men who had little interest in military matters.

As a volunteer military organization with strong fraternal overtones, the National Guard reflected social and cultural trends at work in the larger society. Fraternal organizations experienced an exponential growth after the Civil War, stimulated in part by their effort to replicate the all-male culture of military life through ceremonies and complex hierarchical structures. It is not incidental that the largest Union Army veteran's group, the Grand Army of the Republic, incorporated many fraternal practices when it organized lodges. Most Guard companies resembled fraternal lodges in the way they operated their civil organizations and "selected" new members rather than recruiting them. The emphasis on the armory as a club and the opportunities Guard membership offered for social and athletic activities bore a greater resemblance to the burgeoning fraternal organizations then appearing in cities and larger towns than they did to a regular military system.[18]

Structural changes in the economy that began before 1861 and came to fruition after the Civil War also affected fraternal groups. These changes severed the once predominant physical proximity of home and workplace. Men now spent their workdays in places where women and children rarely intruded. They also more frequently sought their leisure and recreation outside the home, not only in the growing fraternal organizations but in male social and athletic clubs. As E. Anthony Rotundo notes, the world of work and the world of play in Victorian America became "distinctly male realms."[19] A clear separation of male work and recreation from home and family, Rotundo argues, reflected new conceptions of Victorian manhood. In essence, the former cultural emphasis on the restraint of men's natural aggressiveness, competitiveness, and impulsiveness disappeared. Manhood now came to be defined as a life of action and decisiveness rather than of restraint and contemplation.

Rotundo contends that the new version of Victorian manhood identified martial ideals and athletic competition as the best guides for men to follow in the struggles of life and work. Fraternal organizations, social clubs, and athletic teams simultaneously fostered individual competitiveness and the concept of team spirit. For men to be men, they had to cultivate individual skills while simultaneously learning to function effectively as members of an organization. Recruiting appeals by National Guardsmen echoed this late Victorian redefinition of manliness. The emphases in Guard publicity on discipline, physical fitness, moral training, and martial preparedness parallel Rotundo's notion of the "changing standard of masculinity" in the 1880s and 1890s.[20]

Reconstructing a precise social and economic profile of the late-nineteenth-century Guardsman is difficult, but it is possible to sketch in broad detail who served in the Guard and who did not. It is simplest to note who was *not* in the Guard. Few farmers enlisted despite their large presence in the total population. Studies of Wisconsin and North Dakota, two overwhelmingly agricultural states, show that tillers of the soil rarely appeared on the rolls. Virtually none enlisted in Wisconsin, and in North Dakota, a state with only eight incorporated towns with populations greater than a thousand, less than one-quarter of its enlisted men farmed for a living. Exceptions could be found to be sure. Farmers comprised nearly all of Company B, Second Regiment, of Goldendale in the eastern section of Washington, but such a unit was a rarity in any state force. In addition, few recently arrived immigrants appeared in state uniforms. Ohio's Guard was 98 percent native born in 1894, and in North Dakota, where nearly half the population was foreign born in 1890, 80 percent of its officers and men were born in the United States or Canada. As with units dominated by farmers, however, exceptions could be found, such as Milwaukee's Polish Kosciusko Guards company in the Wisconsin Guard. However, in the National Guard era ethnically identified units commonly found in the pre-1861 volunteers became increasingly rare. The absence of a significant number of farming and foreign-born males sharply narrowed the social makeup of the state soldiery.[21]

Unlike the foreign born, African Americans initially found a niche in the National Guard. Surprisingly, given the nature of race relations in the South, nine of the former Confederate states maintained African-American units into the 1890s. Virginia led with twenty-four companies, closely followed by

Georgia and South Carolina, with twenty-two and twenty-one, respectively. In all, Alwyn Barr estimates that Southern states fielded approximately four thousand black Guardsmen in the late 1880s and early 1890s. Outside the old Confederacy, the District of Columbia and Maryland led with the largest number of black units, the former with eight companies, the latter with four. Ohio supported a three-company battalion into the 1890s. South Carolina organized its National Guard units into a brigade commanded by an African-American brigadier general, and Texas briefly maintained a full regiment led by a black colonel in the 1880s. More commonly, states north and south placed African-American Guardsmen in segregated battalions and companies commanded by officers of their own race. Only Massachusetts integrated its single all-black company, Company L, with a line organization, the Sixth Infantry Regiment.[22]

By the early 1890s, as the competition for state funds intensified, states disbanded many black organizations. Texas's regiment became a battalion, and South Carolina's brigade disappeared, with eight of its units surviving as unattached companies. Tennessee and North Carolina slashed their black organizations to only a separate company each, while Georgia and Virginia reduced their black units by two-thirds. Reductions in African-American companies also took place outside the South. Ohio's Ninth Battalion became a single unattached company, and black Guardsmen in the District of Columbia saw two of their three battalions disbanded by 1891. Only in Illinois, where blacks exploited their political influence in the Republican Party, did African-American volunteers enjoy expansion through the organization of the four-company Ninth Battalion (home station, Chicago) in 1896.

Despite an interest and enthusiasm matching that of their white counterparts, African-American Guardsmen fared badly, and discrimination curtailed their development. Mirroring the practice of the Regular Army, the states maintained segregated units but, unlike the regulars, permitted blacks full command of their own units. Within the always financially stringent conditions the Guard faced, black soldiers received the worst of the available state arms and equipment. All Guard units needed to raise their own money to supplement state funding. Here, black units suffered because their low economic status stunted fund-raising efforts. African-American soldiers were forced to hold separate summer camps, usually with little state aid and without the assistance of the Army officers who began to instruct white troops in the mid-1880s. In addition, state adjutants general rarely called on black troops to serve in natural disasters or civil disorders, fearing that their presence would offend the larger white civilian population. It is remarkable that black Guardsmen managed to sustain even the few companies still active in the late 1890s.[23]

By a large margin, the state soldiery drew its members from both native-born and older immigrant white men, groups that encompassed skilled workingmen as well as the upper middle classes. As had been true of the antebellum uniformed militia, National Guard companies and regiments were overwhelmingly an urban phenomenon. After the Civil War, new companies and regiments took root in the growing towns and cities of industrializing America. The Guard fared best in towns of five thousand or more, particularly where rail facilities were readily available. State studies and War Department reports make clear that although small towns attempted to maintain units, "country" organizations usually failed. To succeed, a unit needed a growing economy that provided employment paying sufficient wages and permitting enough leisure time to allow men to indulge in part-time military service. The difficulty many states in the Southern, Plains, and Western regions faced in maintaining effective Guard units stemmed largely from the fact that these regions lacked towns and cities whose economies were tied to activities other than agricultural or extractive industries.

" 'Society is like a barrel of pork—the top and bottom a little tainted,' " Wisconsin's Captain Emil Baensch intoned in 1884. Remove the top and bottom of society, he went on, "and you have some good material left. It is to the middle classes that you must look for the best material." Baensch and other Guard officers liked to think they represented the best of American society, neither the "dude" nor the "rowdy," in his words.[24] Such a view fit well with their contention that when on strike duty state soldiers did not represent the propertied classes, only law and order. Still, the officer corps was a blend of, on the one hand, the older, entrepreneurial, and independent middle class and, on the other, the "new" middle class of managers, accountants, lawyers, and other educated men serving the expanding corporations. Unlike the antebellum volunteers, the Guard rarely commissioned artisans and craftsmen. Now employed as skilled workers, they were far more likely to serve as NCOs.[25]

Captain Baensch's dismissal of the "dude" was a criticism of elite National Guard units, mostly located in the East. Many of these outfits were organized before the Civil War and had long boasted rosters listing the fathers and sons of socially notable families. New York's Seventh Regiment, which had an esprit de corps that its historian Emmons Clark described as "unsurpassed in any military organization in the world," won national acclaim for the splendor of its regimental armory, the skill of its close order drill, and the beauty of its dress uniform.[26] The Seventh Regiment and its crosstown rival, the Twenty-second Regiment, viewed military duty in elitist terms. Neither outfit volunteered for three-years' duty during the Civil War because service as enlisted men was beneath the dignity of their members.[27]

Cities other than New York supported socially prestigious organizations. In Boston, the First Corps of Cadets, organized in 1741, owned its own armory and campground, wore tailor-made uniforms, and claimed three hundred fifty active soldiers and another one thousand honorary members who paid thirty dollars a year to be listed on the battalion roster. In September 1877, following the railroad disorders, prominent businessmen organized Cleveland's First City Troop to protect their property and keep order. Through its first decade, the troop declined to enroll in the Ohio National Guard. If the unit initially took shape to quell disorderly workers, it quickly assumed the trappings of the antebellum militia by adopting a uniform "closely modeled upon a Hussar dress uniform in vogue in the Austrian Army" and indulging in dinners, balls, and parades. The unit finally voted to become Troop A of the Ohio National Guard in 1887.[28]

Socially prominent units were hardly typical of the state soldiery, and their membership profiles are relatively easy to reconstruct. It is more difficult to sketch an outline of enlisted men serving in most states. Secondary state studies seldom examine the rank and file, and contemporary observers rarely commented on them. Despite organized labor's campaign to dissuade workers from joining the Guard, many nonetheless enlisted. Wisconsin's infantry regiments in the 1880s and 1890s included lumber mill hands, clerks, bookkeepers, students, and factory workers—the latter comprising roughly half of all the units. Skilled workers greatly outnumbered unskilled laborers. In 1896, the New Jersey ranks closely resembled those of the Badger State, where 41 percent of the men came from manufacturing and mechanical industries, while another 26 percent were clerks and bookkeepers. North Dakota enlisted railway workers, machinists, tailors, and a few unskilled day workers along with the usual clerks and students. In 1896, the adjutant general of Arizona Territory reported that enlistments had dropped sharply in the last biennium as the "closing down of mines in the outlying towns" had forced miners "to leave their station in search of employment."[29]

Although the profile of enlisted men is impressionistic, it indicates that the National Guard attracted lower-level white-collar workers and industrial laborers. Few middle-class professionals, managers, or entrepreneurs agreed to serve for very long as privates, the military version of unskilled labor. The Guard did offer men in the ranks the opportunity to belong to a recognized community organization and earn the prestige of wearing an NCO's stripes. When coupled with the fraternal associations available at the armory, these attractions led thousands of workingmen to enlist despite the Guard's strike-breaking image.

The fraternal and social club activities of companies kept Guardsmen focused on local affairs. Summer camp, annual state inspections, regimental elections, and the yearly state officers' convention might temporarily shift concerns to the state level, but armory activities occupied unit members most of the time. Along with weekly drill, state soldiers devoted much effort to keeping their organizations financially solvent. Despite the increase in state support after 1877, Guardsmen found that sustaining their units required both personal contributions and an endless round of fund-raising events. Even in states where legislators were the most generous, military budgets proved insufficient to support stable organizations. Contemporary assessments and state studies show that the Guard's greatest liability was inadequate funding. States rarely paid Guardsmen for armory drills, and only a few gave company and regimental commanders money for their administrative duties.

States provided direct cash payments only to cover armory rent or mortgage payments. Units used the funds they raised to pay for utilities, maintenance, and insurance. On average, states distributed between three and four hundred dollars a year for armory rents, allotting larger amounts for urban organizations and for artillery or cavalry units requiring bigger buildings. State aid failed to provide the funds to purchase a decent building. Except in New York and Massachusetts, Guardsmen rented their armories throughout the era. They took what they could afford rather than what was suitable for military drill or the proper security of weapons and equipment. An Army officer inspecting the Ohio National Guard in 1895 reported that the state's yearly two hundred dollars for armory support forced most companies to rent "old roller skating rinks."[30] In Kansas, the commander of Wichita's Battery A complained that his "armory," a single room in a multistory building, included "on one side of us a house of ill-repute . . . below us a 'dive' and above us more 'houses' and a policy shop." He understandably feared that "the unsavory reputation of the building falls on us."[31]

The report was the same whether from California, where state support approached $200,000 in the late 1890s, or from Missouri, struggling along at

$10,000 a year. In the former, an inspector found most armories not "at all suited to the purpose," and in the latter they were found "unsuitable or inconvenient."[32] Guard units in Salt Lake City could use rooms on the third floor of the new City-County Building in 1895, provided they blew no bugles, beat no drums, and damaged no flooring during close order drill. There were exceptions, to be sure. Not surprisingly, Army inspectors found New York City's regimental armories "splendid specimens of such structures," and the Houston Light Guard's three-story building so sumptuous as to not be "an armory, except that it furnishes a rendezvous for the members, there being a social-club feature to the company organization."[33]

States also provided arms, uniforms, and equipment to companies. Most of this matériel came from the annual federal allotment and increased in quantity after Congress doubled the value of the distribution to $400,000 annually in 1887. However, the goods sent to the states, particularly rifles, pistols, and artillery pieces, were older models the Army no longer used. Whatever their condition when sent to the states, arms, uniforms, blankets, overcoats, and canteens were passed from man to man until they wore out. Few states could afford to purchase new clothing and equipment for their men. In the poorer regions, Guardsmen often bought their own uniforms and then sold them to new recruits upon leaving the service.[34]

Many states paid officers and men attending annual training camps. Enlisted men generally received a dollar or two per day, while officers, depending on their rank, earned five to ten dollars daily. Rarely, however, could this money be considered take-home pay, for Guardsmen used their stipends to pay for food and other camp expenses. Moreover, since officers did not receive uniforms and arms from the state and were expected to provide their own horses when in camp, most used their camp compensation to cover the yearly costs of belonging to the Guard. Although as independent businessmen or professionals many officers could afford a week off work, the average enlisted man lost a week's wages by going to camp.

Federal, state, and local support was not enough to maintain the Guard properly. Guardsmen across the nation solicited contributions from individuals and their communities at large for additional financial assistance. For all the largesse of the state and wealth of its members, New York's Seventh Regiment, for example, turned to the city's social elite for donations and bond subscriptions to complete its new armory in 1879. Other elite units such as the Houston Light Guard and Cleveland's Troop A also called on wealthy friends to build their armories and equip their units. Ohio law permitted each company to enroll up to 150 "contributing" or "honorary" members who paid annual dues set by the unit's civil organization. Contributing members did not serve actively but were exempted from jury duty as a reward for supporting their local militia. Most units failed to recruit such a well-known supporter as John D. Rockefeller, Troop A's major coup. However, according to a founder, Columbus's Governor's Guard had the full complement of 150, "each paying annual dues to the amount of twenty five dollars; our own dues were two dollars a month."[35]

Companies of necessity sought other sources of support. They sponsored theatricals, concerts, and dances to raise money. Wisconsin's Colonel Allen Caldwell recommended all these activities. "Make your organizations the leader in social events," he urged company commanders, "and your citizens will patronize you and I venture to say the financial standing of the company will be rated A-1."[36] After inspecting Missouri's First Regiment, in St. Louis, Army Lieutenant William H. Osborne observed that the unit incurred $12,960 in expenses during 1896, but the state gave it only $2,614. Regimental members either had to make up the difference, Osborne said, "or go into the streets and beg for it."[37]

Adjutants general and Army inspectors noted again and again the personal commitments Guardsmen made to sustain their organizations. Self-support began with the monthly dues unit members paid but extended well beyond. For example, the Texas adjutant general estimated in 1891 that his soldiers personally contributed $10,000 for armory rent and $16,000 for uniforms and expenses. He found these expenditures impressive "when it is remembered that the majority . . . are young men and mostly wage-workers with limited means."[38] After inspecting the Minnesota Guard at its 1887 camp, Captain S. W. Groesbeck, U.S. Army, reported that men had bought their own ammunition, uniforms, and mess gear in addition to paying the bulk of their armory rent. He concluded that state aid "makes up but an insignificant portion of the annual expense attending the voluntary effort of the guardsmen."[39] Major John M. Baem, U.S. Army, summarized the Guard's difficulties in an 1886 report: "It requires time, labor and money to make good soldiers and it would seem but reasonable that if the guardsmen furnish the first two" the state should "provide them a permanent camp, uniforms, blankets and sufficient pay to insure them against actual loss during their encampments."[40]

All regions suffered reduced support during the depression of the mid-1890s, but the cuts affected the Plains and West most profoundly. Washington saw its $40,000 yearly budget slashed to $6,000 per annum in 1896 and 1897. Governor John R. Rogers reduced the Guard from sixteen to six state-supported companies. Remarkably, the seven remaining units paid their own expenses while the state continued to provide arms and uniforms. The burden proved to be too much for one Guardsman in South Dakota. When the state reduced its meager $4,000 annual budget to a mere $500 in 1895, Major Lee Stover wrote Governor Charles Sheldon that during his ten-year service "I have contributed liberally all that time from my private funds." Now, he added, "I feel that it is an imposition to expect the National Guard to be further maintained by personal donations" and tendered his resignation.[41]

Financial stringency compounded the problems company commanders always faced. Captains bore the responsibility to recruit men, manage finances, rent an armory, and teach their men the basics of military discipline and drill. The lack of money and the Guard's clublike features hindered company commanders at every turn. Although the civil organizations affected recruiting and fund-raising, the state held the captain responsible for unit strength, condition of the armory, and care of equipment given by the state. A strong captain who demanded strict discipline and rigorous armory drills could face revolt and reelection problems. An effective captain usually succeeded through diplomacy rather than discipline, in addition to his social and business standing in the local community. Under the best of circumstances, captains faced significant challenges in turning volunteer citizens into passable soldiers. In the face of inadequate armory facilities, high absenteeism, and a constant turnover in the enlisted ranks, the task for most company leaders became formidable.

Guard companies ranged in size from fewer than forty to as high as seventy men. As most units maintained a full roster of officers and NCOs—three of the former, ten or so of the latter—the smaller outfits had few privates to instruct or lead even on nights with 100 percent attendance. Captain L. P. Sieker, inspector general for Texas, found "about fifteen" men present in the companies he inspected in 1891 and the "average reported attendance at drills nineteen."[42] Although the Texas example represents an extreme case, absenteeism plagued the Guard. So too did a steady turnover in enlisted men. Guardsmen enlisted for three years, but states readily granted discharges when men left town to work elsewhere. Consequently, company leaders faced the endless task of recruiting and training new men only to see them move on. In the mid-1890s, one-third of Ohio's enlisted men left every year; the rate in Missouri and Arizona Territory reached 40 percent annually.[43]

Companies often failed to survive under the prevailing conditions, particularly in states that offered limited financial support. Adjutant General Wilburn K. King of Texas summarized conditions in his state in 1881, conditions that were to be found elsewhere well into the 1890s. An initial "spasmodic enthusiasm for military organization" leads to new companies, King observed, but "this fervor . . . soon dies out, the officers fail or refuse to act, the men drop off and the company disappears."[44] Unit instability plagued the Texas Volunteer Guard, with forty companies organized and twenty disbanded between 1884 and 1886 alone. A decade later, the Lone Star State saw its Guard drop from sixty-four companies in 1894 to forty in 1896. Company instability afflicted the Guard throughout the South, Plains, and West, except for California. Only the East and Midwest established companies with lengthy tenure at the same home station.[45]

Work at the armory determined the military efficiency of the National Guard. The limited training given at weekly drills, the constant turnover of privates, and the limitations of company officers (most of whom were self-taught in tactics and regulations) severely limited unit effectiveness. By the mid-1880s, state military leaders believed that the best means for improving Guard efficiency was to bring individual companies together in higher units for extended training. The growth of the volunteers from the mid-1870s on and state commitment of money generated calls for annual training camps. Encampments served several functions. Most important, they removed companies from the confines of the armory, in many cases literal confinement, and allowed them to operate as elements of battalions, regiments, and brigades. For hundreds of companies, summer camp was a chance to escape endless close order drill and learn higher-level unit tactics. Encampments also gave field officers the opportunity to command their battalions, regiments, and brigades in tactical exercises. Finally, annual training tested the ability of state headquarters to mobilize and supply their soldiers.

Lieutenant Colonel Jacob Kline of the U.S. Army praised the Massachusetts Volunteer Militia for its performance during its 1896 encampment. "They do well at camp," Kline emphasized, "because they are well prepared in their armories."[46] Few states won such accolades from Army observers or state inspectors. The amateur nature of armory drill became readily evident when companies reached camp and attempted to execute even rudimentary tactical drills. In 1888, the Army's Captain John H. Patterson noted the "indifference, or dullness of comprehension," of several of the company commanders after observing the Minnesota Guard at battalion drill.[47] Army inspectors even found company officers and NCOs of the highly lauded Pennsylvania Guard wanting at its 1896 encampment, observing that among many officers, "the idea that this is a 'go-as-you-please' sort of drill prevails generally."[48]

The close social relations that prevailed between officers and men weakened camp training. Regular officers were appalled by the informality that pervaded the camps and saw the election of officers as the acid that eroded National Guard discipline. Missouri's personnel, Captain J. F. Stretch reported, were intelligent and able but scored low in discipline because the officers "care so much about being popular with their men."[49] Another regular, Major M. P. Miller, observed that in Massachusetts the term *discipline* "has significance more in connection with obedience and soldierly bearing of inferiors on duty." Off duty, however, officers and men dealt with each other on an equal basis.[50]

All too often an air of frivolity accompanied the Guard when it encamped. Many state soldiers saw the annual week in summer camp as an escape from the office, the workshop, or domestic life, not to mention the dull routine of armory meetings. "I am more anxious than ever before to get into camp," Wisconsin's Captain Wallace Greene wrote his adjutant general. "My business now affords no chance for recreation and I am looking forward to the enjoyable week of the year."[51] Guardsmen did not expect to rough it while in camp. States owning their own campgrounds accommodated them by constructing permanent mess halls, showers, and kitchens. New York's camp at Peekskill included floored tents equipped with cots, mattresses, and blankets so as "to make the camp itself as attractive and comfortable as possible," according to an Army inspector.[52] Well into the 1890s, states hired caterers to feed troops rather than make the men cook their own food using the standard Army ration. A regular officer described with incredulity "the impedimenta" at an Iowa Guard camp, which included "bedsteads, banjos, lace curtains, umbrellas, and a heterogeneous collection of other movables."[53]

States that owned their own campgrounds (only eleven in 1893 and seventeen in 1897) fared better than those that did not. States without permanent grounds allowed local communities to bid for the privilege of hosting camps. Desperately short of money but eager for an encampment, the Indiana Legion struck an agreement with civic leaders of Lafayette to hold a camp in 1886 in conjunction with the Barnum Circus. The latter took 60 percent of the gate and the legion the remainder. Major Richard Lodor, U.S. Army, believed the legion's presence in a grand parade with the circus was "derogatory to the dignity and morale of the troops," as was the effect of seeing "officers in full uniform acting as ticket agents."[54] Two years later, the Texas Volunteer Guard participated in a grander affair at Austin. The Guard took part in drill competitions and a sham battle but, according to Christian Nelson, shared time with "band concerts, German singers, an international baby show, rodeo, grand ball . . . and sportsman's tournament."[55]

To attract paying customers and also pique the interests of Guardsmen, states often featured a sham battle as the culminating point of summer camp. At their 1893 camp, Oregon Guardsmen conducted a sham battle "between the troops and a body of Klamath Indians, the Indians being in war paint and following their old methods of attack and defense."[56] An 1889 Texas encampment included not only horse, dog, and Roman chariot racing but sideshows of monkeys and snakes as well as a carefully scripted "nightly exhibition of the 'Fall of Paris.' "[57] Army inspectors condemned the sham battles. One regular inspector described a Missouri Guard skirmish as "a perfect farce from a military point of view."[58]

Competitive drill meets, a vestige of the antebellum volunteer militia, brought forth even harsher condemnations from regular and National Guard officers. Competitive drills were most common in the South during the 1880s although units from other regions occasionally took part. Regular officers understood that the poorer states permitted their Guard companies to take part in competitive drills because there was no money for state-supported camps. Nonetheless, they believed the competitions did more harm than good by perpetuating the worst practices of the old volunteer militia. Companies taking part in the meets gave all their time to perfecting intricate close order drill. More often than not, the drill units appeared in fancy uniforms reminiscent of the antebellum militia. Major E. C. Woodruff reported that at an 1890 meet in Texas "gray, red, and Zouave were mixed with blue within ranks and detracted much from their military appearance."[59]

Worst of all, the most zealous competitors cared only for the prize money, refusing to follow camp routine, ignoring superior officers, and complaining bitterly when they failed to win. An adept drill unit could garner substantial winnings. From the mid-1880s into the mid-1890s, the Houston Light Guard, a premier competitive outfit, took home $30,000 in prize money and trophies valued at $10,000. Following his inspection of an 1885 Mobile meet, the Army's Captain William Powell noted that if the intense effort to win continued, "I fear that companies will be organized on the principles of baseball clubs, and the true military spirit of the encampments absorbed in speculation.''[60] To avoid any appearance that the Army endorsed the meets, Adjutant General J. C. Kelton directed his officers in 1886 to stop serving as competition judges.[61]

Other methods besides annual camps were necessary to improve the Guard in any event. Before 1861, volunteer units dealt with their governments only to obtain legal recognition, commissions for their officers, and federal arms distributed to the states. Following the reorganizations of the late 1870s, however, governors and legislators sought to impose greater control and supervision over their military forces. Governors and adjutants general more readily disbanded units that failed to meet minimum company enrollments or hold the required number of yearly drills. Inspectors general visited local units to examine records, armories, weapons, and company administration. By the late 1880s, nearly all states required newly elected company officers to pass an examination before being commissioned. A smaller but significant number mandated examinations when officers were promoted. If the exams were at times perfunctory, they nonetheless set a minimum standard for holding a commission. Finally, states increasingly came to accept Regular Army regulations and practices as the standard for guiding the National Guard in its quest for effectiveness.[62]

States also increased the power and authority of their adjutants general. More and more, the post became a full-time salaried position. Although the pay was modest, usually from $1,500 to $2,000 annually, it proved sufficient to attract men with National Guard experience who were willing to devote time and energy to invigorating their service. States with larger forces and adequate budgets established small permanent bureaucracies to assist the adjutant general in carrying out his duties. Almost everywhere, the adjutant general served as the governor's chief of staff and ex officio inspector general, quartermaster general, and chief of ordnance.

Any adjutant general was inherently a political personage, appointed by the governor and with a term matching that of the man who appointed him. Yet many were more than political hacks. As the Guard became more firmly established during the 1880s it lobbied successfully for laws that required that the adjutant generalcy go to a man with prior service in the National Guard. Adjutants general could never be nonpartisan given their method of appointment, but few openly used the Guard as a patronage vehicle. Guardsmen came from both major parties, and companies were located in all regions of the states. Only a foolish governor or adjutant general took the risk of offending politically active Guard officers and their local units scattered across the state by subjecting the service to partisan manipulation.

As the only official responsible for regular Guard administration, an able adjutant general familiar with the service could make a significant impact. State studies show that if money was the first factor in determining the effectiveness of a particular state soldiery, strong leadership from the adjutant general came a close second. Governors generally demonstrated only a passing interest in the Guard, usually when civil disorder threatened, and otherwise left the administration of the institution to their adjutants general. A great deal therefore depended on their ability and leadership.

Many states established military advisory boards—usually composed of the governor, adjutant general, and division or brigade commanders—as another administrative means for imposing central control. Some boards simply audited military accounts, but others prepared rules and regulations, approved regimental and brigade organizations, and disbanded ineffective companies. To a lesser extent, divisional and brigade commanders could exert some authority to enhance discipline and efficiency. Their effectiveness depended upon personality and experience as well as the tradition within each state. From its reorganization in 1878, for example, Pennsylvania established a strong role for its division commander, particularly in determining the agenda for summer camps. Elsewhere, where no division organization existed, as in New York, brigade commanders held little power, and the adjutant general set the tone that governed the Guard.[63]

Despite considerable efforts, even the more effectively administered states found it difficult to impose central control over local units. In the 1880s, for example, Wisconsin companies strongly objected to the rigorous inspections and acid commentary of Inspector General Charles King, a West Pointer and retired Army officer. Governor Jeremiah Rusk removed King from the post following many complaints from state legislators and local newspapers. No state could overcome the semi-independence of companies as long as the latter contributed more money for their maintenance than came from the state. Iowa's adjutant general, William L. Alexander, defined the problem succinctly in 1881: "Every man feels a financial interest in [unit] affairs," he commented, "and desires a voice in the management, to the extent of the capital invested."[64]

Strong unit-community connections curtailed centralized control as well. Guard leaders in Pennsylvania recognized the tactical value of the three-battalion, twelve-company regiment, but a statewide reorganization required the disbandment of three regiments and the reassignment of their companies to other regiments. However, such a change "might give dissatisfaction to the Guard" and its local supporters, Army Lieutenant William J. Lyster commented in 1896, and so the state made no changes.[65] Regional rivalries plagued the Oregon Guard, according to Inspector General George F. Telfer. Units from the "country districts" resented reforms, which came largely from officers in Portland's First Regiment. Companies located in the state's eastern region resisted going to camp only "to be 'bossed by and made fun of by a lot of Portland dudes,' " Telfer warned his brigade commander, Charles Beebe. If subjected to strict camp discipline, he added, they would complain, and "we would have a hard time with the next Legislature."[66]

Telfer told General Beebe that he understood the latter's desire to improve the Oregon Guard but advised Beebe "do not try to force matters." Telfer recommended that Beebe personally visit the country companies, give them a "good sharp talk," which "will do more for a company than all the inspecting officers can do in two hours. Talk fifteen minutes to the men—then talk fifteen minutes to the businessmen of the town—and you will start a reform worth having."[67] Telfer's advice, which in any event epitomized General Beebe's command method, says much about the National Guard in the late nineteenth century. Although the Guard established an institutionalized framework more advanced than that governing the antebellum state soldiery, it nonetheless remained a decentralized, locally controlled system governed more by personality than by military regulations and discipline.

The local perception of the state soldiery as volunteers who possessed the right to control their own destiny marked the most enduring connection between the old uniformed militia and the National Guard. Guardsmen resisted centralized control in part because they shared prevailing attitudes toward governmental power of any sort. Morton Keller sees "a period of atrophy" in state administrative affairs in the post–Civil War years, with "a localism and hostility to government that worked against the active state in the North as well as the South."[68] State military officials fared no better than other administrative agencies in extending a strong hand from the capital down to the local level. More importantly, Guardsmen in the companies and regiments resented efforts to centralize control over them because they justifiably believed their organizations were more the products of their own time, energy, and money than of the states'. As long as the onus for organizing and sustaining local units fell chiefly on their shoulders, Guardsmen refused to surrender control to what they perceived to be outside interference.

One element in the state soldiery worked to break ties with the past and make the Guard a quasi-professional service. Composed entirely of officers and difficult to number, they came largely from a small group that made state military service an avocation and cared a great deal for both the friendships they made there and the service they rendered. Compelled by business demands to resign his commission in the Wisconsin Guard after ten years of duty, Captain Joseph M. Ballard lamented in 1898 that "I want to go out and I want to stay in. When I think of quitting the W.N.G. it almost breaks my heart."[69] Ballard's lament reflected the many years he and other Guard officers amassed, which generally encompassed brief service as an enlisted man and promotion through the company officer grades, frequently to field officer level.

Charles Beebe of Oregon began his career as a private in New York's Seventh Regiment in 1871 and retired as a brigadier general and brigade commander in Oregon in 1903. In Wisconsin, Charles Boardman's military career spanned thirty-eight years. He rose from elected corporal in 1880 to brigadier general in the Army of the United States in 1918 and in between served sixteen years as state adjutant general. Boardman's comrade, Charles King, may well have set a nationwide record. King served in Wisconsin for fifty-one years, from 1882 to 1933. Anecdotal evidence confirms biographical detail. The Army inspection report on Pennsylvania, for example, noted that the division's staff officers "are generally officers of long experience, several having risen to be colonels of the line and commanded regiments with distinction."[70]

Long-serving officers pursued an agenda that focused on forwarding the Guard's interests in state affairs, improving its military efficiency, and, ultimately, ridding the service of uniformed militia practices. They did so initially by informal lobbying and after the early 1880s increasingly through state National Guard associations. Guardsmen concerned with furthering the service's interests with the federal government formed the National Guard Association (NGA) in 1879. Associations took shape in the states at the same time. Although the national organization fruitlessly pursued efforts to win a significant increase in federal aid, state groups worked successfully to influence military legislation in their own commonwealths. Guardsmen pushed for revised and codified laws, appointed committees to write the codifications, and lobbied legislators for increased military budgets. These groups led the way in establishing Army regulations and practices as the standard for the Guard.[71]

Guard reformers were particularly intent on preserving the reformed state soldiery for themselves. In part, this meant purging the laws of antebellum militia traditions, notably the appointment of political hacks to the adjutant generalcy, the election of company and field officers with no military experience, and the appointment of socially or economically prestigious men to staff positions and the governor's personal military staff. A New Yorker urged the adoption of laws "whereby the National Guard could be entirely freed from political influences, and all positions in it filled by officers selected by the Guard itself."[72] Wisconsin Guardsmen protested mightily in 1889 when Governor William D. Hoard appointed his political manager to the adjutant generalcy. Although Badger State soldiers failed to amend the law so that only a Guardsman could hold the office, Hoard's successors thereafter selected their adjutants general from the higher ranks of the Guard.[73]

By the early 1890s, nearly all state laws provided that men standing for election as company officers serve at least one enlistment in the ranks before taking a commission. Although Michigan law permitted the governor to appoint any Guard officer as brigade commander, "for many years back it has been customary to promote the ranking colonel," the Military Information Division reported in 1896.[74] As much by custom as by law, Guardsmen came to treat the election of regimental officers and brigade commanders as a question of seniority rather than political popularity. The practice became more common as more men compiled service records of several years and unit stability ensured battalion and regimental permanence. Avocational Guardsmen could then see a promotion path through which they could reap rewards for service in the National Guard.

Finally, long-service Guard officers led efforts to improve their personal professional capacities. Both the national and state Guard associations served not only as lobby groups but as forums for professional discussions. Guardsmen and Army officers regularly lectured on tactics, law, discipline, and other military topics. In his address to the Ohio NGA in 1889, Army Lieutenant A. C. Sharpe discussed "Instruction in Armories" and praised the Ohio NGA as "a most potent agency for your own professional improvement."[75] New York Guardsmen took a prominent role in organizing the National Rifle Association (NRA) in 1871 to promote "scientific riflery."[76]

From the mid-1880s on, articles concerning the state soldiery written by Guard and Army officers appeared with increasing regularity in the burgeoning service journals published by the regulars, most notably the important *Journal of the Military Service Institution of the United States*. The leading military periodical of the period, the *Army and Navy Journal*, included a weekly page on state military affairs and published items of interest and articles on professional matters submitted by Guardsmen. Army officers inspecting state forces in the 1880s as well as those permanently assigned to the states in the 1890s lectured and instructed regularly at the invitation of the Guardsmen.

Guardsmen eager to improve the state soldiery's military efficiency and effectiveness were only partially successful. Stymied by limited state budgets, frustrated by their image as industrial policemen, and constrained by the continuing semi-independence of local units, reform-minded Guardsmen looked to the federal government for succor. Beginning in the late 1870s and with greater energy by the mid-1880s, they sought an increase in federal aid to the states and informal recognition as the reserve ground force for the Army. The reformers encountered congressional indifference and regular Army skepticism, with their only victory the modest increase in annual arms distribution to $400,000 that Congress granted in 1887. Although lack of public interest in military affairs and doubts within the Army partly explain the Guard's failure in these campaigns, the state soldiers bore some of the fault as well. Even the reformers remained at heart volunteer soldiers of the older sort, legatees of the republican citizen soldier tradition. For although they earnestly sought additional federal financial assistance in the name of national defense and promised to serve voluntarily when war came, they did not want to surrender their independence beyond the state level.

5

To Serve the Nation: The Guard's Quest for a Reserve Role, 1880–1898

In 1880, Adjutant General R. C. Drum of the U.S. Army wrote to his state counterparts to solicit ideas to advance "uniformity" between Army and National Guard organizations so that in the event of war state volunteers "could be added to the regular Army without any jarring or confusion."[1] Secretary of War Alexander Ramsey endorsed Drum's actions and also supported legislation pending in Congress to amend the militia law and increase federal military aid to the states. Recalling the chaos of 1861, when Northern militia rushed to defend Washington DC, Ramsey emphasized the need to establish "a trained force, so officered and disciplined as to be ready at once to be added to the regular army" when conflict came. Although General Drum saw state forces as "nurseries" to provide trained officers "to organize and command the volunteer forces," Ramsey backed the reform bill because "it fixes our active militia within practicable limits, makes it an intelligent living force, that can be utilized and controlled."[2]

As the comments of Drum and Ramsey illustrate, the rise of the National Guard in the 1870s revived the question of where the state soldiery fit in national military policy. Interest in the Guard's potential as a reserve for the Army arose prior to 1880. In the early 1870s, the Army's adjutant general and chief of ordnance recommended increasing federal assistance to the states in order to equip their soldiers more adequately for possible national service. The founding of the NRA in 1871, which was largely the work of New York Guardsmen led by Colonel George Wingate of the Twenty-second Regiment, brought systematic rifle shooting to the Guard. Although Wingate's rifle-shooting program initially took root only in the Northeast, by the 1890s its presence could be found in most of the National Guard. Most important, the NRA sought to improve the marksmanship of the citizen soldiery, as organized in the state militia forces, for wartime service.[3]

NRA leaders also played a major role in the establishment of the NGA as an advocate of the reserve function for the state soldiery. Following exploratory meetings in Richmond, Virginia, in late 1878 and in New York City in early 1879, the NGA held its first formal convention in St. Louis in the autumn of 1879. New Yorkers led by George Wingate headed the effort to organize the NGA, and the convention elected Wingate as the association's first president. Representing itself as the voice of "The Volunteers of America," the association asserted that "the wars of this country have all been fought by citizen soldiers."[4] Intent on promoting "military efficiency throughout the active militia," the Guardsmen gathered in St. Louis endorsed a bill to replace the Militia Act of 1792. It was this bill that Secretary of War Ramsey so warmly endorsed in his 1880 annual report.[5]

The Guard's quest for greater federal aid and a recognized reserve role appeared at the same time as its developing role in quelling civil disorder. From the revival of the state soldiery in the mid-1870s to the outbreak of war in 1898, Guardsmen gave equal weight to defense of the nation and constabulary duty as the two major functions of their service. Delegates to the NGA's 1881 convention discussed the reserve role in detail. Massachusetts's adjutant general reiterated the idea in 1882, noting that given the Army's small size, "reliance must be placed on state organizations, the Militia" in time of war.[6] Brigadier General Frank Reeder of Pennsylvania saw the Guard as "a sort of citizens' West Point."[7] Following the Spanish-American War, Wisconsin's adjutant general, Charles R. Boardman, expressed in his annual report for 1898 the predominant view in the state service at the turn of the century: "Deprive the Guard from participation, *as a duty*, in the wars of its country and one of the most important and best reasons for its existence is taken away" (emphasis added).[8]

Guardsmen asserting their institution's role in national defense downplayed the constabulary function. One spokesman argued in 1887 that state soldiers "have been drilled too much as if police work were their only destiny" and urged that the Guard emphasize its reserve function.[9] By the 1890s, Guard spokesmen were affirming more strongly that constabulary duty was not their main mission. Most state soldiers, Illinois's Colonel James M. Rice wrote, would "be very much pained . . . to find that they were only organized to do police duty.'' To serve the nation in war, he asserted, ''is the pride and the life of the National Guard.''[10] Colonel George Graham of Wisconsin took umbrage when a fellow officer maintained that the Guard's chief purpose was to protect property. Graham asked his fellow officers, ''how many of you, gentlemen, are willing to be classed with the police force? . . . I do wish to impress upon you that you are the advance line of the nation's defenders . . . not policemen!''[11]

The War Department endorsed the general idea of the National Guard as a reserve into the 1890s because it assumed volunteers raised by the states would fight the next war. Both former Commanding General William T. Sherman and his successor, Philip Sheridan, urged increasing federal aid to the states in the 1880s to prepare them for war. General Drum and his successor, John C. Kelton, led the effort by supporting militia reform bills that the NGA brought to Congress. They also sought ways for the Army and Guard to work together. Beginning in 1880, General Drum took the initiative when he sent regular officers to inspect the Guard in summer camp whenever state officials requested Army inspection. Drum's office instructed one inspector to develop ''cordial relations'' with the state soldiers, ''remembering that upon the latter our country must ever largely rely in the hour of a general call to arms.''[12] General Kelton sent an officer to New York City in April 1889 to observe National Guard units participating in the centennial celebration of George Washington's inauguration and to ascertain ''the ability of the State authorities to concentrate their militia in times of emergency.''[13]

Kelton's 1889 article in *Forum* magazine, ''Requirements for National Defense,'' offered suggestions for improving the National Guard and bringing it under limited federal control. ''It is upon this force,'' he argued, ''that the defense of the country rests.''[14] In 1890, the inspector general's office of the War Department assumed responsibility for assigning regulars to inspect state organizations. Inspector General J. C. Breckenridge hoped that the state and federal governments would eventually fund the Guard adequately in order to ''maintain a reserve from the militia'' capable of defending the nation.[15] Beginning in 1893, the newly organized Military Information Division (MID) of the adjutant general's office assumed the inspection and reporting function. MID reports became increasingly detailed and instructive and included recommendations and remarks from inspectors on ways to improve the Guard's administrative, disciplinary, and tactical capacities.[16]

After 1880, the Guard and Army came into direct contact through the detailing of regular officers to inspect and instruct state soldiers. Army officers served with the Guard in the 1880s during the summer encampment season, but beginning in the early 1890s the War Department assigned officers to state military headquarters for three- to four-year tours. Commanding Generals Sherman and John M. Schofield in particular supported the detailing of regular officers to state duty to remove them from isolated frontier garrison duty. By the late 1890s, more than forty officers served with state and territorial forces, and during the summer training sessions many more reported for temporary duty to inspect encamped troops.[17]

Regular officers welcomed the opportunity to learn what the state soldiery was doing. Lieutenant C. A. L. Totten reported that he returned to his normal duties following his inspection of Connecticut troops in 1885 "renewed in the confidence of [the] country's inherent invincibility" and deeply impressed that "the states have accomplished so much in the face of odds so great."[18] Another regular noted that working with the Guard provided "officers an opportunity to know thoroughly our future soldiers."[19] War Department cooperation with the Guard represented a view within the Army that one of its chief missions should be to increase its role as a school of instruction. General Sherman believed that one of the Army's major instructional duties was "to mould the militia into a form in which it may be made available when called into active service."[20] Other regulars reiterated the theme. Lieutenant A. C. Sharpe endorsed the Army's teaching role, for he saw the state soldiery as "more than a mere police force. . . . I consider the National Guard as a great school of preparation for the future."[21]

Contact with regular officers detailed to the Guard generated an unprecedented cooperation between state and professional soldiers. New Yorker T. F. Rodenbough, while extolling the volunteer citizen soldiery in Whiggish republican rhetoric, nonetheless accepted that the Guard's "natural instructor and military exemplar is the Regular Army."[22] The Military Service Institution of the United States, founded in 1878 by Army officers eager to promote professional discussion and writing, opened its membership to Guard officers in 1885. Guardsmen thereafter participated in institution meetings and contributed articles to its journal. At an 1886 meeting, General H. C. King, inspector general of the New York National Guard, lauded Guard-Army cooperation. He added, "when *you* come to the front and take us by the hand, it gives a dignity to our work which it never had before, and I can assure you we appreciate it" (emphasis in original).[23]

For all the comity that seemed to govern the relations between the Guard and Army, the legal and institutional relationship between the state forces and the federal government remained unchanged. A succession of congressional bills aimed at amending the militia law and increasing the federal allotment failed to win passage despite War Department support and NGA lobbying. From its initial organization in 1879 through the early 1890s, the NGA tried unsuccessfully to change the national militia law. It first asked Congress to repeal the Militia Act of 1792 in 1879 and to grant statutory recognition of "a volunteer militia," that is, the National Guard, to replace the antiquated eighteenth-century law.[24] Guard reformers also wanted an increase in federal assistance, the suggested amounts ranging from $600,000 to $1 million annually. In addition, NGA proposals called for federal aid, which had always been in kind rather than cash, to include clothing, camp equipment, and general quartermaster supplies as well as weapons. However, other than an 1887 amendment that raised the annual federal allotment to $400,000 and allowed the states to request camp equipment and clothing, Congress refused to amend or repeal the Militia Act of 1792.[25]

The NGA's request for militia reform engendered only passing interest in Congress, a body notoriously indifferent to peacetime military affairs. If the Navy won attention in the later 1880s and increased appropriations thereafter, Washington politicos, the national press, and the general public displayed no interest in reforming the Army or amending the militia statutes. Moreover, some regular reformers proposing programs for change revealed a skepticism toward the state soldiery that belied the apparently genial relationships developing between professional and amateur soldiers.[26]

Ardent Army reformers urged fundamental changes in American military policy because they believed modern warfare and prevailing international relations threatened conflict between the United States and a major European nation. Such a war, they argued, would place the nation in combat against an army equipped with modern weapons and manned by well-trained regular soldiers supported by trained reserves. Reform supporters wanted the Army reorganized to reflect European methods, including a general staff system and a trained reserve available immediately for federal service. Given the traditional American practice of raising a volunteer army only after war had begun, Lieutenant George B. Duncan feared that "a modern war would probably be concluded before [our] embryo armies could be brought into being."[27]

As Duncan's comment illustrates, some Army reformers openly questioned the Guard's value as a reserve. Skeptics fell into two groups. The more extreme reflected the ideas of the era's foremost military thinker, Emory Upton, who excoriated the traditional reliance on untrained state volunteers. Upton believed that only when the nation adopted a military system that placed the organization and direction of war under the control of professional Army officers with a wholly federal reserve force would it overcome what he saw as the military ineptitude of the past. Reformers of the Uptonian persuasion rejected the role of the Army as a school of instruction. Instead, they sought a military system under the control of professionally educated officers pursuing readiness for war in peacetime. Writers echoing Upton saw little value in the National Guard as a reserve. One critic, Lieutenant Arthur L. Wagner, found in the Guard "a sad lack of anything like efficient organization or intelligent instruction."[28] In sum, Lieutenant S. M. Foote asserted, the United States must adopt a "system in time of peace that shall make the Federal government a single supreme power in all matters pertaining to war—certainly in the most important of all, the raising and training of her armies."[29]

A second group of Army reformers was less eager to eliminate the National Guard from the reserve role. Lieutenant A. C. Sharpe argued that while the idea of national volunteers appeared attractive, in fact it would be "wholly and utterly impracticable" given the state soldiery's long history and the nation's traditional distrust of a large regular army. In light of those realities, Sharpe argued, "irresistibly we are drawn to the conclusion" that the Guard was "the true National Reserve—the only practical organization which can be availed of under our form of government."[30] Regulars who viewed the state forces with some favor nonetheless advocated amending federal laws to permit national regulation through the establishment of a National Guard bureau within the War Department. What was needed, Lieutenant Sidney E. Stuart concluded, was to find "suitable constitutional methods" to make the National Guard "susceptible of prompt, combined, and effective employment by the general government."[31]

National Guard officers eagerly entered the reform debate. A minority supported partial federal control largely to counter regular officer suggestions that a federal volunteer reserve be adopted. General Albert Ordway of the District of Columbia National Guard, outlined a plan for dual state-federal control in 1882 that resembled the Militia Act of 1903 (the so-called Dick Act). Ordway favored greater federal "support and instruction rather than attempting the creation of a new force."[32] Another Guard advocate supported a dual oath to make the Guard "in fact, United States volunteers, and, if best, change the name from National Guardsmen to United States Volunteers."[33] By the 1890s, progressive Guardsmen accepted Army reformers' contentions that to become an effective reserve the state soldiery would have to accept at least partial federal supervision. Lieutenant Walter S. Frazier of Illinois reflected the views of many Guardsmen when he wrote in 1897 that "as the prime reason for the existence of the National Guard is and must always be the defense of the nation, national supervision seems not only eminently proper but essential."[34]

The broader outlines offered by Army and Guard reformers for governing state-federal control of the National Guard resembled policies adopted after 1898. There would be no reform in the late nineteenth century, however, partly because state soldiers could not agree on the shape it should take. Differences appeared at the first NGA convention in 1879 when a reform bill supported by the legislative committee's majority limited federal aid to those states maintaining a minimum number of Guardsmen per congressional district, a provision that favored states that kept well-organized forces. The minority report, adopted by the convention, provided that aid be allotted according to each state's population, as had been the case since 1855. More seriously, Guardsmen could not agree on the extent of federal control they were willing to accept. Although it appears that spokesmen from the Northeast were the most ardent in opposing any meaningful federal control, such was not entirely the case. New Yorkers, notably Generals George Wingate and E. L. Molineux, split sharply on the issue, with Wingate willing to accept some supervision while his comrade rejected it outright.[35]

Given the sharp divisions within the NGA, Wingate convinced the third convention in 1881 to state merely that it sought an increase in federal money and recognition of "the volunteer militia as the only active militia." To appease those opposed to federal interference, the convention included a statement in its memorial to Congress that would brand the NGA as an exponent of states' rights to the end of the century. The memorial asserted, "we are opposed to any change in the relative authority now exercised by the Federal and State governments over the militia, and we are opposed to any interference in the existing militia organizations of the States or the creation of a new force."[36]

Yet it is erroneous to see the NGA as a powerful lobby stoutly defending states' rights. The 1881 memorial represented a compromise adopted to win unanimous support for the request for increased aid from Congress. More importantly, at its peak the NGA drew representatives from only eighteen states for its 1885 convention and more commonly reported only fourteen to fifteen states at sessions between 1879 and 1892. Clearly, the NGA did not represent a majority of states, let alone a majority of Guard officers, and it lacked the financial means to sustain a concerted lobbying effort in Washington. In fact, the association met infrequently in the late nineteenth century—only six times from 1879 through 1896. The NGA hardly represented the fearsome interest group some historians contend it was.[37]

Neither is it correct to argue that Guardsmen sought to limit federal authority in an ideological defense of state sovereignty. Their real concern was to ensure that they contributed to the development of national policy and would be given a role in administering reserve affairs. The original 1879 NGA bill included sections requiring the president to establish two boards, one to select a common uniform and another to write a set of rules and regulations for the state soldiery. In each case, Guardsmen were to compose the majority of the boards. A third provision called for an annual inspection to be carried out by a state officer "accompanied" by an Army officer. In 1897 Lieutenant Colonel Walter Frazier of Illinois made explicit what NGA provisions only implied. He favored shared state-federal control and a National Guard Bureau within the War Department. The bureau would be manned by Guardsmen as well as regulars, "but the Guard would be *coordinate* with rather than *subordinate* to the Army" (emphasis added).[38]

When T. F. Rodenbough of New York insisted that Congress must amend the militia law "without encroaching, in the least, upon the prerogatives of any State," he was defending Guardsmen's interests in the companies and regiments they had personally organized and sustained.[39] Ohio's Frank Irvine thus insisted that Guardsmen participate in developing and implementing policy, for they "are best calculated to judge the possibilities of militia organization and efficiency."[40] Guardsmen sought to protect their units and modus operandi from federal interference by reasserting, often arrogantly, Whiggish republican values. As Wisconsin's Adjutant General Chandler P. Chapman argued, the Guard "with every soldier no less a citizen . . . can never be used against the state or the welfare of its citizens," unlike regular soldiers.[41] State soldiers served voluntarily, without pay. "How unlike the Regular!" Colonel James G. Gilchrist of Iowa intoned. "The one does *his* work for a stipulated compensation . . . the other as an act of good citizenship" (emphasis in original).[42] Guardsmen echoed the views found in John A. Logan's *The Volunteer Soldier of America*. Logan boldly contended that "the military power of the Republic has always resided, does now reside, and must continue to reside . . . in the volunteer—the citizen soldier of America."[43] Although Logan wrote about all volunteers, state soldiers appropriated the term *citizen soldier* for themselves. "The young men in the Guard today are of the same stuff as those who crossed the Delaware with Washington and trounced the British under Jackson," the Ohio colonel E. C. Brush claimed.[44] Captain Leroy T. Steward of Illinois, like many Guardsmen, emphasized the ties between the Guard and Civil War veterans. The man tested in "the severe school in '65 . . . has been the inspiration if not the founder of the National Guard today."[45] If, as Colonel Brush of Ohio claimed, "the American Volunteer is the grandest prototype of a soldier ever presented to the world," he was now a National Guardsman.[46]

Wrapped in the mantle of enduring republican values, Guardsmen presented themselves as the institutional embodiment of the volunteer citizen soldier. They believed, with some justice, that as organized state soldiers they represented an improvement on past practice. Unlike volunteers called at large from the body politic in previous wars, Guardsmen were organized, partially trained, and equipped. Given that fact, state soldiers believed they deserved federal financial assistance to better prepare themselves for war. As institutionalized representatives of the volunteer tradition, however, Guardsmen believed they should not be subjected to strict Army supervision lest they lose their special qualities as citizen soldiers.

The refusal of Congress to amend the militia law left the state soldiery in limbo. National laws governing federal use of militia dated from the 1790s and pertained only to presidential calls to execute the laws, suppress insurrection, and repel invasion. They said nothing about calling the uniformed militia to national service. The rise of the National Guard posed a serious constitutional question. Was the Guard a legitimate component of the constitutional militia? Some in the Army thought not. When asked by Adjutant General J. C. Kelton to comment on the legality of the president mobilizing portions of the Guard for war or training purposes, the Army's acting judge advocate general, G. Norman Lieber, deemed "the local and somewhat fanciful name of 'national guard' " an unknown term to the sections of the "Constitution or Acts of Congress defining the militia."[47] On the other hand, Colonel James Rice of Illinois, an outspoken proponent of the Guard as the constitutionally authorized national reserve, argued that the state soldiery was available "for almost any purpose and at any place," with "no territorial restriction as to the use of the militia in the service of the United States." Guardsmen composed "the volunteer army, camping at home in peace, waiting for the bugle call. When war is declared they . . . embark in war. When war is over they return again to their homes."[48]

If constitutional issues caused Army reformers to question the Guard's value as a reserve, so too did the manner in which the states organized their troops. Unit strengths and tables of organizations in the organized militia differed markedly from those of the Army. The Guard not only failed to conform with Army organization, but no two states organized their soldiery in the same way. For example, whereas five states retained the divisional organization in 1895, only Pennsylvania maintained a proper division. Many states formed their regiments in brigades, but each adopted an organizational form to suit local needs. Some states, on the other hand, had more than enough units to organize brigades but did not do so. Finally, diversity reigned rampant in regimental structures both within as well as between states. Eager to provide as many line colonelcies as possible and give regions a regimental identity, states made little effort to maintain a standard organization and supported regiments ranging from six to twelve companies.[49]

To reform-minded regulars and Guardsmen, the state military of the late nineteenth century most resembled the old militia in that it kept elaborate staff systems, including the ubiquitous gubernatorial aides-de-camp selected from a governor's personal friends and political cronies. Although most states provided a full panoply of staff officers, only the adjutant general actually performed meaningful duties. Colonel Edmund C. Brush of Ohio surveyed thirty-six states in 1897 and discovered "a promiscuous distribution of military titles." One unnamed state alone had a staff of 6 brigadier generals, 27 colonels, and 6 majors to oversee a force of 2,000 men. Collectively, the states in his survey claimed 543 staff officers, distributed as follows: 7 major generals, 90 brigadiers, 245 colonels, 143 lieutenant colonels, 45 majors, 5 captains, and a single lieutenant. The number of staff officers, Brush noted, was an embarrassment that "belittles the Guard and belittles rank."[50]

For many Army observers, the Guard's bloated organizational structure and officer corps symbolized the state soldiery's military incapacity. The *Army and Navy Journal* endorsed efforts to develop closer relations between the two services but insisted that "the standard is the Regular Army." Unfortunately, in its eyes, state soldiers "don't want Regular Army methods, as we are often told."[51] An Army correspondent wrote the *Journal* that seeking cooperation with the Guard was futile, for "the majority of officers in the militia know it all and no one can teach them anything."[52] Not surprisingly, such commentary irritated Guardsmen. "It is a little discouraging to us of the 'play-soldier' force," Colonel Winthrop Alexander of the District of Columbia complained, "to have our professional brothers doubt our motives and question our values."[53]

At bottom, the gap between Guardsmen and regulars stemmed from differing perceptions of the nature of military leadership. As expressed in Logan's *The Volunteer Soldier of America*, state citizen soldiers believed that natural talent, love of country, and shared bonds between officers and men produced warriors worthy of their country. The professional view, intensified by the Civil War experience and European military developments, saw soldiering in starkly different terms. In a speech to the Military Service Institution of the United States in 1885, William T. Sherman commented: "I am convinced by actual experience and study that *habit* is a more valuable quality" for soldiers "than what is termed *courage*" (emphasis in original). Indeed, he went on, habit—that is, discipline and training—served better in battle than "even patriotism."[54] Few Guardsmen would have agreed with "Uncle Billy" on the superiority of habit over patriotism in war. The comments of Captain Charles Bentzoni on a Minnesota Guard camp in 1889 encapsulate the differing views of military service. Noting the tactical ignorance of Guard officers, Bentzoni observed that "I was unable to discover any information among them as to the real use of troops, the exercise of organized human physical and psychical force at its highest potence—war." Good men served in the Minnesota Guard, he went on, but they needed to "disenthrall themselves from a slavish belief that parade and review is the highest use to which troops may be put."[55]

The National Guard's military effectiveness and role in national defense remained moot points until 1898. Deteriorating relations with Spain over the fate of Cuba beginning in early 1897 ultimately led Congress to declare war on 24 April 1898. In the month before Congress declared war, President William McKinley's administration at last considered mobilizing a wartime land force, much too late for a reasoned consideration of how to augment the Army. Congress eventually named the National Guard as the main source for volunteers. Selection of the ill-prepared state troops led to a chaotic mobilization and the calamities of disease and death that swept the camps where state soldiers concentrated. These well-accounted events need no detailed treatment here.[56]

Mobilization in 1898 gave the National Guard an opportunity to meet its claim that it could provide effective soldiers ready for war. In the eyes of the Army, and many historians, the Guard failed miserably. Admittedly, state soldiers worked against War Department efforts in late March and early April to win legislation enlarging the Army to one hundred four thousand men by the addition of seventy-five men each to existing regiments. Sponsored by Congressman John A. T. Hull, the bill represented the efforts of Army reformers to rationalize and centralize wartime manpower policy and curtail the role of state military systems in the conduct of war. Hull's proposal immediately encountered opposition in Congress as well as from Guardsmen and governors. Congress rejected the Hull bill and approved a manpower bill on 22 April that allowed the Guard to volunteer as units.

In the ensuing mobilization, the state soldiery displayed much incompetence, but the greater failure in 1898 was a systemic one—a failure of public policy. Augmenting the army with a hastily mobilized and untrained state-recruited volunteer force complicated the conduct of an overseas war in an age dominated by steam and steel navies. Fears of a Spanish fleet attacking American coastal cities or delivering troops to Cuba pushed the McKinley administration to send an expeditionary force to the island well before the land forces were properly organized. Institutional myopia in the Army and National Guard contributed to the flawed mobilization. During fifteen years of debate and discussion neither regulars nor Guardsmen had explored ways to overcome the barriers to military reform. War Department plans to bypass the Guard were ill conceived because they ignored the Guard's prewar quest for the reserve role. Strong state opposition culminating in the Hull bill's defeat should not have surprised military leaders. On the other hand, the Guard's peacetime refusal to conform to Army unit tables of organization or adopt realistic training practices complicated mobilization and brought to federal service a mass of men unprepared for military duty.[57]

The Army's most grievous error was to ignore history and tradition. Reformers proposing the Hull bill failed to anticipate the widely popular demand to volunteer, an enthusiasm that potentially threatened the National Guard as much as it contributed to the destruction of the expansible army idea. From the sinking of the USS *Maine* in Havana harbor on 16 February 1898 well into June, men eager to serve inundated President McKinley and governors with tenders of service. Military enthusiasts most commonly offered themselves as candidates for Army or Guard commissions, but some also tendered companies and regiments they were ostensibly in the process of organizing. As commander in chief of the Army, McKinley more easily fended off the volunteers, although ultimately he had to satisfy the most bumptious of them all, Theodore Roosevelt.

Governors faced a more formidable challenge. Given the manpower law and the wording of President McKinley's telegram assigning quotas to each state—"regiments of the National Guard or State Militia shall be used"—the majority of governors called on the Guard to volunteer.[58] Some state leaders, however, refused to disregard tenders of service from friends and allies eager to gain commissions. Governor Murphy J. Foster of Louisiana slighted his State Guard by naming two political associates to command the state's two regiments. Protests from the Guard compelled Foster to permit Guard officers to elect the colonel of the Second Louisiana Volunteer Infantry. Missouri's governor, Lawrence V. Stephens, also created a furor when he had to choose between the Guard and volunteers from the larger body politic. Since Missouri maintained only four peacetime regiments, Stephens had to recruit two other units at large to meet the state's quota. He ignored the tender by self-appointed "Colonel" Louis A. Craig of an independent Kansas City regiment and earned the condemnation of the Kansas City press in the process. Stephens also offended Guard officers when organizing the Fifth and Sixth Missouri regiments by selecting state staff officers to command the units rather than line officers.[59]

Governors usually fended off private military aspirants by noting that they had no choice but to use the organized militia and citing President McKinley's mobilization telegram. One veteran of the war, Jones Palm, recalled that he and others from tiny Evansville, Minnesota, "organized a company of 50 young men," then sought "recognition from the governor and the officers of the state militia." State officials denied recognition and encouraged the enthusiasts to enlist in an active Guard company, which Palm and several others did.[60] In North Dakota, Governor Frank Briggs and his private secretary, George H. Phelps, commiserated with those seeking commissions but gratefully took refuge behind what Phelps described to one correspondent as "that infernal military code" governing the National Guard.[61]

Governor John Leedy of Kansas, a Populist, distrusted the Guard and believed that volunteers direct from civil life made the best soldiers. Leedy organized four infantry regiments, one composed entirely of African Americans, including officers. He allowed Guardsmen to enlist and be elected as officers by volunteers but otherwise bypassed the existing regiments. Of the 167 officers in the four Kansas regiments, only thirty had served in the Guard and only two of those at field grade level. By good fortune, Leedy selected the able Frederick Funston to command the Twentieth Kansas Volunteer Infantry. After Theodore Roosevelt, Funston would become the most famous and successful of all the 1898 volunteers. Funston conceded that much of his success with the Twentieth Kansas in the Philippines was due to the presence of some three hundred Guardsmen in the regiment.[62]

No other governor so blithely defied the president's request to rely on the Guard, but it is clear that Leedy's actions represented a broad cultural preference for localized voluntary participation in the war effort. Tell A. Turner, chaplain and historian of the Fifteenth Minnesota Volunteer Infantry, described his outfit as a "purely volunteer organization" because it did not come from the National Guard. Minnesota recruited the regiment from the general population to meet its quota of four regiments because the Guard maintained only three active units. According to Turner, "the other three regiments, having belonged to the National Guard were, necessarily, not so largely creatures of the Executive, nor were they so thoroughly representative of the State."[63] James E. Payne, chronicler of the Fifth Missouri Volunteer Infantry, which like the Fifteenth Minnesota was raised from the population at large and possessed just as undistinguished a wartime record, boasted of the "superlative excellence of the American volunteer."[64] Payne compared the low casualty rates suffered by European armies in wars of the 1860s and 1870s with those endured by both sides during the American Civil War. He argued that the much higher American casualty rates demonstrated conclusively that "American soldiers have withstood punishment that no trained armies of Europe ever have" because the volunteers possessed "endurance and fighting qualities" unseen in overtrained European armies.[65]

Historians critical of the Guard's role in 1898 fail to take into account the widespread support for voluntarism, localism, and informality that so profoundly affected the state response to President McKinley's call. If the volunteer tradition at its best produced a Frederick Funston, at its worst it brought forth an enduring American tendency toward braggadocio that transformed Theodore Roosevelt's brief brushes with combat into majestic military feats and led the Fifth Missouri's Payne to rank a state volunteer regiment the equal of a Prussian division. How else is one to explain Chaplain Turner's perception that Minnesota's organized militia units "belonged to the National Guard" and not to the governor or the people of the state and that by virtue of its amateur status the Fifteenth Minnesota "would have been good warriors" had they only been given the chance?[66]

Gerald Linderman situates the volunteer phenomenon within the local community that served as the primary focal point for loyalty and attachment, a focus that fostered a sense of familiarity and security in the face of war. It was the sort of localism that led community leaders in Florida to organize home guards without state sanction to defend the Atlantic and Gulf coasts against Spanish raiders. It was the kind of provincialism that defied the state of Pennsylvania when it attempted to place experienced Guard junior officers and NCOs in command of newly recruited companies raised to give existing Guard regiments a third battalion. The National Guard lost that struggle, its adjutant general reported, because "the localities from which the companies were taken exacted that officers as well as men should be from the same locality."[67]

Beginning in early 1898, state military leaders expected that their men would serve and began to prepare them for a call. Adjutants general in Massachusetts, Pennsylvania, and Wisconsin, for example, acquired more equipment and informally surveyed units to see how many men would volunteer. In Massachusetts, Governor Roger Walcott ordered Adjutant General Samuel Dalton "to make all necessary preparations for war, without seeming alarmist."[68] Dalton called the entire Massachusetts Volunteer Militia to an armory inspection on January 15 to assess the condition of his troops. From late January to mid-March, Guard officers wrote Wisconsin's adjutant general, Charles Boardman, asking him how to prepare for war. Boardman advised them to recruit to full strength and particularly to reenlist former Guardsmen. He wanted to demonstrate "to those outside [the Guard] that if they desire high positions they must first show their worthiness by serving a term during peace in the Wisconsin National Guard."[69]

Massachusetts and Pennsylvania sent military representatives to Washington before the declaration of war to find out how state troops were going to be used generally and to ensure specifically that the War Department would call for their Guardsmen. Early in March, General Boardman urged his political ally, Wisconsin's Republican congressman, John H. Davidson, to protect the interests of the National Guard. Boardman convinced Davidson to vote against the Hull bill because there was a "general feeling among all the boys that it was a blow to the National Guard."[70] It is hardly surprising that the bill met ready defeat, for Guard leaders like General Boardman had indicated weeks before war came that they were taking action to win the right to fight.[71]

Having won the privilege to volunteer, the Guard then had to meet the demands of mobilization. State units assembled in their armories or state camps where companies and regiments were then asked to volunteer as units. The vast majority of Guard units agreed to become United States Volunteers, although some Guardsmen did not opt to volunteer for personal, family, or business reasons. Nearly everywhere, large numbers of Guardsmen failed their physical exams. State officials recruited new enlisted men and supervised the election of replacement officers, then saw their men mustered into federal service by a U.S. Army officer. The mobilization and muster-in of the state volunteers proceeded at varying rates, depending upon how well states had supported and administered the Guard before 1898. States that equipped their men well and regularly sent them to camp faced few difficulties while mobilizing. In states where the Guard formed an effective lobby, with active officers in both parties and a permanent presence in capital cities through the state military bureaucracy, the Guardsmen were transformed into United States Volunteers relatively easily. Regimental and company officers, and most NCOs, remained essentially unchanged and formed the leadership cadre of volunteer units. The effective mobilizations in these states indicated that state funding, above all other factors, determined the efficiency of the only reserve the United States possessed.

States in the Northeast and Midwest, as demonstrated by Massachusetts, Pennsylvania, Ohio, and Wisconsin, mobilized their units quickly. In these states, Guard officials made preparations to feed and house their men prior to receiving their manpower quotas and moved them to mobilization camps upon the president's call. Governors worked closely with Guardsmen to recruit volunteers and demonstrated little rancor in making officer assignments, choosing to appoint peacetime line officers to command the volunteer regiments. In instances where military spending fell short of peacetime needs, as in North Dakota, a close-knit officer corps convinced the governor to allow it to determine the makeup of North Dakota's volunteer organization.[72]

On the other hand, commonwealths that neglected their soldiery in peacetime experienced disorganized mobilizations accompanied by gubernatorial interference in the selection of officers and rancorous disputes among unit officers. For example, confusion marked mobilizations in Florida, Missouri, Louisiana, and Texas. Governor Charles A. Culberson of Texas mobilized his Volunteer Guard by company but kept for himself the right to appoint regimental officers. The latter came from the Guard but rather than selecting line officers Culberson gave colonelcies to his adjutant general and other staff officers. Missouri's governor, Lawrence Stephens, nominally allowed the four Guard regiments to form volunteer outfits but continually interfered in officer appointments and angered everyone when organizing the state's Fifth and Sixth volunteer regiments.

In Florida, Governor William Bloxham delayed mobilization between 28 April and 23 May while he dithered in selecting which of the state's twenty companies should constitute the single twelve-company regiment asked for by the War Department. In the end, Bloxham accepted companies according to when they first entered state service. His decision offended the eight not chosen, most of whom refused to volunteer as individuals. Bloxham then permitted the companies to elect their regimental officers. An unseemly and fractious election campaign ensued and generated more bad feelings within the already splintered First Florida Infantry. Louisiana State Guard officers in New Orleans read about the call for volunteers in local newspapers. Members of the city's three infantry battalions dashed to Baton Rouge to save at least one of the state's two regiments for New Orleans Guard members. Disputes over company and battalion officer assignments notwithstanding, Elmer Ellsworth Wood, a leading New Orleans Guardsman, won the colonelcy of the Second Louisiana Volunteer Infantry.[73]

Troops from these states were poorly fed and housed while in state camps and entered federal service poorly equipped. With no substantive military budget or emergency fund, Missouri's Governor Stephens left his volunteer regiments at their home stations as long as possible in hopes he could convince the federal government to pay for a mobilization camp. Stephens's ploy failed, delaying by at least a week the concentration and muster-in of volunteers in St. Louis. Colonel Wood bluntly described Louisiana's commissary department as being "in a deplorable condition" and its quartermaster department as "a complete failure." When Wood marched his newly formed regiment from its battalion armories to the New Orleans fairgrounds his troops wore "every known costume the civilized world can witness."[74] As Guardsman Colonel Milton Moore organized the Fifth Missouri he turned to the people of Kansas City to provide his men with blankets. Another Missouri commander, Colonel William Coffee, Second Missouri Infantry, lamented that his unit was "inadequately provided with uniforms and equipment." When his boys arrived at Camp Thomas, Georgia, "many heads hung ashamed because of the miserable appearance we presented."[75]

Elsewhere, states organized their volunteers to their own dictates but relied on the Guard for officers and men, if not on units currently in their state service. New York accepted nine standing regiments and, in deference to its many separate companies, organized three volunteer regiments from these units. Several states faced the difficult task of organizing a single regiment from state organizations larger than their quota. West Virginia simply allowed its eighteen companies in two regiments to draw lots, the twelve winners forming the volunteer unit. In Oregon, the State Military Board, composed of Guardsmen and Governor William P. Lord, consolidated both state regiments and relied on seniority as the method for awarding regimental and company commands. Governors in Colorado and Washington directed the consolidation of peacetime units into single regiments, to the chagrin of those Guard officers left out. Interestingly, both governors named regular Army officers to command their volunteers. Finally, Utah's governor attempted to please both Guardsmen *and* civilian volunteers. Assigned a quota of two light artillery batteries and a troop of cavalry, the governor called on his small contingent of gunners and troopers to volunteer, ignored the existing infantry battalion, and welcomed volunteers at large to fill up the batteries and troop. Displeased with the governor's decision, the infantry Guardsmen refused to enlist.[76]

The call for volunteers inspired African Americans to demonstrate their willingness to fight and use their political influence to serve in state-sanctioned units on a broad scale for the first time in American history. North and South, black Guardsmen demanded the right to volunteer. If they failed in Pennsylvania, Texas, and the District of Columbia, they succeeded elsewhere. Four African-American state units, led by their own officers, served in 1898: the Eighth Illinois Infantry, the Twenty-third Kansas, the Third North Carolina Infantry, and Ohio's Ninth Battalion. White officers commanded two other black infantry regiments, the Third Alabama and Sixth Virginia. Company L, Sixth Massachusetts Volunteer Infantry, was the only black unit to serve as an element of a white outfit, much to the Army's displeasure. With the exception of Massachusetts, governors organized black units while Guard leaders demonstrated little interest in them.[77]

Including black volunteers, the state military systems provided approximately 200,000 of the 275,000 who served during the Spanish-American War. The vast majority of state soldiers entered service with little or no training. Taking into account the number of enlisted men who refused to volunteer or failed the Army physical examination, at best only one-quarter of Guard units contained men with prewar training. The majority of state volunteer regiments were organizations led by National Guard officers and NCOs but manned by volunteers direct from civil life. Even units from states with adequate military budgets were ill equipped for extended field duty and carried weapons unfit for modern combat. State officers exhibited limited command and administrative skills, while Guardsmen of all ranks demonstrated an appalling ignorance of camp sanitary practices. Finally, once it became evident that few state units would serve in combat, many state volunteers immediately demanded their discharges, all the while defying Army discipline.[78]

Historians critical of the Guard's 1898 weaknesses measure its failures against an imaginary force—the expansible army called for in the rejected Hull bill. It is more useful historically, however, to compare the National Guard's performance with state forces mobilized in 1846 and 1861. The 1898 state effort, for all its flaws, proceeded more effectively than had been the case earlier in the century. Between 25 April and 20 May, the states placed over one hundred thousand organized men in federal service. Although only two state regiments played a direct role in the brief Santiago campaign in Cuba, volunteers made possible the campaigns in Puerto Rico and the Philippine Islands. The expeditionary force to Puerto Rico led by Commanding General Nelson A. Miles included ten infantry regiments, eight of them state units. Before the end of May, state regiments were on their way to the Philippine Islands. Guardsmen contributed fifteen infantry regiments to the Eighth Corps, representing a majority of the land forces in the Pacific. These volunteers remained well beyond the legal limits of their enlistments to fight the first months of the ensuing Insurrection. Most did not return to the United States until May or June 1899.[79]

Guardsmen preferred to emphasize their 1898 accomplishments rather than dwell on obvious failures. Henry A. Courses, colonel of Pennsylvania's Thirteenth Regiment, stressed that those who saw the Guard "largely as holiday soldiers" and expected "a great thinning out of the companies" when the volunteer call came were compelled to admit the Thirteenth had lived up to its promise to serve.[80] Noting that citizen soldiers had long been "the nation's pride," W. D. B. Dobson, official historian of the Second Oregon Volunteers, contended that "volumes" would be written on the war. "These volumes will be simply the history of the National Guard organizations that were converted into the volunteer army of 1898."[81] Frank Edwards of the Sixth Massachusetts Infantry asserted that "the Spanish-American War of 1898 was the justification of the Massachusetts Volunteer Militia." Edwards believed that the great "strength which entered into the make-up of the army was the 'moral' force of men having volunteered. There was no half-hearted obedience from drafted men, but the willing response of soldiers who offered freely and willingly their services . . . for their country."[82]

Idiosyncratic interpretations of the volunteer principle illustrated what Edwards and many other Guardsmen meant by "freely and willingly." Some elite units, the best known and most publicized being New York's Seventh Regiment, initially refused to volunteer under the misapprehension that they were joining the Regular Army. New York officials turned a deaf ear when the Seventh Regiment belatedly pleaded to be allowed to volunteer and promptly disbanded Brooklyn's Thirteenth Regiment following its refusal to enlist. In Texas, the Houston Light Guard, the nation's most successful competitive drill outfit, rejected the call for volunteers on the grounds that they were militia sworn only to defend their city, county, and state. Debates within the Light Guard also suggested that many members saw military duty as being beneath the dignity of men of quality. Ultimately, a splinter group partially salvaged the Light Guard's reputation by reorganizing the outfit and volunteering to serve.[83]

In Pennsylvania and Massachusetts, state officials made it clear that no member of the National Guard was obligated to volunteer. In his orders mobilizing the Guard, Pennsylvania's governor, Daniel H. Hastings, noted that no Guardsman should "consider himself bound . . . to enlist . . . if such enlistment shall impose on him personal sacrifices."[84] At the Mount Gretna mobilization camp, Ralph L. Bitting of the Sixth Pennsylvania's Company D recalled that "most old members and family men were returned to their homes" at the encouragement of their officers.[85] Regimental officers in Massachusetts carefully screened volunteers to find men with pressing family or business obligations. In the Second Massachusetts Infantry, "officers candidly and kindly dissuaded" these men "from putting their names on the enlistment rolls," its historian wrote. So too did officers in the state's First Heavy Artillery Regiment.[86]

The individual's right to refuse to volunteer was implicit in the ethos of the nineteenth-century republican citizen soldier. By its very definition, volunteering was an act of conscience and patriotism, not an obligation. To ask a man to feel *obligated* to volunteer contradicted the essential nature of the principle and likely produced a poor soldier as well. Leaving to Guardsmen the decision whether to withhold their services as a "personal matter with them," a historian of the Second Massachusetts Infantry wrote, made the 1898 mobilization "a volunteer movement purely and simply and the Second was in the highest sense of the word a volunteer regiment."[87] That trained officers and men were lost through such acts of conscience bothered Guardsmen far less than it concerned Army reformers. The latter saw little value in spending federal dollars to train and equip men—then prepare mobilization plans to use them—when the decision to serve remained in the control of individual Guardsmen. The most ardent state soldiers saw no problem in this, for the regiment or battalion would turn out when called, and avid volunteers would rush to fill the vacancies left by men of conscience. Many had done so in 1898. Guardsmen assumed they would do so in the future and returned to the states confident that their regiments, the real volunteers of 1898, had redeemed themselves.

6

National Guard Reform,

1899–1915

The disorderly mobilization and logistical failures of 1898 prompted President McKinley to reorganize the War Department when the Spanish-American War ended. In August 1899 McKinley selected Wall Street lawyer Elihu Root to serve as secretary of war. Root turned to reform-oriented regular officers for ideas on how to alter the Army, but he also intuitively grasped the need for basic changes in the service as well as in national policy. The initiatives he began in 1899 led to the adoption of a general staff system in 1903, the creation of an advanced Army educational system, the abandonment of the Army's traditional constabulary role, and the adoption of the preparation for war as the Army's chief peacetime activity. He also recognized the nation's need for a trained reserve. With advice from regular officers, he supported the idea of making the state soldiery a nominal reserve force through increased financial aid and partial federal control. A redefinition of the state soldiery's relationship to the federal government thus became a major element in the new secretary of war's reforms.[1]

Root could not have ignored the National Guard even had that been his inclination. Guardsmen had lobbied for the reserve role and more federal money since the early 1880s, and they had renewed the campaign as their regiments demobilized in the autumn of 1898. W. B. Crawford, the assistant adjutant general of Colorado, put the state view in late 1899: "I am one of those who believes our National Guard . . . should be a . . . school in Military training. That it can be done if the National Government will give it proper support. In that case the State troops would realize that they were truly a 'National Guard.'"[2] Colonel Edward E. Britton of New York, a prize-winning essayist on National Guard reform, argued that although the Guard suffered many deficiencies it was wiser "to take the existing force as the basis for reorganization" than to create "an entirely new force, such as a National Reserve."[3] In 1901, Britton distributed a pamphlet that reported the opinions of state adjutants general on a proposed Guard bill closely resembling the militia act approved in 1903. Well before Congress acted, then, the key provisions of the law were widely discussed. Indeed, General Albert Ordway of the District of Columbia had proposed the basic outlines in 1882. Given the prevalence of these views, Root's task was to encourage agreement among Guard leaders and garner support in Congress.[4]

Root's support for an NGA proposal for more aid led Congress in 1900 to increase federal funds shared by the states from $400,000 to $1 million annually. In the same year, Root created a board of officers within the Army to study reform and appointed Lieutenant Colonel William Cary Sanger, a New York Guardsman and future assistant secretary of war, to the board. The board agreed to invite "prominent and proficient Militia officers" to its sessions "and take part in deliberations" affecting the state soldiery.[5] Root conferred frequently with NGA leaders and Representative Charles W. Dick (Republican-Ohio), long-time member of the Ohio National Guard and chair of the House Militia Affairs Committee. Because of Root's careful cultivation of support, a militia bill moved through Congress without significant opposition and became law early in 1903.[6]

The Militia Act of 1903 repealed the antiquated Militia Act of 1792, although it retained the obligated militia of able-bodied men between the ages of eighteen and forty-five. The statute divided the state soldiery into a Reserve Militia and an Organized Militia, with the latter identified as state units receiving federal allotments provided by section 1661 of the Revised Statutes (hereafter referred to as R.S. 1661). It set the terms whereby the president could "call forth" the organized militia for up to nine-months' service to repel invasion, suppress rebellion, or enforce federal law. The sections implicitly made the Guard a reserve, a fact reinforced by a clause providing that the law to organize volunteers for the war with Spain would govern formation of future volunteer armies.

Amendments in 1908 eliminated the nine-month limit, changed section 5 to read that the president could set the term for militia service, and added that state troops could be used "either within or without the territory of the United States." Furthermore, section 5 stated that the Organized Militia should be called "in advance of any volunteer force which it may be determined to raise." A 1914 national volunteer act ensured the Guard's first-line reserve status by requiring that all Organized Militia units be given the opportunity to volunteer before any national volunteers could be organized.[7]

Financial aid represented the most significant element of militia reform. The 1903 act appropriated a one-time $2 million grant to give the Guard modern arms and ordnance equipment. More importantly, it allowed states to use R.S. 1661 funds (formerly restricted to issues of weapons, clothing, and camp equipment) to transport, subsist, and pay state soldiers attending summer training camps. Use of federal money to pay for training camps relieved the states of the largest item in their operating budgets. Congress doubled R.S. 1661 funds to $2 million in 1906 in response to Guard lobbying. Two years later, the NGA gained a separate $2 million annual disbursement when Congress amended the 1903 law, making total federal aid $4 million annually. Money from the new account allowed states to draw standard regular army arms, uniforms, and equipment according to their enlisted strength and to requisition army issue stores, office supplies, and publications to equip armory and state-owned camp facilities.

Federal aid also underwrote the National Guard indirectly. Guard officers could attend Army service schools funded by money from Army appropriations. Beginning in 1903, the War Department paid for joint Army-Guard maneuvers and instruction camps, with Congress providing $1 million for extensive maneuvers in even-numbered years through 1912. Special appropriations to equip the National Guard with modern field artillery, automatic pistols, and other equipment added to federal support. The government assumed an additional indirect cost under a 1911 law that added two hundred officers to the Army to serve as inspector-instructors with state troops. The government spent approximately $60 million directly on the Guard from 1900 through 1915, an average of $4.3 million yearly for the 1903–10 period, and just over $5 million during the next five years. By 1908, the nation had increased by more than tenfold the yearly aid available to the Organized Militia in the 1890s. Contrasted with the support provided in the nineteenth century—$22 million from 1803 through 1899—federal aid to the National Guard in the early twentieth century was generous indeed.[8]

State soldiers assumed new responsibilities and obligations in return for federal recognition and money. They obligated themselves to answer a presidential call, subject to court martial, and, after 1908, to serve overseas. The law's most immediate impact stemmed from provisions under which the

Guard qualified for federal aid. As had been the case since 1887, to receive funding a state had to maintain a minimum of one hundred enlisted men for each member of its congressional delegation. In addition, state units had to participate in practice marches or camps of instruction for at least five consecutive days each year, meet for drill or target practice at least twenty-four times annually, and undergo a yearly armory inspection. Section 14 permitted states to use their allotments for summer camp but only if an Army inspector found their troops "sufficiently armed, uniformed, and equipped for active service." Finally, states accepting R.S. 1661 funds obliged themselves to conform the organization, armament, and discipline of their Organized Militia to that of the Army within five years of the passage of the law. The 1908 amendment extended the conformity requirement to 21 January 1910.

The amended Militia Act of 1903 represented the most important national legislation in militia history. In prescribing a legal relationship between state and federal forces, the law gave the state soldiery a statutory place in public policy. It incorporated the National Guard in the nation's military system and obligated the federal government as much as it imposed requirements on the states, a fact often neglected by zealous general staff officers seeking to revamp military policy.[9] However, because it was written in general terms, the law did not precisely define the Guard's role in national defense. In the ensuing decade, state and federal soldiers contended with each other to give concrete meaning to the law's vague terms, a struggle that engendered an increasingly acrimonious relationship between the National Guard and the War Department.

Prior to 1903, the War Department dealt officially with the states only to arrange the meager annual weapons allotment. Informal relations followed Adjutant General R. C. Drum's offer to assist the Guard in the early 1880s, but to the end of the century the War Department had no statutory role in militia affairs. Approval of the 1903 act created an official relationship between the states and the War Department. From 1903 through 1907 the Adjutant General's Office managed militia matters under the general oversight of Assistant Secretary of War Robert Shaw Oliver and the direct administration of Lieutenant Colonel James Parker. Parker believed that "much of the success of the administration of the law will depend upon the manner in which it is presented to the people," and he solicited opinions from state adjutants general on how to implement the act.[10] Under Parker, a spirit of comity governed federal relations with the states. Through 1907, the adjutant general's office treated Organized Militia affairs largely as a matter of bookkeeping, collecting and reporting statistical information on the state forces, and overseeing distribution of the annual allotment. When the NGA sought an extension of the requirement for states to conform to Army regulations, from January 1908 to January 1910, the War Department assisted the NGA in amending the militia law.[11]

In 1908, the War Department altered its administrative oversight of the Organized Militia at the suggestion of Oliver. Oliver wanted to centralize management of the increasingly complex state-federal military relationship. Several War Department agencies took part in militia administration, but no single office coordinated militia affairs. Secretary of War Luke E. Wright established the Division of Militia Affairs (DMA) in January 1908, appointing Lieutenant Colonel Erasmus M. Weaver of the Coast Artillery Corps, who had served as lieutenant colonel of a Massachusetts infantry regiment in 1898, to be the first DMA chief. Henceforth, Wright noted, the chief of DMA would "be the channel of communication between the Secretary of War and the adjutants general of the States."[12] The DMA supervised the distribution of arms and equipment to the states, assessed National Guard training and discipline, coordinated the state role in joint maneuvers and instruction camps, and represented the Organized Militia in general staff planning discussions.[13]

The advent of the DMA created an office headed by Army officers committed to rationalizing military policy and bringing the state soldiery more firmly under War Department control. Unlike the generally benign reports issued prior to 1908, the annual DMA report became a combined primer on military efficiency and a report card on the Guard's annual performance, couched in the paternalistic tones of professional wisdom. Colonel Weaver observed in his 1909 report that military efficiency rested on the trinity of organization, equipment, and training. The amended militia law provided the equipment and prescribed unit organization. The DMA would henceforth scrutinize Guard training to determine if the state forces "may be considered worthy of the designation 'Organized Militia.' " His "duty," Weaver emphasized, was to define "what the federal standards are."[14] Sadly, the Guard fell short in nearly every category. Reports from Army inspectors and instructors serving with the states indicated that armory instruction, performance at summer camp, officer preparation, the care of federal property, and the condition of local armories all failed to meet DMA standards. Weaver reminded Guardsmen a year later that federal funds were not spent "for the purpose of providing a summer's entertainment for officers and men" but to offer "an opportunity for instruction in their field military duties," an observation many Guardsmen took as a gratuitous insult.[15]

Far sharper criticism came after Chief of Staff Leonard Wood reorganized the general staff in 1911. Intent on making the chief of staff the authoritative voice within the Army, Wood also sought to create a general staff able to develop military policy and prepare the nation to fight a war. He established four coordinate divisions within the staff, each headed by a general officer. As one of those divisions, the DMA gained a stronger voice within general staff mobilization planning. Previously, several staff offices had conducted mobilization studies, but they rarely coordinated their work with agencies supervising Organized Militia matters. By elevating the DMA's position within the general staff, Wood's managerial reforms substantially altered War Department–National Guard relations.[16]

Brigadier General Anson L. Mills, the longest-serving chief of the DMA, proved a stern critic of the state soldiery. In 1913, for example, he observed that despite much hard work, "it remains a fact that conditions on the whole are far from satisfactory."[17] More fundamentally, the new emphasis on preparation for war that followed the Wood reorganization altered the DMA's function. The role of the DMA, General Mills noted, was to create "a militia that may be counted upon in time of federal need as a strong and efficient service prepared for active service in the field."[18] Mills used his annual report to enumerate state failings and ensure full compliance with the law and Army standards. He also issued a series of circular letters to enforce War Department regulations. Circulars sent out between 1913 and 1915, for example, outlined how states should conduct their training. Their intent, Mills noted, was to replace "order and system for random effort and more or less aimless methods of instruction."[19] In the Army, circular letters carried the same force as regulations. Although the states could ignore the cajolery aimed at them in annual DMA reports, they had to comply with the circulars.

State leaders resented, and some resisted, what they saw as unconstitutional federal interference in their affairs. The Constitution permitted Congress "to provide" for "disciplining," that is, training, the militia but left to the states the right to *conduct* training according to those provisions. Mills realized he was encroaching on state prerogatives but lamented that the Guard would never achieve tactical efficiency "as long as the influence of the War Department is merely advisory."[20] Captain M. C. Kerth, a DMA staff officer, suggested in 1910 that achieving Guard efficiency was "a question of dollars and cents. Full pay for value received." He recommended that the War Department withhold summer camp pay unless state soldiers demonstrated competence and compliance with federal regulations. [21]

Although the law permitted the secretary of war to deny R.S. 1661 funds when states did not comply with it, the War Department approached the withholding of funds with caution. It first refused to release militia money to Arkansas in 1912 because the state could not account for $115,000 worth of federal property. The DMA announced that in the future states that neglected federal property would be denied funds and added that those violating other federal regulations would lose federal aid as well. For example, the law provided that federal funds could be allotted only to state units found by an Army inspection to be armed and equipped for field service. A 1914 circular threatened to deny funds to units failing that inspection. The nation gave states military funds, General Mills emphasized in 1915, to gain "a force of trained and partially trained men" capable of defending the nation. Units unable to meet that responsibility had no claim on national support. [22]

The imposition of stringent regulation by administrative fiat introduced a new element into militia affairs. The national government had never interfered with the operations of the state soldiery in peacetime but now increasingly did so. At first only those specific states directly affected by DMA regulatory action protested. Wider reactions came when War Department policy affected the entire state soldiery. The first major conflict came in 1912. In contemplating the probability of an American intervention in revolution-torn Mexico, general staff planners became concerned about the availability of the Guard for such an operation. Secretary of War Henry L. Stimson asked the Army's judge advocate general, Enoch H. Crowder, to study the question. Crowder concluded that the National Guard was not a legal substitute for a volunteer army but merely the militia under a different name. He also asserted that Congress erred in 1908 when it amended the militia law to permit use of the Organized Militia outside the United States. Stimson forwarded Crowder's views to United States Attorney General George W. Wickersham for a formal legal opinion. Wickersham ruled that the president could not order the Organized Militia to serve in a foreign country as an occupation force "under conditions short of actual warfare." [23]

Attorney General Wickersham's opinion effectively meant that the president could not order state forces overseas while they remained in their status as militias. In the eyes of the War Department, the ruling destroyed the Guard's value as a reserve and led Secretary of War Stimson to withdraw his support for a federally funded pay bill pending in Congress. As a *National*

Guard Magazine editorial suggested, many Guardsmen believed the general staff was deliberately trying to bypass the state forces. They saw the Wickersham decision as another War Department "monkey wrench" thrown in to disrupt the Guard's hopes of taking its place in national defense.[24] One leading Guardsmen, General Henry C. Clark of Missouri, argued as late as 1916 that Stimson had raised an "abstract proposition of law" aimed at a "purpose not altogether compatible with perfect frankness," that is, with the intent of killing the pay bill.[25]

General staff efforts to create a permanent military policy and prepare contingency war plans also challenged state independence. The staff decided to organize the National Guard into divisions, even though the Army did not keep up divisions in peace, in order to facilitate joint Army-Guard maneuvers and mobilization planning. Plans in 1910 to create a provisional First Field Army, to be composed of New England and New York units brigaded with Army regiments, came to naught because many regulars disliked mixing Guard and Army regiments in the same brigades or divisions. The War Department's publication of "Organization of the Land Forces of the United States" in 1912 had a lasting effect. The plan stressed the Army's intention to develop a "unified military doctrine" that permeated "the entire National Army" so as to avoid the old "problem of extemporization" when war came. The general staff called for a mobilization force of 112,000 regulars in a field army of four divisions and auxiliaries and 348,000 Guardsmen organized into four field armies of twelve divisions. Each division would contain combat and support troops in proportion to its role in modern war.[26]

The War Department encountered problems when it tried to create the twelve balanced divisions out of existing state forces. Unfortunately, it could not compel states to comply with the plan because the militia law did not give the federal government the power to tell states what types of units they should organize. Hence, while approximately 80 percent of the Guard was organized as infantry, DMA hectoring failed to convince the states to organize other unit types to fill out the divisions. In addition, ten of the twelve Guard divisions involved two or more states, a fact that complicated War Department efforts, for no state wanted to organize noncombat support units. Assistant Secretary of War Oliver's 1912 letter to the governors urging them to conform to the divisional plan, so "the General Staff and the Army War College will be able to put all war plans on a more permanent and satisfactory basis," failed to win the states' cooperation.[27]

The War Department could not order states to organize specific units, but it could force them to form existing ones according to Army tables, as the law had required since 1903. Because the "Organization of the Land Forces" placed Guard divisions at the center of staff mobilization plans, it was essential that the states conform their units to Army standards, the DMA noted in 1912. The report emphasized that conformity to Army organizational tables would be "a requisite for participation in Federal funds."[28] To achieve this end, the DMA issued Circular No. 8 in August 1913. The circular required all state organizations, from headquarters staff and divisional officers to battalions, to conform to Army regulations or disband. Units and their personnel not in conformity on 1 January 1914 would be denied federal recognition and funding.[29]

The circular directed states to dismantle their bloated headquarters staffs; denied recognition to purported divisional organizations in Illinois, Pennsylvania, New Jersey, and Missouri; and called for the disbandment of brigades in many states. Moreover, infantry regiments of less than twelve companies were to conform to that standard within six months or lose federal funding. General Mills realized that Circular No. 8 would generate opposition from the National Guard. Well aware of the hostile reception awaiting him, Mills nonetheless attended the 1913 NGA convention to explain the reasons for imposing conformity. He acknowledged that Circular No. 8 left supernumerary many founders of the modern Guard but emphasized that the action "marks the final step in the welding of the several state armies into a National Force."[30] Furthermore, Mills believed "an implied agreement" existed when states accepted federal funds. Taking the money meant "federal desires should be absolutely decisive" in the development of military policy.[31]

The Guard's persistent quest for federal armory drill pay further strained relations between the states and the War Department. In 1910, the NGA initiated a six-year effort to win congressional approval of a pay bill. The *National Guard Magazine* solicited the views of Guardsmen throughout the year. A Connecticut officer lamented that "since the annual outings of the old guard have gone into history and the real work in camps has been established, the men are not there."[32] Major John Bersey of Michigan contended that with War Department requirements demanding greater efficiency, the federal government "should foot the bill."[33] The 1910 NGA convention unanimously endorsed a federal pay proposal to be introduced in the next Congress. As the *National Guard Magazine* noted, "remember—this pay bill means more to the National Guard than anything else which has been proposed in many years.''[34]

Guardsmen saw the pay bill as a simple matter of partial compensation for work already rendered. The War Department viewed the matter differently. Secretary of War Jacob M. Dickinson refused to support the NGA proposal unless the law legally obligated Guardsmen to serve and guaranteed that all state units were properly trained and organized. As Dickinson's successor, Henry Stimson, noted, "there is no objection to militia pay, provided the National Government receives an adequate quid pro quo.''[35] Finding an acceptable quid pro quo was not easy. Throughout 1912, the ramifications of the Wickersham decision kept the War Department from supporting the bill. Stimson and the NGA reached a tentative agreement on a pay proposal that imposed federal standards on Guard officers and units, obligated Guardsmen to serve when called, and made state soldiers available for overseas duty. By the autumn of 1912, a pay bill seemed feasible, but a Democratically controlled House rejected the plan. The fall elections then produced a Democratic administration indifferent to military reform and unwilling to appropriate more funds for the National Guard.[36]

In late 1913 and early 1914 the NGA resumed efforts to revive congressional interest in a pay bill. Although representatives of the war office and the NGA agreed to the outlines of a bill, Congress continued to ignore it. Meanwhile, Secretary of War Lindley M. Garrison became increasingly reluctant to support federal pay. By 1915, he refused to endorse any pay bill "unless the Government is given the most absolute control of the discipline and other essentials of efficiency.''[37] More significantly, the outbreak of war in Europe reinforced a growing preparedness movement that had emerged in 1913. Preparedness supporters called for a larger Army and Navy and a more effective reserve system. Some even advocated compulsory peacetime military training. Garrison and general staff officers who had never reconciled themselves to the Guard's first-line reserve role saw preparedness agitation as the opportune occasion for revising Army policy completely. Garrison introduced a new plan in 1915 and published in full a *Statement of a Proper Military Policy for the United States* in its entirety early the next year. In brief, the Statement called for a Regular Army and reserve of five hundred thousand men and a volunteer federal reserve of a half million men to be called the Continental Army. The plan restricted the Organized Militia to its three constitutional uses and called for the repeal of laws that gave Organized Militia first preference in a volunteer war army.[38]

The political furor attending War Department efforts to revise military policy drastically in 1915 marked the culmination of militia reform after 1899. Garrison's proposal engendered a political struggle that saw relations between the National Guard and the War Department reach their nadir. In part, this may be seen as a struggle between two services seeking to defend and extend their institutional interests. Parochialism played a part in the contention, but the differences between the Guard and the Army were more complex than mere self-interest. State and federal soldiers differed profoundly over what the nation's military policy should be, who should determine that policy, and what made an army effective. The differing perspectives had existed since the 1880s, but they generated public debate only after the militia law and the general staff act won approval in 1903.[39]

The establishment of a general staff had given the Army an agency to plan for war and create policies to ensure the combat readiness of its soldiers and the National Guard. Overburdened with multiple assignments, however, the Army lacked the men and money to organize peacetime divisions or conduct field maneuvers. More fundamentally, the regulars could not fight even a small war without immediate augmentation by either the Organized Militia or volunteers. Given the condition of the Army, then, the general staff had little choice but to rely on the National Guard. Early in the century, staff planners saw some promise in the Guard despite their misgivings. Following a review of the militia's historical failings, a 1906 Army War College study nonetheless contended that the 1903 act marked "a great advance in militia legislation and organization."[40] A study carried out two years later asserted that the Army's principal peacetime duty should be to "furnish a model for the organized militia," then train and educate "the militia for war purposes."[41] Through the publication of the "Organization of the Land Forces," the War Department maintained a public posture that the Organized Militia could become an efficient reserve available for any military purpose.[42]

The more the planners planned, however, the more displeased they became. Close scrutiny reinforced doubts most regular officers had long held about the state soldiery. DMA reports from 1910 on listed Guard shortcomings, but much harsher criticisms appeared in staff studies and planning documents. When Captain George Van Horn Moseley examined the militia law in 1912, he found it so flawed that he concluded that never had the "militia system been so perilous to the public safety as it is at present."[43] In an extraordinarily sharp critique, Captain William Mitchell described the Organized Militia as so inept that "if they were ever turned out against a well organized and trained enemy [they] would serve principally as 'food for shrapnel.' "[44] The general staff's harshest assessments came in planning studies prepared by the War College Division and the DMA to support the *Statement of a Proper Military Policy* of 1915. After reviewing the documents, General A. L. Mills, chief of the DMA, concluded that the Organized Militia did "not provide a suitable force of citizen soldiery to meet our probable need in time of war."[45]

Yet the general staff could not escape reliance on the states. For instance, mobilization plans assigned governors the responsibility of selecting and preparing mobilization camps and gave state adjutants general the task of actually calling up the Guard. The general staff disliked the decentralized nature of the scheme, but the War Department lacked the necessary camps and personnel to carry out a centralized mobilization. This reality was reflected in the 1914 volunteer act, which specified a state role in the mobilization of United States volunteers. Regulations for that law called for governors to supervise the mobilization and even allowed them to recommend men to be appointed as federal volunteer officers. This complex system, General Mills lamented in 1915, left "a widespread and serious degree of uncertainty" in mobilization planning.[46]

The greatest uncertainty remained when staff officers attempted to make plans premised on the use of state volunteers. Their studies emphasized that past wars demonstrated the fickleness of citizen-soldier volunteers. Although Guardsmen were legally obligated to answer a president's call to federal service for the three constitutional purposes, they were not obliged to volunteer for overseas duty even though the law gave first preference to state units when Congress authorized a volunteer army. General Mills of the DMA maintained that a "moral obligation" bound Guardsmen to offer their services, but the *Statement of a Proper Military Policy* argued that "a promise made in time of peace . . . cannot be legally binding, and should therefore be neither given nor accepted."[47] The unpredictability of state volunteering posed a fundamental problem for mobilization planning, the Statement stressed. Because it was impossible to estimate how many Guardsmen might volunteer, "no definite plans can be made . . . for the actual employment in war of any individual or organization of the Organized Militia."[48]

From Elihu Root's first proposals to reform the military system in 1899 to congressional approval of the National Defense Act of 1916, manpower policy centered on the volunteer tradition. Root had wanted to bypass state forces as the *constituted* volunteers, consistently stressing that the Organized Militia should serve as "the great school of the volunteer soldier."[49] For anything other than the constitutional purposes, he argued, Guardsmen should serve as volunteers as provided by the law of 2 March 1899 that organized volunteers to fight in the Philippines. That force remained the Army's ideal, as a 1906 staff study indicated: "Taken as a whole the United States has probably never put in the field a more efficient force of volunteers than those organized in 1899" because those volunteers had been recruited independently of the states.[50] Neither Root nor his successors, however, managed to duplicate the 1899 force or dislodge the Guard because the amended 1903 militia law and the 1914 volunteer act reaffirmed tradition by giving the Guard first preference as volunteers.

Despite the law, general staff officers sought to divorce the state soldiery from the volunteer tradition. Echoing Emory Upton, staff studies asserted that Congress authorized volunteers through the constitutional raise-and-support clause and that past recognition of state militia forces as volunteers by Congress and presidents had been unconstitutional. Studies claimed that state forces serving in the Mexican War, Civil War, and Spanish-American War were not militia but national forces.[51] Unable to cajole state cooperation and prevented from imposing its will on the Guard, the general staff lamented its inability to establish a viable military policy. Even a sympathetic 1908 staff study observed that if the Guard failed to become "a certain and reliable force" then it would be necessary to resort to "a larger standing army or to the conscription and training of a force equal to national needs."[52] Captain William Mitchell reflected a harsher view in a 1913 study that concluded that "it might be better and cheaper to make entirely new U.S. Volunteer regiments for a war than to try to do anything with militia."[53]

A minority of War Department officials spoke favorably of the Guard. These observers displayed a more finely tuned sense of history and American political culture than did the centralizers. Secretary of War Stimson told one correspondent that while he favored a fully federalized Guard he expected that "such a federal force would encounter very widespread and deep-rooted prejudice."[54] Enoch H. Crowder, the Army's judge advocate general, told a friend that Chief of Staff Leonard Wood's efforts to overhaul military policy began as a comedy but "ended in something of a tragedy. Neither Wood nor his cohorts are able to appreciate that this Republic of ours is going to maintain a republican army."[55] Even the DMA's General Mills accepted, at least until 1915, that political reality dictated that the Army either work with the Guard or have no peacetime reserve at all. Captain James Romayne, the only staff officer to object to the adoption of the *Statement of a Proper Military*

Policy, asserted "that the National Guard is not worthless." Although the Guard fell far short of perfection, Romayne stressed that "any policy which does not in some way recognize the National Guard" was almost doomed to fail.[56]

John McAuley Palmer, an officer more favorable to citizen soldiers than most of his cohorts and the principal author of the "Organization of the Land Forces" of 1912 explained that military organization had two aspects, one dynamic and the other political. The dynamic aspect applied to purely technical questions, but "the form of military institutions must be determined on political grounds, with due regard to national genius and tradition."[57] Army reformers gave greater attention to technical military matters, but one element of their "dynamic aspect" failed dramatically. Thoroughgoing military reform could only be achieved if its supporters could convince Congress and the public of its necessity. Reformers repeatedly argued that the United States lay open to immediate invasion. Reflecting over a decade of general staff thinking, the *Statement of a Proper Military Policy* justified its adoption on the assumption that one or more European powers might invade the United States. This scenario forced the conclusion "that we must be prepared to resist a combined land and sea operation of formidable strength."[58]

The unpredictability with which modern war came and the rapidity with which it was fought, reformers argued, required an Army and reserve able to mobilize and deploy almost simultaneously. The general staff's efforts to improve the National Guard's efficiency, and then to replace it with the Continental Army, proposed in late 1915, stemmed from these assumptions. The abstract nature of these conjectures lacked urgency and specificity when they did not generate incredulity. Certainly in the midst of the Great War, the *Statement of a Proper Military Policy* scenario of a possible European invasion of the United States raised questions of credibility. General Crowder noted that planners knew full well that England, "with her 30 mile wet ditch," had avoided invasion for centuries. Yet, he went on, they failed to consider that the United States had a three-thousand-mile "wet ditch" to the East and a five-thousand-mile one to the West, "separating us from every formidable international foe."[59] An abstract argument that the National Guard needed to conform to Army standards rang hollow when planners could not explain to what end that conformity was aimed.

War Department concerns about National Guard availability for overseas duty seemed even less convincing when staff planners argued that the most likely military threat to the nation was an invasion of the continental United

States. Whatever the Guard's liabilities, tradition, the law, and the Constitution allotted the state soldiery a clear role in repelling invasion. Among the many political misjudgments Garrison and the general staff made in the *Statement of a Proper Military Policy* certainly the most egregious was relegating the Guard to a mere home defense role and not including it in the forces assigned to repel invasion. Neglect of what Major Palmer called the "political aspect" of military policy plagued the War Department throughout these years. It consistently failed to anticipate state resistance to reform.

The inability within the Army generally and the general staff specifically to understand why the NGA and individual Guardsmen opposed attempts to rationalize and centralize military policy appears puzzling. Many regular officers had served with the states as inspectors in the 1880s and 1890s, and a greater number had done so since the approval of the 1903 Militia Act. Many had also commanded or served in state regiments during the Spanish-American War. Many more served with former Guardsmen in the thirty-five United States Volunteer regiments recruited in 1899 for two years' service in the Philippines. Moreover, most regulars understood that promotion was sure to come their way in any future volunteer army formed from National Guard regiments. Despite familiarity with the Guard and the possibilities for increased command opportunities leading state forces, regulars were caught unawares when Guardsmen vehemently opposed extended federal control.

Moreover, National Guardsmen had made it plain since the Spanish-American War that they expected to serve in the nation's future wars. Approval of the 1903 Militia Act sanctioned the 1898 mobilization in the eyes of most Guardsmen. To them, the new law was an end, not a beginning, a codification of American tradition under which the National Guard and the volunteer army became synonymous. From 1903 on, Colonel James M. Rice of Illinois argued, Guardsmen "should be considered by others as they generally consider themselves, the first contingent of the Volunteer Army, already enlisted, examined, mustered, disciplined and equipped and awaiting orders."[60] The state perspective remained unchanged over the next decade. Senator Charles Dick, author of the 1903 act, noted in 1910 that the Guardsman was "practically in the service of the United States when he takes his oath of office or . . . enlistment."[61] A Massachusetts soldier, Walter M. Pratt, wrote that the 1903 law "killed the 'Tin Soldier' " image of the state soldier. "The Organized Militia is no longer considered by the government a kind of State Police Force. It is the secondary force of the United States Army for national defense."[62]

Unfortunately, Guardsmen failed to see that state-federal relations would undergo substantive change following the approval of the 1903 law. Much of the rancor attending War Department efforts to reshape the Guard under the law stemmed from National Guard assumptions that past practice would continue. Colonel Edward E. Britton of New York advised the War Department to consult with state soldiers when devising regulations for implementing the 1903 act before taking suggestions from Army officers. The War Department, he added, should not require anything of the states that was "not thoroughly practicable and consistent with conditions as they exist."[63] Among National Guard officers, widespread attitudes such as these largely explain why the states resisted growing federal authority.

As a result, after 1910, Guardsmen saw War Department regulation as an unnecessary, sometimes illegal, interference in state military affairs. The department's refusal to support a pay bill in Congress unless the federal government gained expanded control of the Guard provoked angry retorts. Major General Edward C. Young of Illinois, chairman of the NGA's executive committee, informed Chief of Staff Leonard Wood that he opposed provisions in the Army's version of the 1910 pay bill because "I do not believe that many States will be willing to release all coordinate control over the National Guard."[64] The *National Guard Magazine* protested three years later that successive War Department pay proposals were "rehashed and loaded with 'riders' and infected with 'sleepers' until we wonder 'where we are at' and whether the Department really wants to help any at all."[65] Guardsmen disliked the Army's demands for detailed legislation. Although the 1910 NGA pay proposal contained six simply worded sections, a 1914 Army version included fifty-four detailed sections prescribing the obligations of officers and men. The NGA resented these provisions and revived the brief 1910 bill, because, as General Young argued, it covered the "essential principles" and eliminated "extraneous subjects which in fact have little or no relation to it."[66]

State soldiers deeply resented the DMA's efforts to create balanced divisions and its concomitant promulgation of Circular No. 8 as unwarranted intrusions in state affairs. The latter issue dominated the 1913 NGA convention, at which delegates resolved "that the control over the Militia in time of peace must not be taken from the State directly or indirectly."[67] General Young pronounced the circular "not only illegal, but manifestly unjust and unfair."[68] Circular No. 8 particularly irked Guardsmen because the Army itself lacked the men to maintain divisional organizations according to regulations cited in the circular. *National Guard Magazine* expressed the bitter feelings surrounding Circular No. 8 by damning a "narrow, vacillating, bigoted, self-contained, short-sighted War Department" that managed the Army poorly and "let the National Guard take its chances with the Devil and the hindermost."[69]

Beneath the vitriolic rhetoric lay the National Guard's fundamental objection to War Department actions. The advent of the general staff gave the Army its first modern management system. Charged with shaping military policy and developing war plans, the staff relied on study groups to assess and shape policy, then used its executive powers to implement decisions. That is, it functioned as a central bureaucratic management agency that rarely asked its constituent parts for ideas. Guardsmen chafed under the regulatory control the War Department sought to impose, a control governed by regulations, circulars, and legal decisions written by staff officers, secretaries of war, and attorneys general. In the old days, not even state governments had deigned to exert such authority over their military forces.

Guard supporters argued that despite increased federal aid, the state soldiery had a right to participate in policy decisions. Even before Congress approved a militia law, the *Northwestern Guardsman* boldly asserted that Guard officers were "thoroughly competent to draw up their own laws."[70] The *National Guard Magazine* contended in 1912 that Guardsmen were "just perniciously conceited enough to think we know what we want, what we are entitled to, and how to get it; that this is our affair."[71] Gardner Pearson, adjutant general of Massachusetts, insisted that "men who have made a success in their own business and a success in handling organizations of citizen soldiers can qualify as experts in regard to such soldiers."[72] Guardsmen sought a part in policy formation, the *National Guard Magazine* stressed, because "the National Guard has problems the Army knows not of and that the Guard as a *de facto* part of our military establishment should have at least as much recognition in [War] Department councils . . . as the Army does."[73] Because the two services differed so greatly, most Guardsmen believed the War Department ought to consult state military officials before adopting new policies.

In the wake of Circular No. 8, the issue of unfettered federal control of the National Guard produced some of the most vitriolic rhetoric of the pre–World War I years. General Young opened the 1913 NGA convention by proclaiming that "the most important problem which this Association should face squarely . . . is whether the Organized Militia shall be under Federal or state control in time of peace."[74] Convention speakers damned the War Department for ignoring the National Militia Board, established in 1908. The board, composed of leading National Guard officers, was to advise the secretary of war when that official saw fit to convene it. He rarely did. Led by General Young, the NGA resolved the following: "It is the sense of this convention that the governing of the Organized Militia should rest in the States in time of peace, as provided for by the Constitution of the United States."[75]

Young's staunch states' rights defense of the Guard earned him the chiding of General Walter Harris of Georgia, who argued, "there is no state militia . . . we are a national militia."[76] Although a few other delegates joined Harris to oppose General Young, the convention adopted a series of recommendations that sought greater independence from the War Department. Young defended local control of the Guard and questioned regulation by a Washington agency that was "bound to lose entirely the personal equation which is so essential to the citizen soldier."[77] Ohio's General John C. Speaks earned applause from convention delegates by asserting that the "leaders of the National Guard are better prepared to outline and present a military policy for this country than are the gentlemen of the Army alone."[78]

General Young hoped that the Guard could attain "some legal method by which the Organized Militia may be represented in the councils of the National Government."[79] Some Guardsmen saw the national legislature as the authority that would rescue the state soldiery from War Department regulators. General Charles W. Harris of Arizona, among others, argued that "Congress should fix an organization by law and not leave the matter to regulations."[80] Yet little came from the protests launched at the 1913 NGA convention. The Guard failed to win War Department support for a pay bill, gain reversal of Circular No. 8, or stop the War Department from withholding federal funds from states that failed to comply with DMA regulations. The NGA thus proved to be an ineffective lobby group. It never achieved 100 percent membership of all states and territories and was plagued by financial stringency. In 1913, a crucial year, the NGA collected a mere $1,337 in dues. Between 1910 and 1916, the NGA's official journal, the *National Guard Magazine*, consistently urged Guardsmen to use their local political connections to convince congressmen to vote for a pay bill. The campaign failed.[81]

Internal disagreements weakened the Guard's efforts to thwart the War Department. Some Guardsmen, though how many is unclear, welcomed federal control. At the 1913 NGA convention, eight state delegations voted against the states' rights resolutions. Individual Guardsmen from across the nation turned to the service journals to express support for War Department efforts to regulate the state soldiery. Captain Richard Stockton Jr. of New Jersey spoke for all of them when he noted that "the Guard as a whole" did not endorse the action of the 1913 NGA convention, and most advocated "the need for an entirely Federal, rather than State, citizen soldiery."[82] In 1914, the adjutant general of Massachusetts called for "a Federalized militia . . . raised, armed, organized, equipped and paid by the United States government."[83]

Public and congressional indifference toward military affairs spurred the NGA to adopt a more conciliatory approach toward the War Department. In 1914 the association replaced General Young with the more moderate General J. C. R. Foster of Florida as chairman of its executive committee. The *National Guard Magazine* presented a more cooperative stance in the next two years and featured editorials favoring greater federal control of the Guard. Reacting to the growing preparedness movement, Guard spokesmen dropped the rhetoric of state control out of fear that obstructionism could damage the interests of the state soldiery once Congress acted on military matters.[84]

Conciliatory Guardsmen were unprepared for the War Department's *Statement of a Proper Military Policy* and Secretary of War Lindley M. Garrison's Continental Army plan. When Garrison met with the executive committee of the NGA on 29 October 1915 to discuss yet another pay proposal, New Jersey's adjutant general, Wilbur F. Sadler, reported Guardsmen's astonishment that Garrison "contemplated the extinguishment of the National Guard."[85] According to the *National Guard Magazine*, the secretary of war also stated that he had never favored putting Guardsmen "on the national payroll as if they were national soldiers."[86] General Sadler urged Joseph Tumulty, private secretary to President Woodrow Wilson, "for God's sake don't let the President" endorse the plan. Sadler warned Tumulty that he had always supported the president, but "if he adopts the Continental Army plan, I simply cannot follow him."[87]

Neither could other Guardsmen. The *National Guard Magazine* launched an editorial campaign mocking the Continental Army and berating Garrison for his betrayal. Although the National Guard vigorously fought the Garrison plan, congressional opposition, not Guard lobbying, doomed the proposal. Congressmen opposed the idea for a variety of reasons: it was too expensive, it smacked of militarism, there seemed no reason to support preparedness. Garrison sought Woodrow Wilson's support throughout 1915, but the president showed little interest in preparedness until early 1916. When the president at last took up the preparedness question, the redoubtable secretary of war still failed to win Wilson's endorsement of the new military policy. Democratic leaders in the House, led by James Hay, chair of the House Military Affairs Committee, rejected the proposal. Garrison and Assistant Secretary of War Henry Breckinridge resigned on 10 February 1916 when President Wilson refused to exert any effort to save the policy. Hay and other congressmen, fearful that the general staff might next call for conscription, saw a more thoroughly federalized National Guard as a palatable alternative to the hypothetical Continental Army. The National Defense Act of 1916 (1916 NDA) would emerge from this conclusion.[88]

The *Statement of a Proper Military Policy* proposed to replace a policy in place since 1903 and a tradition as old as the nation. Congress rejected it because the National Guard retained first claim on the concept of the volunteer citizen soldier, although under the provisions of the 1916 NDA the act of volunteering came upon enlistment in the Guard, for federal pay, and not, as before, upon the outbreak of war. The *National Guard Magazine* mocked the Continental Army idea, boasting that the Guard could "claim to have had a little experience in the matter of enlisting, organizing, and training the citizen." Admittedly, the Guard had weaknesses: "We point to our past and present difficulties in securing recruits, the limited . . . training time, indifference or opposition of employers and fellow workers and the total lack of favorable public opinion as the reasons for our failure to measure up to the highest standards of military efficiency."[89] These "difficulties" had affected the state soldiery since its rebirth following the Civil War. They persisted through 1915 and profoundly affected not only the National Guard's efficiency but how Guardsmen perceived their service and defended it.

7

The National Guard Dilemma: Serving the States, Serving the Nation, 1899–1915

The National Guard remained oriented toward state and local affairs even though the Militia Act of 1903 redefined the state-federal relationship. Although federal authority increasingly affected how states managed their military affairs, more so by 1915 than a decade earlier, the average Guardsman remained largely untouched by the furor surrounding the NGA's disputes with the War Department. State soldiers continued to oversee routine regimental and company affairs—recruiting men, drilling in the armory, planning summer encampments, and administering the force—much as they had in the 1890s. That fundamental fact underlay the War Department's frustrated efforts to create a uniform state soldiery. When they attempted to impose general rules to govern the entire system War Department reformers too often ignored the fact that no single entity could be described as the National Guard. The diversity that permeated the state soldiery during the late nineteenth century persisted long after 1900.

States welcomed federal aid. The $1 million first appropriated in 1900 and the special allotment to rearm the Guard in 1903 reanimated poorly funded forces left moribund after the Spanish-American War. Federal funding was particularly valuable to state soldiers in the South and Plains regions as well as parts of the West. Although the Northeast and Midwest had historically supported its soldiers more substantially than elsewhere, federal dollars meant a great deal to particular states. In Missouri, for example, the adjutant general reported that federal money allowed his men to attend summer camp in 1903 and receive the first camp pay in the state's history.[1]

Of course, the War Department used federal aid to force compliance with federal regulations. Guardsmen clung tenaciously to unit tables of organization that did not conform to Army provisions or were too large for their states to man and fund. The War Department began to withhold money when states failed to conform to proper tables of organization. In 1915, for example, the DMA forced all states to adopt the twelve-company regiment. By compelling states to maintain only those units they could man properly, the War Department both rationalized state military forces and contributed to unit stability. When coupled with federal aid, the policy contributed to the permanence of local companies, troops, and batteries. Unit stability was one of the most successful results of militia reform, an achievement the War Department failed to perceive.

The DMA's efforts to cajole states to create units from which balanced divisions could be created proved less effective. Although the Guard's force structure underwent some change between 1903 and 1915 (the proportion of infantry, for example, fell from 86 to 79 percent), the state soldiery failed to field the units required for balanced divisions. New coast artillery companies largely replaced the disbanded infantry units, and states continued to neglect the organization of artillery, cavalry, and combat support units. States emphasized infantry units largely because they were inexpensive to maintain and relatively easy to train. Moreover, most states resisted organizing support units because their men wanted to serve in the combat arms. Few could support full artillery or cavalry regiments but insisted on retaining one or two cavalry troops or field artillery batteries. As was common during the previous century, each commonwealth wanted its own little army, with all the combat arms organized to meet its needs, interests, and traditions.[2]

Not all Guardsmen were indifferent to the War Department's desire to organize the National Guard in the Army's image. Massachusetts, which had set the standard for progressive militia policy since the 1840s, readily conformed to the 1903 requirements. Its adjutant general described relations with the DMA as "most harmonious" and stressed that the state cooperated "to the fullest extent with them."[3] Washington's adjutant general, James A. Drain, abolished his state's ineffective brigade in 1903 and reorganized his soldiery to meet Army standards. Poorly funded states also made efforts to cooperate. Since Missouri's divisional organization failed to conform with federal law leaving the Guard with "a multitude of officers of high rank," reform-minded adjutant general John B. O'Meara disbanded the organization in 1914.[4] In Alabama, where a perpetual shortage of funds and persisting nineteenth-century ideas about the militia prevailed, Adjutant General Joseph B. Scully mustered out a weak cavalry squadron in 1911 and boldly disbanded the inefficient Third Infantry Regiment a year later.[5]

The efforts of Generals Drain, O'Meara, and Scully indicate that most Guard leaders saw the state soldiery as the guard of the nation and downplayed its state functions. Few deliberately sought to obstruct War Department policy. At the same time, however, many failed to appreciate the general staff's concern for planning, rationalizing of the force structure, and centralizing command. The state soldiery had always functioned informally, each unit state adapting its *modus operandi* to its own tastes and local circumstances. Indiana's adjutant general, Franklin L. Bridges, reflected the Guard perspective when he disbanded ten infantry companies that lost federal recognition in 1915. Although Bridges mustered out an entire regiment, he did so grudgingly and complained to the DMA that "it is not a question of these companies being less efficient, it is because the government is more strict in its requirements."[6]

It is doubtful that General Bridges meant to be disingenuous, but his criticism of War Department strictness failed to take into account the National Guard's inability to improve its military efficiency after twelve years of federal support. Guardsmen explained at length why their service failed to become more efficient. Despite the increase in federal aid after 1900, state soldiers stressed that inadequate funding was their major problem. However self-serving the Guardsmen's arguments sounded, they were essentially correct. The lack of money mattered a great deal, for Guardsmen could not meet militia law requirements with the funding the nation and their states provided. Historians have neglected the financial needs of the National Guard before World War I and have focused instead on the War Department's struggle to extend control over the state soldiery. The issue of how much control the national government should exert over the Guard was not an insignificant one. Disputes with the War Department often arose, however, because states lacked the money to comply with federal requirements. The shortage of funds, not mere local institutional defenses against an outside intruder, more often than not provoked these arguments.

Federal assistance unquestionably proved valuable to the states. It covered all expenses for sending men to state camps as well as joint Army-Guard maneuvers. National militia funds supplied the same arms, uniforms, and equipment issued to the Army. Federal aid rescued desperate states and territories from military penury and bolstered all but the richest commonwealths.

Table 14 Combined Federal and State Appropriations, by Region, 1903

	Federal	State	Combined
Northeast	$273,276	$1,689,375	$1,962,651
South	279,261	183,000	462,261
Midwest	267,295	796,850	1,064,145
Plains	84,621	137,050	221,671
West	64,932	242,500	307,432
Totals:	969,385	3,048,775	4,018,160

Sources: SWR 1903; SWR 1904.

Table 15 Combined Federal and State Appropriations, by Region, 1913

	Federal	State	Combined
Northeast	$1,283,192	$2,849,783	$4,132,975
South	1,097,026	468,961	1,565,987
Midwest	1,024,549	1,609,699	2,634,248
Plains	409,545	290,054	699,599
West	358,931	529,695	888,626
Totals:	4,174,243	5,748,192	9,921,435

Source: DMA 1914, 302–6.

Appendixes 1 and 2 detail federal and state spending state by state, while tables 14 and 15 summarize the impact of federal aid from a regional perspective.[7]

The tables and appendixes demonstrate two crucial aspects of the reform-era National Guard. First, some states relied far more than others on the federal government. In 1903, eighteen states and territories (marked by an asterisk in appendix 1) received half or more of their combined military budgets from the War Department. Eleven of thirteen states in the South belonged to this category as well. Arkansas and Nevada operated with no state support at all, and Oklahoma drew over 90 percent of its support from Washington. Ten years later, the number had risen to twenty-eight, as indicated by asterisks in appendix 2. In 1913, twelve southern states and seven of eight in the Plains region depended more on federal dollars than on funds provided by their own legislatures, but all regions had at least three states that relied on that aid for more than 50 percent of their military budgets. The South remained the most

Table 16 Percentage of Federal Funds in Combined Appropriations,
1903 and 1913

	1903	1913
Northeast	14.0	31.0
South	60.0	70.0
Midwest	25.0	39.0
Plains	38.0	58.5
West	21.0	41.0

Sources: SWR 1903; SWR 1904; DMA 1914, 302–6.

dependent region. Arkansas took its entire 1913 budget from Washington, while five other states drew more than 80 percent and three over 70 percent.

Second, all states had become more dependent on federal assistance by 1913, as table 16 shows.[8] State operating budgets roughly doubled in these years, from $3 million in 1903 to $6 million in 1915, but state spending failed to keep pace with federal aid, which quadrupled between 1900 and 1908 from $1 million to $4 million. In 1913, only four states—Massachusetts, New Jersey, New York, and Ohio—provided 75 percent or more of their money to the combined appropriations.

Although the states became more reliant on the national government, federal aid did not bring forth a new millennium. The War Department allotted R.S. 1661 aid ($2 million) according to each state's congressional delegation, in other words, by population. Assistance under section 13 of the militia law ($2 million) was based on the enlisted strength of each state force. Although theoretically states might gain greater federal assistance as their populations grew or they recruited more men, in fact neither option prevailed. Congressional delegations were determined according to the last census, and so R.S. 1661 allocations were set for a ten-year period. More importantly, from 1908 on federal appropriations remained fixed at $4 million. However, the National Guard added nearly nineteen thousand new men between 1908 and 1915, which meant that federal assistance in dollars per soldier actually declined.

The effect of national aid was also limited because, except for camp and maneuver costs, it came in material form, not cash. State appropriations remained essential to National Guard operations and, far more than federal support, determined the quality and efficiency of individual Guard organizations. States paid the costs to house Guardsmen and their equipment, train and educate soldiers, and administer the state soldiery, expenses that rose substantially after 1903 to meet federal requirements. State appropriations totaled roughly $3 million for operating costs in 1903, exceeded $4 million in 1911, averaged $5.5 million in the ensuing three years, and approached $6 million by 1915. Legislatures also approved special appropriations for expenses not covered by the operating budget. In 1909, for example, the DMA noted that while the states allocated $4.2 million for "general expenses," in all, appropriations totaled $9.4 million, with over $2.5 million for armories alone. Major D. W. Ketchum of the DMA estimated that state and local governments expended roughly $12 million in 1912, of which $5.3 million was allotted for operating costs.[9]

Funds for armory construction accounted for the largest nonoperating expense. Massachusetts spent $3.2 million between 1900 and 1915 to put all its units in state-owned armories. By the latter year, only three companies remained in privately owned buildings. Only New York matched the Bay State in its financial commitment to armory construction, with the New York City Armory Board alone owning armories and land valued at $20 million. Other Northeastern states spent millions to build armories. Pennsylvania, for example, appropriated $1.5 million between 1905 and 1912, while Connecticut opened a million-dollar building in Hartford in 1909. In the Midwest, Ohio initiated a program in 1910 to build armories around the state, and Illinois began a similar effort a year later. On the West Coast, Washington allotted nearly $400,000 for armories in its major cities, while California approved a $420,000 armory for San Francisco in 1910.[10]

States not building armories gave annual grants from their operating budgets to offset rental fees or mortgage payments for individual units. Armory aid varied greatly among the states. Pennsylvania gave $1,500 yearly for field artillery and cavalry armories and $500 for the infantry. Iowa's armory support rose from $600 annually to $1,000 between 1908 and 1913. The South trailed the rest of the country. Virginia allotted $10 per man, which meant the average infantry company received $450 per year. Alabama allotted $200, Texas $180, and Georgia $120 annually to each unit. Arkansas and Mississippi provided nothing.[11]

Few states supplied sufficient funds to assure decent armories. In 1905, the secretary of war reported that "very few states have proper and adequate armories," an observation repeated almost verbatim in the DMA's 1910 report.[12] The DMA observed in 1915 that 55 percent of over two thousand armories suffered major deficiencies. States were well aware of their problems. West Vir-

Table 17 Regional State and Combined Appropriations, per Soldier, 1903 and 1913

	1903		1913	
	State	Combined	State	Combined
Northeast	$39.75	$42.00	$61.00	$88.00
South	6.30	15.90	18.35	61.25
Midwest	28.50	38.00	54.12	88.75
Plains	17.33	28.00	36.25	87.45
West	33.30	42.22	61.00	102.36

Sources: SWR 1903; SWR 1904; DMA 1914, 302–6.

ginia's adjutant general described his armories as "a great and lasting disgrace to the State."[13] The inability of states to provide decent armories severely hindered recruitment and training and remained a singular weakness in the state soldiery.[14]

Armories represented the largest expenditure but not the only one. States also purchased campgrounds and rifle ranges to meet federal requirements. Administrative costs, including salaries for adjutants general and clerks, expenses incidental to inspecting troops and examining officer candidates, and maintenance of state arsenals absorbed from 5 to 10 percent of annual operating budgets. A few states offered drill pay, the kind of support Guardsmen most eagerly sought. Utah enacted the nation's most liberal provision in 1911, offering enlisted men $1.50 per drill and captains $200 a year. One-third of the Massachusetts budget in 1914 went to drill pay, an average of $32 a year per man. Other states were not so accommodating. West Virginia paid its enlisted men ten cents a drill while Iowa promised the same amount per hour but set a limit of twenty cents per drill![15]

The demands of the militia law required state contributions much greater than those provided in the 1890s. Appendixes 1 and 2 indicate that some states responded more generously than others. Table 17 illustrates the extraordinary variance in the manner in which states supported their soldiers.

Most clearly, federal dollars contributed to higher combined appropriations per soldier by 1913 and particularly benefited the South and Plains regions. Per-soldier appropriations, which are regional averages, mask crucial intraregional differences. The most dramatic differences appear in 1913. For the Northeast, the per-soldier state rate ranged from Delaware's $31.33 to

Massachusetts's $104.19. In the South, six states allotted less than $10.00 for each man, while in the Midwest Iowa's $80.36 contrasted sharply with Missouri's mere $18.46. Montana provided only $16.39 for each of its soldiers, while Colorado spent $50.48 in the Plains. Out west, a generous Utah legislature appropriated a nation-leading $122.99 for each of its 354 National Guardsmen. Despite that assistance, the widely scattered Utah force could not recruit enough men and disbanded its two companies in 1914 under DMA orders.[16]

With rare exceptions, combined state-federal military budgets remained insufficient to sustain the National Guard as an effective organization. State leaders repeatedly appealed to their own legislatures and to Congress for more money. Brigadier General Henry C. Clark, Missouri's brigade commander, observed a year after the militia law passed that it was "imperative" for the state to increase its support "if the advantages contemplated by the law are to be obtained."[17] In 1910 California's adjutant general turned his eyes to Sacramento for money to purchase new uniforms to meet militia law requirements. He noted, "this clothing will have to be purchased with State funds, as the allotment to California from Federal appropriations is inadequate."[18] Georgia's adjutant general put the case well for underfunded states like his own. "Radical changes and readjustments are absolutely necessary" in state funding he reported in 1914. His state spent 75 percent of its annual budget on armory support, leaving Georgia with less than $10,000 to meet yearly operating costs, including "expenses imposed by the U.S. Government." The Georgia Guard needed twice its current appropriation to comply with federal requirements. Although the "fetich [sic] of State's Rights versus Centralization of Power" hovered over the Guard, he personally favored its total federalization.[19]

General A. L. Mills of the DMA believed inadequate state funding could be boosted if Congress amended the militia law to require that the federal allotment be "proportionate to that which the state is willing to appropriate itself."[20] The suggestion died aborning. Some states continued to neglect their military forces even in the face of the loss of federal aid. In 1913, the Arkansas legislature refused to approve money for its Guard. Governor George W. Hays preserved the federal allotment by appealing to local governments and private individuals for enough funds to keep the Guard functioning. West Virginia faced the same problem in 1915 when its governor vetoed the military appropriation. Adjutant General John C. Bond also turned to local civic groups and municipalities as a last resort.[21]

Calls for local help were not unusual. Local governments and private citizens had traditionally assisted the Guard. Some states required municipalities or counties to provide armory aid, and, as in the 1890s, Guardsmen raised armory funds through private subscriptions. Units rented their armories to community groups and hosted dances, dinners, and theatricals to earn money and win support from local civic leaders. A Pomona, California, company produced a play to meet those ends. "This play was a grand success," a correspondent wrote *National Guard Magazine*, "and the company is now free from debt."[22] Smaller towns turned to local businessmen. Frankfort's Ambulance Company Number 1 of the Indiana National Guard, for example, invited businessmen to pay dues to use its armory as a club and gymnasium. Finally, Guardsmen personally bore an undetermined but substantial amount of the costs that sustained the Guard. For example, during the 1909–10 biennium, Missouri needed $183,000 to maintain its Guard. The state paid $120,000, while Guardsmen and their friends supplied the rest, according to its adjutant general, "in order that the State may . . . secure their share of the Federal appropriation."[23] Determining the total amount of state, local, and private money raised to support the National Guard is impossible. Whatever the total might have been, it greatly exceeded federal assistance. Yet combined federal, state, local, and private support was not sufficient to make the Guard as a whole an effective force. The striking disparity in state appropriations created a state soldiery of a decidedly mixed quality. Southern troops suffered the most from financial stringency, but they were not alone. The less populous states in the Plains and West also faced dire circumstances, but every region claimed more than one poverty-stricken organization. Disparity in state financial support created a major gap in the quality of troops from state to state. The varying differences in the training and equipment of state soldiers weakened the National Guard's assertion that all state soldiers were of equal value to the nation. As the War Department well knew, it was a hollow claim, and the general staff's decision to seek a federal reserve to replace the state soldiery reflected this fact.

Guardsmen complained that stringent War Department standards and biased Army inspectors tainted the DMA's assessments of Guard efficiency, yet state adjutants general recounted the same failings in their own inspection reports. The Guard's commonly shared weaknesses could be listed in detail, region by region, state by state. Suffice to say that federal and state reports as well as scholarly studies confirm the pervasiveness of National Guard military inefficiency in the years before World War I. Regionally, the South and

Table 18 National Guard Strength, Selected Years

	Total	Gain/Loss from Previous Year listed
1899	106,339	
1903	116,547	+10,208
1905	111,057	− 5,490
1907	105,213	− 5,844
1909	118,926	+13,713
1915	129,398	+10,472

Source: MBR 1916, 59–60.

Plains states, where dispersed rural populations and woeful state budgets predominated, demonstrated the most inefficiency, but the Guard suffered weaknesses in all regions.

The state soldiery faced a major problem simply maintaining its strength. Ironically, the immediate impact of the 1903 law was to reduce the Guard's size, as table 18 shows.[24] State forces suffered severe losses in the four years following approval of the law. By the end of 1907, the nadir of Guard strength in the pre–World War I years, 11,334 men had left the service. Following a dramatic rebound in the ensuing two years, moderate annual growth continued through 1915. For the entire period, the states added 12,851 soldiers, an 11 percent increase. The Guard's inability to enlist more men dismayed many in the War Department, who already viewed the state soldiery with skepticism.

Declines in state strengths were not distributed evenly across the country, as table 19 shows.[25] Southern states took advantage of the new law to purge their forces of black Guardsmen. By 1906, Alabama, Georgia, South Carolina, Texas, and Virginia had disbanded black units both to avoid sharing federal aid with them and to remove African Americans from their military in an era of hostile race relations. Because of the disbandments, the South lost more than any other region between 1903 and 1907, nearly eight thousand (70 percent) of the over eleven thousand who left the Guard overall. It was the only region not to regain its 1903 strength by 1915, and in that year both Georgia and South Carolina counted nearly two thousand fewer men. The disbandment of Southern African-American Guard units greatly reduced the number of black men in the Guard. Prior to World War I, Illinois's Eighth Infantry was the only all-black regiment in the Guard. The District of Columbia and Ohio supported separate black battalions, and four states kept up individ-

Table 19 National Guard Strength, by Region, Selected Years

	1903	1907	1915
Northeast	42,497	43,595	48,821
South	29,057	21,788	26,957
Midwest	27,936	26,284	31,245
Plains	7,908	5,960	9,492
West	7,292	5,789	10,039
Hawaii and District of Columbia	1,867	1,787	2,942
Totals:	116,547	105,213	129,398

Source: MBR 1916, 59–60.

Table 20 Regional Gains or Losses from 1903 through 1915

Northeast	+6,224
South	−2,100
Midwest	+3,279
Plains	+1,584
West	+2,747

Source: MBR 1916, 59–60.

ual companies. Efforts in New York City to establish an African-American regiment did not succeed until the spring of 1917.[26]

Other regions sustained strengths that reflected patterns established in the late nineteenth century. The Northeast grew moderately throughout the period, while its proportional strength in the National Guard remained the same. New York and Pennsylvania contributed 75 percent of that region's growth; the Empire State alone claimed 21 percent of all the Guard's expansion through 1915. The Midwest held its own through 1907, then expanded steadily, while the Plains and West suffered some loss before experiencing healthy growth, as table 20 shows.[27]

Presenting regional developments in gross numbers is deceiving, however, for intraregional growth and loss were not evenly distributed. For example, Alabama, Georgia, South Carolina, and Texas accounted for some six thousand of the eight thousand Southerners, mostly African Americans, who left the Guard between 1903 and 1907. Minnesota and Missouri raised two-thirds of the Midwest's expansion; Colorado and Kansas predominated in the

Plains; Oregon and Washington led in the West. States that fielded the largest forces in the 1890s—New York, Pennsylvania, Illinois, Massachusetts, and Ohio—held the same distinction in 1915. Conversely, Nevada, which reported 140 men in 1903, disbanded its military force altogether in 1906. Delaware, Utah, Wyoming, and Montana, none with more than seven hundred men, represented the smallest organizations in the National Guard.

The extra demands of the new militia law drove indifferent men from the Guard. New requirements also hindered the recruitment and retention of enlisted men. Recruitment had never been easy, but unlike the old days states could no longer maintain companies with only a few enlisted men. Units lost federal recognition and money when they fell below minimum strength, especially after 1913, when the DMA began to enforce minimum standards. In official and unofficial commentary, state officials repeatedly complained of how difficult it was to convince men to enlist. Adjutant General Wilbur F. Sadler Jr. of New Jersey spoke for all when he noted that the demands of federal regulations "have tended to greatly retard recruiting."[28] Guardsmen saw federal drill pay as the answer to the recruiting problem. Captain C. F. Rodgers of Ohio observed that most of his men were "working boys, many not getting over two or three dollars a day." He believed "it was a disgrace to the state and to the National Government" that his men were not paid for voluntary military training.[29] Adjutant General A. J. Leon of Georgia bluntly stated the case for pay: "Patriotism is a good stock in trade for the militiaman, but in time of peace it becomes dry and needs a lubricant . . . all work and no pay makes a dissatisfied, disgruntled and inactive militia."[30]

Officers believed that they too deserved federal compensation. Attitudes changed quickly following approval of the 1903 law. In 1906, Minnesota's Colonel A. W. Wright observed without cynicism that the Guard depended upon men "whose only pay is the love of blue clothes and brass buttons."[31] Wright's view did not endure long. Adjutant General J. Clifford Foster of Florida initially opposed the pay proposal but came to believe that with the duties imposed by the law "it is clearly necessary that some compensation must be given."[32] Guard officers lamented the amount of time they spent working on military administration and studying. From 1912 on, adjutants general and Guard commentators reported that many officers were resigning, and fewer men were indicating an interest in taking commissions. Proponents of drill pay particularly stressed the responsibility borne by company commanders. Captains faced the challenges of recruiting, planning weekly drills, and maintaining discipline in a service long governed by informality. They were personally liable for federal military equipment held by their units and responsible as well for the financial management and maintenance of their armory. According to Oregon's adjutant general, William E. Finzer, "the amount of work required of captains of companies can hardly be appreciated."[33]

Holding a commission also imposed personal costs. Officers had to purchase their own uniforms, sidearms, and field glasses and provide their own horses for summer camp. Many gave their own money to cover incidental armory expenses. One disgruntled company commander detailed at length the burdens of his position to the *National Guard Magazine*, closing with the comment: "Written by a captain at midnight after the men had gone home from drill and company business had been attended to and typewritten by an enlisted man paid out of the captain's pocket."[34] New York Major General John F. O'Ryan viewed the pay bill as compensation for money already spent by officers and men to support their organizations. If these men had not "gone into their pockets for the necessary funds to cover all these matters," O'Ryan wrote to Congressman J. F. Conry, "we would have no National Guard today."[35]

General O'Ryan stressed that the Guard had "ceased to be an organization primarily for the purpose of providing recreation and mild exercise."[36] The increased time and effort devoted to field training became particularly demanding. Joint Army-Guard maneuvers and instruction camps, which began in 1903, dramatically revealed the Guard's lack of preparedness for extended field duty. The joint training exercises did little to enhance comity between the Guard and the Army, as the former generally found the latter haughty, overly demanding, and punctilious. On the other hand, regulars complained that the state soldiers were neither physically fit nor tactically prepared for field duty. The Guard's poor performance in joint camps led the DMA to institute annual officer instruction camps in 1910 to improve the tactical proficiency of Guard officers and prepare them for training with the Army. Although officers received Army pay during these summer sessions, the extra week to ten days in camp meant yet more time away from families, businesses, and occupations.[37]

More importantly, the Guard's ineffective performances spurred the DMA to take a closer look at how Guardsmen trained at state encampments. In 1912, the DMA issued a circular that prescribed a specific course of instruction to be followed by the states after it found that Guard camps "were as a rule inferior in instructional value to the camps conducted by the War Department."[38] The DMA presented a three-year training program in 1914. During the first year, the Guard would train at the company and battalion level, then conduct regimental training in the second year. Only states following the program would be invited to attend Army instruction camps in the third year. Closer DMA supervision of state training inevitably eroded the long-standing tradition of viewing Guard camps as a combined vacation and fraternity outing occasionally interrupted by a few drills and a sham battle.

Army inspector-instructors extended the War Department's efforts to educate the National Guard. Although the 1903 Militia Act authorized the assignment of regular officers to state duty upon a governor's request, the undermanned Army could not meet state requests until a 1911 law expanded the officer corps. Thereafter, the DMA posted officer inspector-instructors and sergeant instructors to all the states. At the discretion of state officials, the regulars inspected local units, instructed Guard officers, advised adjutants general, and oversaw summer camp training.[39]

One of the striking contrasts in the pre–World War I years was on the one hand the endless state bickering with the War Department and at the same time the effective collaboration between Guard and Army officers in state armories and camps. Most Guardsmen welcomed the inspector-instructors, respecting their professional expertise and delighting in having one officer, paid by the federal government, who devoted all his time to the improvement of their service. The program's greatest weakness, New York's Major General O'Ryan complained, was the War Department's "inability to provide the necessary inspectors-instructors."[40] In 1914, for example, eighty-two regular officers were on duty with the states to serve nearly 130,000 Guardsmen. Not all states, of course, welcomed the inspector-instructors, many of whom were unsparing in their inspection reports. After four years of state duty, Army Lieutenant Fay W. Brabson advised his brother officers to use tact and patience with Guardsmen and to be as "wise as a serpent and as harmless as a dove."[41]

Under the inspector-instructor system, Guardsmen and regulars learned to work together and even developed friendships. Captain George Van Horn Moseley kept in touch with several Illinois Guardsmen after his stint as an instructor with that state's First Cavalry Regiment. His most frequent correspondent was the regiment's colonel, Milton J. Foreman. Foreman asked Moseley in 1914 if he wished to serve again as cavalry inspector-instructor. "It will be a bully place for you," Foreman wrote, "and put you right where you could do the most good for yourself and for us."[42] Another Illini soldier praised Moseley for displaying "the rare tact of correcting without humiliating or hurting the other man's feelings."[43] Roy C. Vandercook, Michigan artilleryman and adjutant general from 1912 to 1915, maintained contact with several former inspector-instructors who had instructed his battery and battalion. He solicited their advice on how to train his gunners and improve the Guard overall. One former inspector-instructor, Captain Frank Wells, wrote Vandercook that if he were to serve in that capacity again, "I'd much rather go to Michigan than anywhere else."[44]

Guardsmen welcomed the advice of Army officers at every opportunity. Nearly every state NGA meeting featured regulars as lecturers. Some states sought to improve their military professionalism by commissioning Army officers in the state service, an effort endorsed by the DMA in 1912. Officers of Oregon's Third Infantry Regiment elected Army Major Charles H. Martin to be its colonel in 1913 following his two-year stint as inspector-instructor for Oregon. After two months of legal study and general staff discussion, the War Department allowed Martin to assume command of the Third Oregon.[45]

Cooperation with Army officers reflected an effort to improve Guard leadership. The amended militia law did not directly affect National Guard officers, but states increasingly imposed stricter examinations before commissioning or promoting officers. More significantly, progressive states took bold steps to end the hallowed tradition of electing officers, as Wisconsin had done in the late nineteenth century. Washington acted first in 1903 by granting commissions to enlisted men who performed well on competitive examinations. Promotion to other ranks came by seniority and through examinations. In the same year, New York adopted a law that permitted the election of second lieutenants, with promotion above that rank based on seniority; Texas curtailed its election process; and Kansas abolished elections altogether. The election tradition persisted in many states, however. With so many other attractions of Guard service disappearing, Guardsmen were unwilling to surrender a practice with deep roots in militia history that provided one of the few attainable rewards.[46]

Spurred in part by DMA suggestions and more so by reform-minded adjutants general, state forces developed programs to educate their officers. Most relied on correspondence schools. Inspector-instructors often created and supervised the programs, which were modeled on Army garrison schools. More ambitious states, for example, Massachusetts, New York, and Wisconsin, adopted modified versions of the Army's branch schools and staff college curricula at Fort Leavenworth or used course material provided by the Army War

College. Massachusetts developed the most thorough educational system when it established its Service School in 1906. The school provided combined correspondence and residence courses for all ranks and military specialties. In 1913, the Bay State initiated its Training School to prepare promising enlisted men for commissions.[47]

Many Guard officers took their work seriously. Within the limitations imposed by inadequate financing, curtailed time, unenthusiastic enlisted men, and public indifference, dedicated officers worked to make the Guard more effective. They lobbied successfully to ensure that state laws required governors to select adjutants general from line officers. An increasing number of officers, largely Spanish-American War veterans, pursued a second career in the Guard. Paul M. Pruitt Jr.'s brief biography of Alabamian Walter E. Bare, for example, illustrates how a successful business executive struggled to balance his occupational interests with the thirty-five years he devoted to the National Guard. State studies invariably feature long-service Guardsmen just as committed to their military avocation as Bare. Few enjoyed the luxury given to New York's division commander, Major General John F. O'Ryan. In 1913, the Empire State granted O'Ryan an $8,000 annual salary and $3,500 expense account to supervise daily operations.[48]

Despite the Guard's effort to professionalize its officer corps and Guardsmen's admiration for the expertise of their Army tutors, a cultural gap persisted between the two services. Michigan's Roy Vandercook, a friend of many regulars, articulated the differences upon his retirement as adjutant general: "National Guard officers confront problems which do not enter into . . . the . . . Army. Handling the financial affairs is of no small importance . . . and when this is coupled with the difficulty of recruiting and keeping men . . . a burden is imposed on the national guard officer of which the regular army officer knows nothing."[49]

Along with raising money to supplement insufficient state and national support, recruiting and retaining reliable enlisted men posed a major problem for the pre–World War National Guard. Although the War Department demanded that the Guard abandon the informal social and fraternal ways by which Guardsmen had long governed their own affairs, state soldiers resisted surrendering the old practices. They resisted not merely out of recalcitrance, although that impulse played its part, but because an emphasis on the traditional social and fraternal aspects of their service seemed the best way of solving their recruiting and financial difficulties.

The challenges of finding new men in the 1900–15 period differed little from the problems company commanders had faced twenty years earlier. As in the past, recruiting solicitations assumed many guises, few of which pertained to military service, and were aimed not only at potential recruits but at their parents, employers, and civic leaders as well. In Grand Rapids, Michigan, a battalion commander held "Publicity Month" at his armory, and "during that time everything possible was done to get the public to visit headquarters. Entertainment was provided in abundance."[50] Some recruiters stressed that the Guard inculcated moral and civic virtues. Captain John T. Sintzler of Ohio assured his fellow citizens that he did not tolerate "profanity, dissipation or gambling" and commended "sobriety, chastity and other Christian and gentlemanly virtues."[51] Guard leaders also offered recruits the opportunity to take part in athletics, social affairs, and off-duty recreation. Major P. L. Hubler of Ohio listed thirty reasons to enlist. Two items on his list bore on military duties; the remainder related to improving the enlistee's physical fitness, occupational success, political opportunities, and social life. In sum, Hubler concluded, military service appealed to strong men eager to prepare themselves "mentally, morally and physically to fight life's battles," be they civil or military struggles.[52]

Retaining hard-won recruits proved as difficult as enlisting them. Many armories were not attractive men's clubs but dank, cramped, unpleasant buildings. Weekly armory meetings, featuring repetitive close order drills, quickly became monotonous and prompted many men to quit. Estimates given by state adjutants general and the DMA of the annual turnover ranged from one-third to one-half. A South Dakota company commander reported that he enlisted 130 men over a three-year period, but 78 of them left during the same span. And a Michigan officer found that over a five-year period only one-quarter of the men he enlisted served out their full three-year term. Virtually no state compelled men to honor their enlistment contracts. To do so would have violated the volunteer concept and would have almost certainly deterred recruitment.[53]

Absenteeism also plagued the Guard. Absentee rates at the annual federal armory inspection reflect the difficulty Guard officers confronted when convincing their men to take armory work seriously. Although the inspection was crucial—it determined whether a unit would retain or lose federal recognition—few states presented a full roster on inspection day. From 1903 through 1905, absentee rates averaged 21 percent. Absenteeism declined to an average of 14 percent for the next three years, but thereafter the number of men missing federal armory inspections climbed steadily, averaging nearly 20 percent from 1912 through 1915. The inability of states to present a majority of their men at federal armory inspections demonstrated a fundamental ineffectiveness.[54]

Officers gave as much attention to solving the absentee problem as to recruitment difficulties. Unit commanders offered prizes and sponsored contests between company squads for best attendance. The methods rarely worked for very long. Most captains, therefore, emphasized athletic events and social activities. The sporting aspects of Guard service extended back to the antebellum years and persisted well into the twentieth century. Every state sponsored a rifle team to compete in national and international target-shooting contests. Units organized baseball, basketball, and track teams that vied against other Guard and civilian teams. Chicago's First Regiment hosted an annual open track meet that attracted athletes from the Universities of Chicago, Illinois, and Notre Dame. Better supported armories included gymnasiums, and the most substantial also provided bowling alleys, swimming pools, and billiard rooms. A Guard company providing such amenities ensured better unit participation by restricting its facilities only to soldiers in good standing.[55]

To retain enlistees, Commanders also emphasized the Guard's social-fraternal traditions. Although the increased demands of militia service inevitably eroded the social side of Guard life, the latter nonetheless remained well entrenched, and unit commanders relied on the club features of the Guard to retain enlisted men and ensure their participation in military activities. A popular means of luring men to drill nights involved some social activity after training. A Pennsylvania battalion commander permitted dances after drills. His regimental commander praised the idea and asserted that "a well developed social side in armory life would have almost more effect than the pay for drill bill in increasing attendance."[56] In Michigan, Roy Vandercook's former artillery battalion earned kudos from the *Detroit News* for its monthly supper. The word *banquet*, the *News* opined, "is associated in each soldier's mind with 'lots of fun'" and so "keeps the men in the ranks."[57] Finally, some Guard outfits looked for female assistance by organizing ladies' auxiliaries, composed of Guardsmen's relatives and sweethearts, to encourage and support their citizen soldiers. An enlisted man's club in Ohio held a monthly "ladies night" at the armory in hopes it would become an important town social affair and lead young women to use "their influence with the fellows to enlist."[58]

Table 21 Aid to Civil Authorities, 1900–1908

Racial incidents	82
Protection of prisoners	64
Miscellaneous	40
Labor disorders	28
Disaster relief	28
Total:	242

Note: Two states, Kentucky and North Carolina, did not report to the Army War College.

Source: Report AWC 9744-C, "Duty Performed by the Organized Militia in Connection with Domestic Disturbances from 1894 to 1908," RGI65.

Some Guardsmen objected to the social emphasis. Lieutenant Dwight M. Green of Indiana argued that such affairs "detract from the purely military" aspects of state service.[59] New York City Guardsmen were unhappy with General O'Ryan's plan to rehabilitate the Forty-seventh Infantry Regiment armory. O'Ryan proposed tearing out the wooden drill floor and replacing it with a concrete floor covered with dirt in order to conduct realistic training. According to the *National Guard Magazine*, O'Ryan's decision would cause "many social activities, including dancing" to be banished.[60] One Guardsman argued that dances and banquets did "more harm than good," for they opened "social chasms that membership in the Guard does so much to bridge or close up" and too often divided "the officers and men into cliques and groups."[61]

Retention of its constabulary function also challenged the Guard. An Army War College study, covering the years 1900 through 1908, provides the only general source on state active duty for the period. When combined with state reports and secondary works, however, the study permits a broad assessment of the Guard's constabulary duties (see table 21).[62]

Governors frequently used their soldiers for purposes not easily classified. In 1900, for instance, Minnesota sent a Duluth company on a three-hundred-mile trek to the village of Koochiching on the Canadian border to quell a dispute over the sale of liquor to Indians. The trip included a twenty-seven-mile forced march across bog land that the doughty Guardsmen completed in twenty-four hours. Cleveland's Troop A, the poshest outfit in the Ohio National Guard, spent two weeks in May 1908 patrolling the Ohio River to prevent Kentucky night riders from crossing the river and destroying tobacco plants. Beginning in 1911, states along the Mexican border mobilized Guardsmen to keep marauding revolutionaries from entering the United States. Arizona, California, and Texas turned out troops for this purpose, the Texas troops alone performing this duty on fourteen occasions between 1911 and 1915. Governors turned to the Guard for assistance during fires, floods, tornadoes, hurricanes, and epidemics far more often after 1900 than in the century before.[63]

As was the case in the late nineteenth century, civil officials most frequently used the Guard to prevent the lynching of jail prisoners or to stem the disorder that followed them. Black men remained the chief target of lynch mobs, which were, as in the past, largely confined to the South. For the period 1900–1908, Texas (42 instances), Georgia (33), Virginia (28), and Mississippi (22), accounted for over half of all Guard mobilizations in this period, regardless of cause. Sixty instances were clearly racially connected, and forty others were categorized as protecting prisoners. Not all the lynchings occurred in the South. Indiana soldiers fought an Evansville lynch mob in July 1903, killing at least six and wounding over twenty. The shooting broke up the mob, but in the aftermath Evansville citizens condemned the Guard, and several Guardsmen lost their jobs for performing their military duty. Three years later, Missouri Guardsmen arrived too late to prevent the hanging and burning of three African Americans in Springfield. Elsewhere in the Midwest, Illinois troops quelled two race riots, at Eldorado in 1902 and at Springfield in 1908.[64]

Southern Guardsmen usually acted quickly and responsibly to prevent lynchings. Alabama soldiers, for example, failed only once to protect black prisoners from lynch mobs in over thirty instances between 1900 and 1911. State Guardsmen were equally effective in Texas and Virginia. Use of Southern troops in lynchings fell sharply after 1910. Georgia's interventions declined largely because in 1912 the legislature repealed a law that permitted judges, mayors, and sheriffs to call out troops, granting that power solely to the governor. More importantly, governors increasingly acted more forcefully to stem the vicious practice by mobilizing troops before local officials requested state aid and by condemning local tolerance of lynching. Mob hangings occurred less frequently as a result. In Alabama, for example, Guardsmen responded nine times to lynching episodes during the 1909–10 biennium but only once thereafter through 1916. Texas and Virginia soldiers witnessed similar declines.[65]

Calls for the National Guard to serve during labor-related disorders also decreased. For the years covered in table 21, Guardsmen spent less than 15 percent of their active service time on strike duty as opposed to nearly 30 percent in the late nineteenth century. Half the states did not police a strike between 1900 and 1908, although all regions witnessed some industrial duty. The South experienced more strike service than it had in the previous twenty years. The diminishing frequency of the Guard's role as industrial constabulary was not the consequence of a reign of peace in labor relations. Urban industrial conflict grew in the mass industries of the early twentieth century, while an intensified employer effort to weaken or destroy unions through the open shop campaign as well as the appearance of the militant Industrial Workers of the World (IWW) provoked violent confrontations in industrial cities. Finally, the number of strikes and workers involved in them increased sharply between 1910 and 1915.[66]

Despite these conditions, strike duty declined, partly because urban police forces and Pennsylvania's state police, created in 1905, assumed a larger role in controlling strike disorder. Indeed, policemen largely assumed the role Guardsmen had played in the late nineteenth century in controlling and breaking major strikes. Moreover, governors became increasingly cautious about sending troops to a strike scene at the first call of local law officials. For all that, Guardsmen still intervened in labor disorders, usually, although not exclusively, in rural areas when mining, lumbering, or railroad workers walked off their jobs. Governors and Guardsmen still faced the dilemma of maintaining order and enforcing the law while attempting to remain neutral in employer-worker disputes.[67]

Confrontations between strikers and soldiers during this period differed from the upheavals of the Gilded Age. Gubernatorial attempts to appear impartial and an effort by labor leaders to keep their followers from resisting Guardsmen reduced the potential for violence. So too did the Guard's effectiveness. Militia reform produced a more disciplined, better commanded state soldiery. State military leaders convinced governors to quickly commit large numbers of troops in order to ensure that the Guard was neither overwhelmed nor left exhausted from trying to do too much with too few men. National Guard intervention during the labor disputes that preceded World War I seldom witnessed the indiscipline and indiscriminate violence that state troops sometimes displayed in the 1870s and 1880s. Although Guard interventions usually led to labor defeats, most neither provoked disorder nor attracted national attention.

Table 22 Major Labor Conflicts, 1912–1914

Place	Event	Dates of Occupation
Lawrence, MA	Textile strike	15 Jan. 1912–26 Mar. 1912
Kanawha Valley, WV	Coal strike	25 July 1912–1 May 1913
Copper country, MI	Copper strike	23 July 1913–23 Feb. 1913
Colorado coal area	Coal strike	26 Oct. 1913–20 Apr. 1914
Butte, MT	Copper strike	31 Aug. 1914–28 Dec. 1914

Source: AWC 9744-C.

From 1912 through 1914, however, a series of upheavals highlighted the Guard's role as a strike police. Strikes led by the militant Western Federation of Miners (WFM) and its ardent offspring, the IWW, brought out Guardsmen in California, Massachusetts, Michigan, and Montana. An equally determined United Mine Workers (UMW) called coal strikes in Colorado and West Virginia that engendered extensive violence. Most important, with the exception of a brief 1913 IWW agricultural dispute in Wheatland, California, these bitter conflicts entailed lengthy Guard occupations as well as the imposition of martial law in Colorado, Montana, and West Virginia. Table 22 summarizes these disputes.[68]

Occupying a strike district for an extended period of time posed serious challenges for state officials. Powerful corporate officials demanded that their property be protected and order maintained so nonunion employees could work. At the same time, labor insisted that it had the right to act collectively to save workers' jobs. All the while, the general public simultaneously demanded order and the conservation of their tax dollars. Massachusetts's adjutant general, Gardner W. Pearson, assured his fellow citizens that soldiers in Lawrence acted "solely in the interests of law and order, and not in the interest of any class."[69] Although the Massachusetts Volunteer Militia harassed the Lawrence strikers by banning parades, public meetings, and the gathering of small groups on the street, the IWW won a wage increase. West Virginia's governor, William E. Glassock, erred grievously, however, by allowing Guard officers to assist coal operators in organizing mine guards and openly aligning themselves with employers. The Guard's actions embittered miners and perpetuated the strike for another six months.[70]

Unquestionably, the role of the National Guard in Colorado's violent Southern coal fields marked the most egregious use of state military power in a labor disturbance to that time. The Colorado Guard had established a reputation as an ally of employers, as it had demonstrated in the coal strikes of

1903–4. During the 1913–14 intervention, Guard officers—many tied to the mining industry—openly collaborated with mine owners. Adjutant General John Chase imposed martial law, deported strike leaders, and enlisted privately employed mine guards and detectives into state service. The intervention ended in a paroxysm of violence on 22 April 1914, when Guardsmen attacked a miners' tent colony at Ludlow. Two women and eleven children hiding in tents died when the canvas caught fire. A running weeklong gun battle between soldiers and miners ensued while much of the nation, including many Guardsmen, damned the Colorado state soldiery for its brutality. The shooting war ended only after President Wilson sent federal troops to Colorado at the end of April.[71]

In Michigan, the efforts of Governor Woodbridge N. Ferris and Adjutant General Roy C. Vandercook to maintain impartiality during a lengthy copper strike—even though both distrusted the WFM and its largely foreign-born membership—illustrated the dilemmas of industrial constabulary service. Governor Ferris did not want the Guard to act as strikebreakers or appear to favor the employers. He asked Vandercook to dissuade off-duty officers from "hobnobbing with the employers at their clubrooms." Ferris also refused to meet with the manager of the largest mine in the copper country lest he be charged with "courting their favor." The governor also fretted about the background of Houghton County deputies, who were largely "strikebreakers or so-called gun men from outside."

Vandercook, initially more amenable than Ferris to the employers' cause and more skeptical of the strikers, came to see that the governor's advice had led the adjutant general to "maintain a better balance" on the situation and "guard against prejudice." The general spent a good deal of time in the Upper Peninsula supervising the operation and appreciated the frequent letters from the governor. Vandercook agreed with Ferris about the dubious background of the deputy sheriffs and that the "strikers really need protection from these bruisers." He added, "if riots occur" it would be due to the actions of "these alleged officers." In late September 1913, Vandercook was pleased to report that "there is a better feeling between the strikers and the National Guard" and that the miners had come to see that "we are acting as fairly as possible." In all, the general lamented, "such clashes between capital and labor are awful." Michigan troopers managed to prevent violence in the remote Upper Peninsula. Nonetheless, the WFM did not win its wage demands, and although employers did not destroy the union once the strike ended the WFM lost many members and was ruined financially.[72]

Strike duty compounded the recruitment difficulties the state soldiery already confronted. Organized labor intensified the campaign it had initiated in the late nineteenth century to deter workingmen from enlisting. Union opposition to the Guard affected enlistment to varying degrees. An Army inspector reviewing Pennsylvania soldiers noted that two infantry regiments in Pittsburgh, "the very home of unionism," suffered from the "intense antagonism of mine labor organizations."[73] Another reported that in parts of Illinois the "hostility of many of the labor unions" made it very difficult "to keep their ranks full of desirable men."[74] Washington state's adjutant general found that in some places the union campaign was "so intense as to render it almost impracticable to . . . successfully maintain organizations," though it was less effective elsewhere.[75] On the other hand, a Maryland regimental officer observed that in his state the labor boycott could be "represented by zero as far as the National Guard is concerned."[76] Union boycotts hurt companies in some localities, but overall the labor effort failed to keep workingmen out of the National Guard.

National Guard officers stoutly defended their service against charges that it was the tool of industry by stressing that most of the Guard's rank and file came from the working classes. Anecdotal evidence demonstrates the prevalence of workingmen among enlisted men. Contemporary observers referred over and over to the presence in the ranks of "laboring men," "workingmen," or men from "the trades." Since recruiting had already faltered under the more demanding federal requirements, Guard leaders eagerly sought ways to avoid having to police strikes. In 1915 and 1916, Colorado offered a prime example of a bitter strike intervention that led to unit disbandments and declining enlistments. A growing chorus of Guardsmen suggested that the state soldiery be relieved of strike duty. Lynn Naftzger, a retired Indiana officer, put the case succinctly. He argued that an effective state soldiery could not be maintained "so long as the Guardsman is a target for the jeers and sneers of many from the class of which rank and file of the Guard must largely come."[77] Former Secretary of War Henry Stimson feared that as long as the Guard remained "liable to this kind of police duty it will be difficult if not impossible to keep its numbers full."[78]

National Guardsmen, Army officers, and editorialists argued that the citizen soldiery could ease recruiting problems if state police or constabularies assumed the riot duty role. Although mentioned occasionally in the 1890s, the idea gained greater impetus after 1905 when Pennsylvania established a statewide constabulary force with the policing of strikes as one of its key duties. Commentators believed that the state police idea was the best way to eliminate organized labor's hostility toward the National Guard. Creation of state police forces would result in "the disappearance of that prejudice entertained by labor unions and other organizations" against the Guard, an Illinois officer argued.[79] In Michigan, officers of the Grand Rapids battalion sent a resolution to the state legislature calling for a state police because the "mixing of the troops in strike work is a serious handicap to the growth and popularity of the military arm."[80]

State and federal soldiers also found the idea appealing because they believed strike duty hindered the Guard's efficiency and detracted from its reserve function. Early in the century, Captain Herbert Barry of New York wrote that Guardsmen believed their service had "a higher destiny than . . . to aid in suppressing domestic disorders." That destiny was to serve with the Army as "one of the defenders of the Nation."[81] A Minnesota captain argued in 1906 that the Guard should focus on military training, for "we have taken to 'world powering' . . . and the young manhood of America must be prepared."[82] Later, the *Army and Navy Journal* argued that strike duty put the Guard to work "for purposes really foreign to the basic principles underlying its organization and maintenance."[83] Given the Guard's "raison d'etre" as a reserve, Army Lieutenant Charles H. Mason argued that if performing strike duty "stands in the way of discipline . . . then that . . . duty must be terminated."[84]

There would be no relief from strike duty. No other state emulated Pennsylvania by organizing a state police before America entered World War I. To this day, the Guard remains the force of last resort when state and local law agencies cannot quell civil tumult. Guardsmen were also disappointed that federal aid did not alleviate their most pressing financial problems. Burdened by the demands of new federal requirements, the seemingly stringent supervision of the War Department, and the all too frequent calls to police a turbulent society, the Guard suffered a drop in recruiting while officers grumbled or resigned. In his study of the South Dakota National Guard, Richard Cropp observes that after 1903 federal aid was "enough assistance to be a . . . decisive help, and yet not enough to do away with the spirit of independence and self-reliance that was such a characteristic of the Guard."[85] Under these circumstances, the National Guard clung to its local ties, its traditional social and fraternal activities, and its reliance on state, local, and private financing. Although the Militia Act of 1903 placed the state soldiery under federal supervision for the first time, the Guard remained closely integrated with local communities, an informal institution familiar to all and remarkably resistant to centralized control.[86]

8

The National Guard in

Federal Service, 1916–1920

From the Spanish-American War through 1915, Guardsmen sought increased federal financial aid, statutory recognition as the nation's first-line reserve, and retention of their central role in manpower policy. At the same time, they defended long-established rights to select officers and organize units as they saw fit and asserted a right to make military policy when it affected the state soldiery. From June 1916 through May 1917, Congress and President Woodrow Wilson resolved the question of where the Guard fit in national defense policy. The resolution was not what ardent Guard defenders desired. Although state soldiers won enlarged federal aid they lost their central place in manpower policy, and the right to determine unit structure and officer qualifications. State soldiers also failed to win a substantive role in determining reserve component policy.

Through 1915, the War Department opposed the Guard's quest for federal drill pay unless state soldiers accepted stringent federal control. Events unrelated to the dispute between the Guard and the War Department broke the impasse and moved Congress to approve the National Defense Act of 1916 (1916 NDA). Pressures resulting from agitation over preparedness, deteriorating American relations with Germany, and, above all, the Mexican Revolution led Wilson to push Congress to enact national defense legislation. The 1916 NDA not only affected the Guard but reorganized the Army, created an Organized Reserve Corps, and established the Reserve Officers Training Corps.[1]

Approximately half of the 1916 NDA, sixty-two sections, pertained to state-federal military relations. By far the larger part of this redefinition granted greater control to the federal government. The law allowed the president to prescribe the branch or arm of service each state organized, and to assign units to brigade or division organizations involving more than one state. It established a uniform enlistment contract for enlisted men and required commissioned officers to pass federal tests to determine their "physical, moral, and professional fitness." In addition, the law doubled the required annual armory drills to forty-eight and tripled the annual summer training requirement to fifteen consecutive days. Most important, the 1916 NDA required enlisted men and officers to take a dual oath upon entering the Guard, one to the state and a second that bound each state soldier to obey the president of the United States. A further provision allowed the president, upon congressional authorization, to draft Guardsmen into U.S. service.[2]

In return for accepting expanded federal control, the state soldiery won greatly increased federal aid, notably for armory drill and summer training camp pay. The act authorized Congress to appropriate sufficient annual sums to equip, supply, and pay state forces rather than allot a fixed yearly amount as had been the case from 1900 through 1915. In addition, federal funds were to be apportioned "in direct ratio to the number of enlisted men" in each state force. The Guard apparently won a concession through the establishment of a Militia Bureau to function directly under the secretary of war. Although an Army general would serve as militia chief, the secretary could assign Guardsmen to the bureau temporarily. State soldiers believed that if the agency was removed from the general staff and Guardsmen served in it, the state soldiery would receive fairer treatment in War Department plans and policies.[3]

Preparedness advocates and Army reformers saw the act as a capitulation to the state soldiery and a continuation of a decentralized military policy that threatened national security. The 1916 *Militia Bureau Report* conceded that Congress had greatly expanded War Department control over the state soldiery, notably the power to form tactical divisions, compel unit conformity, and impose federal standards for enlistments and commissions. Nonetheless, acting bureau chief Colonel Jessie McI. Carter questioned the viability of the legislation. Should the law fail, he observed, it would be due to "defects inherent in the militia system which are beyond correction by legislative action."[4] More fundamentally, Carter emphasized that the voluntary nature of the National Guard left the nation unable to plan for a war that might require an army larger than the currently enrolled state soldiery. Under modern conditions, he concluded, only "a system of universal liability to military training" would ensure proper military preparedness.[5]

Despite the skepticism, the law represented a reasonable policy that fit American military traditions, contemporary political attitudes toward centralized governmental power, and the nation's security needs. Lindley M. Garrison's Continental Army scheme, which was simply a federal version of the localized National Guard, stood little chance of winning congressional acceptance. Although the Continental Army merely seemed superfluous, calls for compulsory universal military training to ensure military preparedness confronted one of the nation's most entrenched military taboos. Americans had always despised military conscription. The inability of colonial and state officials to compel obligated militiamen to participate in compulsory peacetime training led to the demise of the regular militia and the rise of volunteer uniformed units. Universal military training as an alternative to the National Guard was wholly unacceptable in 1916.

Contemporary and scholarly critics contend that the law represented a National Guard victory, but the 1916 NDA can be described as a state triumph only in the sense that the Guard avoided being eliminated from military policy. When the provisions of the law are compared with the goals state soldiers pursued after 1899, a Guard victory appears less evident. In financial terms, the National Guard gained the most in that the law relieved states of all military expenses except administrative costs and armory support. The Militia Bureau demonstrated the full import of the financial provisions of the new law by comparing 1916 appropriations, which approached $6.5 million, with funds it requested for fiscal year 1917, which exceeded $57.5 million—a nearly ninefold increase in federal support.[6]

The National Guard fared less well in other areas. Hereafter, the federal government determined organizational structure and set standards for personnel. The president, through the secretary of war, prescribed the rules and regulations governing unit branch, organization, strength, and armament. As the Militia Bureau conceded, federal control of state organizations was now "absolutely complete."[7] If informality in the National Guard did not disappear after 1916, neither did many of the social activities that had prevailed so long in the state service. Although Guardsmen might continue to elect officers and recruit enlisted men according to club rules, new soldiers now had to meet the same standards the Army used in commissioning and recruiting men. Finally, hopes that a Militia Bureau separated from the general staff and partially staffed by Guard officers would lead to more sympathetic War Department policies proved a chimera.[8]

The state soldiery's most fundamental loss in 1916 was its central place in the nation's war armies, although that was not evident when Congress approved the law. Since the law provided that the Guard's strength would increase to nearly 430,000 over the next five years and with the Volunteer Act of 1914 still in effect, it could be assumed that state soldiers would form the heart of the next war army. Few Americans in the spring and early summer of 1916 envisioned circumstances that might lead the United States to intervene in World War I. Guardsmen had failed to anticipate that the nation's next war might demand an army of millions of men or that the general staff might raise that army through conscription.

Before that war came President Wilson called the National Guard to federal service as part of his efforts to influence the Mexican Revolution. In 1914, the United States had blockaded the Mexican Gulf ports of Tampico and Vera Cruz, then sent soldiers and Marines to occupy the latter. On 9 March 1916, the revolutionary general Francisco "Pancho" Villa raided Columbus, New Mexico, killing several American civilians and soldiers. The attack came as retaliation for President Wilson's recognition of Venustiano Carranza, one of Villa's rivals, as the legitimate leader of Mexico. A week after the Columbus raid, Brigadier General John J. Pershing led an expeditionary force into Mexico in pursuit of Villa. Even as Pershing's force met and fought regular Mexican forces during the pursuit, other armed Mexican bands threatened the border. Since the Army lacked the men to protect the long boundary from Brownsville, Texas, to San Diego, California, Wilson mobilized over five thousand Guardsmen from Texas, Arizona, and New Mexico on 9 May. The forces proved insufficient, however, and on 18 June 1916, the president called the rest of the state soldiery to federal service to reinforce the border watch.

As the first federal use of state soldiers since the Spanish-American War, the Mexican border mobilization tested fifteen years of National Guard reform. Many state forces barely earned passing marks, and some failed miserably. First and foremost, their units reported for federal service woefully under strength. In addition, state soldiers appeared at muster-in inadequately armed, uniformed, and equipped. Few units were sufficiently trained to conduct battalion or regimental tactical maneuvers. Most officers displayed at best an elementary knowledge of Army administration, discipline, camp management, or tactical proficiency. On first impression, the Guard's 1916 performance appears to differ little from its 1898 record. For Army officers, the millions of federal dollars spent on the state forces seemed a monumental waste that put the nation's security at precarious risk.[9]

The Guard's border service requires more than a general assessment, however. Mobilization not only tested the Guard's military effectiveness but the essence of the American military ethos—reliance on volunteers. States were notified at the mobilization call that their units were to be mustered in at minimum peace strengths, then recruited to war levels as soon as possible. Infantry regiments, the most common of state units, for example, were to provide 990 at muster-in and 1,915 at full strength. Few states met the minimum strength at muster-in, and at least nine never reached that level during their entire active service. Only two, Washington and Rhode Island, came within 2 percent of their war strength. Furnishing some 158,000 officers and men—59 percent of war strength—the Guard's inability to fill units to war strength demonstrated a serious weakness.[10]

States found it difficult to meet their strength requirements in part because many Guardsmen did not understand the obligations that enlistment in the National Guard entailed. Oklahoma Guardsmen, for example, believed the federal government had no authority to send them out of the state, let alone order them into extended federal service. Some governors and adjutants general displayed a similar ignorance about the legal obligation to report for duty upon a presidential call. State officials frequently discharged men from the Guard prior to muster-in because duty on the border would have created severe family or business hardships. Prior to the 18 June order, the enlisted strength of the Guard totaled 95,000. Half of those men did not appear on the muster rolls after state units were sworn in. Nearly 24,000 of the 47,600 men not on the final rolls failed the Army physical exam. The remainder either never reported to their armories or found other means to avoid being sworn into federal service.[11]

Recent approval of the 1916 NDA created further confusion. The call for border duty came just two weeks after Congress approved the act, and few states had conformed to the new legislation. Many state organizations remained Organized Militia and therefore bound by the amended 1903 law, while others had become National Guard under the 1916 law. Soldiers in some states refused to take the dual oath required by the NDA when asked to do so at their mobilization sites and further contended that since they were Organized Militia they were not bound to go to the border. Unit commanders occasionally released Organized Militiamen under the same misunderstanding. The War Department compounded the confusion by issuing mustering-in regulations that failed to differentiate between Guardsmen and militiamen. Nonetheless, because President Wilson worded his call to the states in terms of repelling invasion, both the Organized Militia and National Guard were obligated to report.

In any event, many men avoided duty along the border by refusing to report, by obtaining an illegal discharge before muster-in, or by taking advantage of the confusion over the obligations of the Organized Militia versus those of the National Guard. The War Department faced the delicate problem of how to treat thousands of militiamen who failed to report or were illegally excused. Secretary of War Newton D. Baker told one congressman that his department did not want "to bring about wholesale courts-martial" but expressed the fear that if the presidential call went unenforced "chaos will result."[12] In the end, the War Department decided it was the better part of wisdom not to send out federal marshals to arrest Guardsmen who had shunned their duty. Published reports and internal documents make clear, however, that soldiers and civilians in the War Department viewed the avoidance as unseemly, even craven, behavior.[13]

For some state soldiers, the legal obligations that accompanied enlistment or commissioning in the state service conflicted with the traditional definition of the volunteer soldier. As demonstrated in 1898, the volunteer idea held that American men should decide to offer their military services to the nation when war came. If family and business responsibilities dictated that a man should not go to war, then he was not obliged to volunteer even if he wore the uniform of the state military. The volunteer tradition also allowed a man to decide whether the political ends of a conflict requiring military service met his approval before he served. Whatever the circumstances, the final decision to perform military duty lay with the individual. That conception was alive in 1916, and it affected the way Guardsmen responded to the call and reacted to duty on the border. The volunteer idea sometimes led men to behave pettily. When the War Department requested that West Virginia provide only one regiment its adjutant general selected the Second Infantry on the basis of seniority. Deeply offended members of the neglected First Infantry refused to transfer voluntarily to the Second Regiment to bring it up to the peacetime minimum.[14]

Finding new men to fill up the regiments offered major challenges. Recruiting posed no problem in the early days of the mobilization and while units remained at their home stations. Once companies left their armories for state mobilization camps enlistments dropped and fell even more sharply as units departed for the border. Furthermore, as Oregon's adjutant general noted, "interest in military service ceased" once it became apparent there would be no war with Mexico.[15] The Army took over recruiting from 1 July through 31 October with the assistance of National Guard officers. That four-month effort produced only fifteen thousand men for both the Guard and the Army. "The ancient theory that patriotism would always provide enough men for America's armies is unsound," Massachusetts's adjutant general lamented when the volunteers failed to come forth.[16]

Service on the Mexican border in 1916 also eroded the traditional volunteer conception of duty. State soldiers had never been federalized to serve as an instrument of foreign policy short of war. Wilson's policy of "watchful waiting," wherein most of the Army and National Guard remained in the United States while General Pershing pursued the illusive Pancho Villa, left Guardsmen in an emotional limbo. Most believed they had been called to fight Mexicans, either to drive them out of the United States or to invade Mexico along with Pershing. That they were to remain in the United States to patrol the border and deter regular or irregular Mexican forces from crossing it blunted the enthusiasm with which many Guard members greeted the initial 18 June call. When it became evident by early July that duty along the border actually meant extensive training under Regular Army tutelage, the desire to render federal service faded even more rapidly.

Many Guardsmen resented being called from civil life to intimidate Mexican banditti or to serve the political ends of a president seeking reelection. Upon the unit's return from the border, New York's *Seventh Regiment Gazette* editorialized that the Guard was intended for use only in "a real national emergency."[17] In the editor's opinion, the 1916 episode was not an emergency, and he predicted more service like that would destroy the Guard. A North Dakota officer, fearing financial losses in his mercantile business, requested a furlough from border duty. He explained that "this service is only nominal and if war was declared would be glad to join his colors."[18] Guardsmen everywhere expected a quick, victorious war with Mexico and a glorious return home. When no war ensued, they chafed under Army control. Duty in the Guard training camps scattered from Brownsville, Texas, to Nogales, Arizona, seriously weakened the volunteer tradition.[19]

As soon as units arrived at their state mobilization sites, officers submitted resignations and enlisted men sought discharges. Most contended that dependent relatives relied on them for basic support. The requests for release from military duty increased once Guardsmen arrived in Texas and Arizona. For a time, the War Department accepted officer resignations and allowed enlisted men to apply for hardship discharges. In early September, however, in light of the steady loss of officers and experienced NCOs, the War Department re-fused to approve most resignations and hardship discharge requests. Con-gress approved a law in August that provided a monthly allotment to enlisted men based on the number of their dependents. Thereafter, men with depen-dent families and personal business obligations remained in service, unhap-pily for the most part, although Nebraska's adjutant general sympathetically observed that they battled "a condition that is harder than war."[20]

High school and college students in the Guard represented another group of enlisted soldiers likely to be lost. State officials had found college cam-puses to be fertile recruiting grounds, especially for such technical branches as engineers, artillery, and signal corps. Colorado alone mobilized two engi-neer companies, a cavalry troop, and an artillery battery composed of college students. As the summer progressed and no sign of demobilization appeared, parents, educational leaders, and the young men themselves demanded that students be sent home. In early August, the chief of the Militia Bureau in-formed state adjutants general that units made up of students would be mus-tered out after 1 September 1916. In all, nineteen organizations totaling just over fifteen hundred men were released. The Militia Bureau also approved a policy that permitted high school and college students to apply for discharge after 1 September. Secretary of War Baker rescinded the provision, however, once the War Department learned that thousands of students served through-out the Guard and that their release would therefore paralyze it. In Oregon's Third Infantry Regiment, for example, the discharge of students, a total of 250 men, would have cost the regiment 15 percent of its strength.[21]

The National Guard's inability to meet its manpower requirements re-flected peacetime recruiting practices. Guard recruiters rarely told new re-cruits that along with athletics, dances, and target shooting enlistment in-cluded a federal obligation. Nebraska's adjutant general lamented that some men joined the Guard knowing they might be called in an emergency, but others unfortunately neglected "to consider what [enlistment] might mean to their families or their business affairs."[22] In a similar vein, the adjutant gen-eral of Massachusetts noted that nearly fifteen hundred of his soldiers sent south were married men with dependent families "who should not have gone to the border at all."[23] Neither man discussed why their services enlisted such men in the first place. States were equally irresponsible in enlisting men who fell short of Army physical requirements. Nearly 19 percent of Guardsmen mobilized for the initial 18 June call failed the Army physical exam prior to muster-in, leaving most state units well below peace strength.[24]

A desperate need to meet DMA requirements had led state officials to recruit students, married men, and businessmen, among others, whose peacetime pursuits and responsibilities would pose serious problems if a federal mobilization came. The military subculture of the National Guard before World War I did little to inculcate the sense that the state soldiery represented a reserve component of the Army in the modern sense of that term. Guardsmen continued to see themselves as volunteer soldiers who would, as their predecessors had in 1898, determine for themselves when, where, and under what circumstances they would render military service to their nation.

Peacetime modes of operation shaped the effectiveness of the Guard's mobilization in other ways. States that provided their soldiers with adequate financial aid mobilized readily, concentrated their troops quickly, equipped new men easily, and moved to the border promptly. On the other hand, poorly funded states encountered innumerable mobilization problems. Oklahoma, for example, owned no state campground and took five days after the 18 June call even to select a mobilization site. Less well supported states, with a greater number of understrength peacetime units, enlisted large numbers of raw soldiers who had to be fully equipped and given rudimentary training. Alabama, Colorado, and Georgia forces, for example, were so poorly manned, organized, trained, and equipped that they remained in state camps up to four months before the War Department deemed them fit for border duty.[25]

States that had refused to organize their forces to fit the twelve-division plan as prescribed in DMA Circular No. 19, issued in 1914, found that not all their units would be mobilized. The War Department required states to provide troops according to Circular No. 19. States that had not followed the provisions of the circular found that many of their units would be left behind. Three of Pennsylvania's infantry regiments, for example, were not called. The Keystone State belatedly converted its Second and Ninth Infantry Regiments to artillery units to conform to the details of Circular No. 19, and the converted units were then mobilized. Virginia did likewise by changing its well-known Richmond Light Infantry Battalion into a cavalry squadron. Obviously, neither Pennsylvania's newborn gunners nor Virginia's raw troopers were of much immediate value to the Army.[26]

The National Guard confronted an unprecedented situation in 1916. For the first time, mobilization placed the state soldiery on active duty at the full disposal of the War Department in peacetime. The implications of the 1916 NDA now became evident. Under the law, the Army asserted control over nearly every aspect of Guardsmen's personal and institutional lives. War Department and general staff officers determined which units were mobilized and which Guardsmen were obliged to serve. Once the mobilization was completed, the War Department dictated where Guard units would be stationed, what they would do while along the border, and how long they would remain in federal service. Inevitably, this assertion of federal authority over the state soldiery during peacetime engendered a clash of military cultures, a clash that previously had taken place largely in military periodicals, NGA conventions, and the popular press.

Provisions of the twelve-division plan governed the mobilization. Unlike past calls for state troops, the federal government did not set a numerical quota of men for each state. Instead, it informed governors what kind of units, that is, combat units or auxiliaries, and at what level of organization, for example, battalion, regiment, or brigade, they were required to provide. The twelve-division plan gave the War Department a means to fend off old-style independent volunteer offers and offended Guardsmen not originally chosen to serve. The Army's adjutant general, Henry P. McCain, sent a standard response to all tenders from putative volunteers or unhappy Guardsmen. McCain stressed the divisional plan and noted that "any departure from this plan would throw the entire mobilization into confusion."[27]

Mobilized Guardsmen first reported to their armories and then moved to state mobilization camps where they were fully equipped, given rudimentary training and Army physical examinations, and mustered into federal service. Army inspectors either deemed units sufficiently equipped and organized to be sent to the border or recommended that poorly prepared battalions and regiments remain in state camps for extended training before going south. State units first reported for duty on the border on 1 July, but it soon became evident that there would be no war and the Guard would not be sent into Mexico.

Nonetheless, the Wilson administration did not think the border situation permitted a quick demobilization. Appalled by the Guard's inefficiency and lack of training, the Army saw the mobilization as an opportunity to subject state soldiers to rigorous instruction. Over the next six months, Guard units underwent a program ranging from individual training through company and regimental exercises to, by November, division maneuvers. Guardsmen served in the Army's Southern Department, commanded by Major General Frederick Funston. Funston warned his superiors in late June that three months of patrol and training "will be the limit of the National Guard." Kept any longer than that, he noted, and "there will arise such a storm of protest and complaint that it will have to be heeded and these troops returned to their homes.''[28] Funston understood volunteer state soldiers well but overestimated how long they would tolerate Army tutelage without complaint. The demands from the border camps, state capitals, and hometown newspapers that the boys be sent home offered most regulars yet another example that the state soldiery would never make a reliable reserve.

Indeed, the mobilization confirmed doubts professional soldiers had expressed for a decade and a half. Captain Horace P. Hobbs, a former inspector-instructor and officer in the DMA, oversaw the mobilization and muster-in of the District of Columbia Guard. The exercise ''only strengthens my belief the militia is worthless.'' As Hobbs saw these soldiers off to the border in early October, he thought ''the Lord help such troops if they ever have to go against trained regulars.''[29] Another regular, Lieutenant Colonel Eli Helmick, of the inspector general's office, recalled that he did not expect the Guard's field training to be of a high standard, ''but I was not prepared to find the disciplinary training to be of such a low order.''[30]

Army inspectors reiterated dismay, approaching disgust, in report after report. Officers from the Southern Department's inspector general's office presented a stark picture. Lieutenant Colonel Helmick sent inspection teams to review every regiment and brigade closely. The teams found little to praise in the Guard other than its remarkably good health. Helmick concluded that the Guard ''has proved a hopeless failure,'' but, he added, Guardsmen were not at fault, for ''the defective system to which they are bound is responsible.''[31] The Militia Bureau asserted that state leaders, with ''rather crude ideas'' of what constituted first-line troops, erred in viewing the state soldiery as a viable reserve. The mobilization had proved otherwise, the Bureau concluded, and with a note of professional smugness added ''the sooner this idea is abandoned the better it will be for all concerned.''[32]

The Army, however, was hardly without fault in its execution of the mobilization. From the publication of the ''Organization of Land Forces'' plan in 1912, War Department agencies had emphasized the need for states to organize their forces according to the twelve-division plan. General staff plans for using the Guard in troubles with Mexico, first considered in 1912 and given greater attention in 1914, assumed that the divisional scheme would govern any mobilization. When the 1916 call came, the War Department abandoned this preliminary preparation and merely used the twelve-division format as a guide for calling up specific state combat and support units. The War Department ignored the twelve-division tactical organization and simply sent well-prepared regiments to Texas or Arizona as soon as they were mobilized and mustered in, regardless of their divisional assignments. The Militia Bureau later contended that little was lost by not calling Guard divisions because they were incompletely organized, and state units were woefully inefficient. However, the Army actually had no detailed plans to use the National Guard for a national emergency, and the mobilization and deployment of state troops evolved in an ad hoc, decentralized fashion. Commanders of the four geographic departments conducted the operation, supervised the mustering-in process, and ordered troops southward, each according to his own priorities.[33]

State military leaders stressed the flaws in the mobilization process. Missouri's adjutant general lamented that the failure to follow DMA plans generated great confusion. It was not clear "whether the mobilization was being managed by the Central Department, the Militia Bureau, or the War Department." Conflicting directions from these agencies confused both the Army mustering officer and Missouri officials.[34] Massachusetts reported that the Eastern Department had made no provision to care for state-leased horses once its field artillery regiment and cavalry squadron left for the border. After the regiment and squadron boarded their trains, the horses were left to fend for themselves despite "the protest of every army officer on duty with the state." Several animals died and many were hurt.[35] Virginia's new cavalry squadron, the recently converted Richmond Light Infantry Blues battalion, spent four months in a state camp as a mounted unit with no horses and no training.[36]

Army department commanders agreed that War Department supply bureaus failed to deliver uniforms and equipment to state mobilization centers. An obsession with paperwork and an overly centralized supply system, with two depots for the entire nation, delayed the delivery of needed supplies to Guard units that had doubled in manpower in less than a month. General Funston of the Southern Department concluded that most of the disarray accompanying the call-up could have been avoided had the War Department adhered to the original divisional plan. As it was, all phases of the mobilization were confusing, plagued by unnecessary paperwork and inflexible regulations. Captain George Van Horn Moseley, temporarily a National Guard colonel and chief of staff for Pennsylvania's Seventh Division, wrote to Secretary of War Baker that many of the Guard's difficulties could "be traced to our own supply system."[37]

Once state units reached the border, General A. L. Mills, chief of the Militia Bureau, urged that they be assigned to provisional brigades and divisions for training and instruction. Mills also proposed that regular officers command the provisional organizations and serve as divisional chiefs of staff and colonels of provisional Guard cavalry, artillery, and engineer regiments. From the onset of the mobilization, General Funston urged the War Department to promote Army officers to higher temporary ranks. He wanted to ensure that the Army obtained "the best men" rather than have politically influential National Guard officers made brigade and division commanders. More importantly, Funston argued, without temporary Army promotions "it is difficult to see how brigadier generals of the regular army are to be kept from being superseded in command by Major Generals of organized militia."[38] National Guard major generals commanded only two of the ten Guard divisions, the Sixth Division from New York and Pennsylvania's Seventh Division.

Guardsmen did not unthinkingly object to regular officers assuming command of state units. Three Army officers, all selected by state governors, commanded Guard brigades, and regulars also led several state regiments and battalions following election or gubernatorial appointment. However, the assignment of regulars to serve as provisional commanders of Guard divisions, brigades, and regiments as well as divisional chiefs of staff reflected the gulf that had long existed between professional regulars and part-time volunteers. Generals Funston and Mills believed that state soldiers could learn to soldier only under the firm command of Army officers. Viewing the state soldiers with disdain, the professionals displayed little interest in teaching volunteers of all ranks the skills needed to lead their men in battle and moved quickly to put their own kind in command of higher-level state organizations.

Captain Moseley personally experienced the culture gap between regulars and volunteers while traveling on a train in Texas. Wearing a uniform with Pennsylvania National Guard insignia, he encountered several junior Army officers. The young men were polite to the "Guard Colonel," but after a lengthy conversation Moseley "got a very distinct example of the real patronizing attitude of the Regular Army officer toward the National Guard officer—and it was very illuminating to say the least."[39]

Few regulars would have agreed with Moseley's judgment that the mobilization "clearly demonstrated that the Regular Army is no better prepared to meet an emergency . . . than the National Guard."[40] The Army applied abstract standards in evaluating the Guard's performance in 1916, standards that many elements of the regular service could not have met. Colonel Helmick's officers inspected the Guard in September and October to determine if it was capable of fighting a modern, well-organized army. Not surprisingly, the inspectors found few state units "ready and fit for active field service against a well-trained enemy."[41] One regular, Brigadier General James Parker, commander of the Brownsville district, differed with the Militia Bureau. He reported early in 1917 that his troops were "fit to take the field against a fairly well trained enemy or to act on the defensive against well-trained troops."[42] Moreover, as General Pershing's struggling expeditionary force in Mexico demonstrated, the Army itself fell well short of modern military efficiency.[43]

The National Guard, in any event, was called to the border to deter Mexican intruders and relieve regular troops ordered to support Pershing's expedition, not to fight a well-trained enemy. The assignment placed the Guard in camps across Texas, New Mexico, and Arizona where, as the Mexican threat diminished, the Army implemented its training program. Service on the border put clashing military subcultures in close proximity and reinvigorated enduring animosities between regulars and volunteers. State soldiers, in the hallowed volunteer tradition, traveled to the border expecting to engage and whip unruly Mexicans and then go home. Resentful Guardsmen kept on the border saw little purpose in their training and much to dislike in an Army seemingly obsessed with paperwork and snobbish protocol.

On the other hand, the Guard's woeful performance in 1916 led the regulars to try yet again to eliminate the state soldiery from national defense policy. "The entire mobilization," Major General T. H. Barry stressed, "emphasizes the absolute necessity of some form of universal training," with all the nation's military forces "under sole Federal control."[44] Army Chief of Staff Hugh L. Scott urged the abandonment of the volunteer system and directed the War College Division to prepare a universal military training and service bill for congressional consideration. War with Germany intervened before Congress acted on the bill, but the border incident, especially the difficulties the Guard and Army faced in recruiting volunteers, paved the way for wartime conscription. Through February and March, the Wilson administration remained undecided whether to rely on volunteering until it faltered or adopt conscription immediately. President Wilson and Secretary of War Baker at last opted for a draft, but Congress waited for more than a month after war was declared before approving the Selective Service Act of 18 May 1917.[45]

War with Germany found the National Guard in disarray. The border mobilization delayed the implementation of the 1916 NDA and state reorganization once forces came home from the border. Although some states demobilized as early as October 1916, most organizations were not mustered out until January or February. Even then, thousands of Guardsmen were still on active duty when the United States declared war on 6 April. Some forty thousand more were federalized in late March and early April to prevent sabotage to communication lines, harbor facilities, and railroads. When war came, eighty thousand Guardsmen were already in federal service. In the interim between border demobilization and the declaration of war, the Guard lost men through resignations and the termination of enlistments. To compound state problems, the Militia Bureau directed that all Organized Militiamen, that is, men who had refused to take the dual oath required by the 1916 NDA, be dropped from the National Guard.[46]

The state soldiery was ill prepared for a second mobilization when war came and yet was left idle from April through August. Despite the strong emphasis it had placed on planning since 1910, the general staff had not anticipated American intervention in the war and lacked plans for mobilizing a mass army. Admittedly, the War Department had been occupied with the Mexican problem, and President Wilson had said little about his intentions toward Germany. Still, in April planners found themselves at war with few ideas about how to meet its demands. That failure created problems that plagued American action to the end of the war. The Army would face serious difficulties organizing, supplying, and transporting a fighting force to France in large part because it had never considered the likelihood of having to do so.[47]

Approval of the Selective Service Act allowed mobilization plans to be prepared. In late May, the War Department announced that the Army would be recruited to three hundred thousand men by the end of June, with the National Guard to be federalized in mid-July and "drafted" into federal service two weeks later. The "National Army," that is, draftees, would be called to the colors beginning in early September. In the meantime, the Guard was to recruit to war strength and prepare itself for duty. The states moved quickly to recruit new men and acted just as rapidly to take advantage of the authority granted by the War Department to organize units sanctioned by the 1916 NDA. That law provided enough men to field sixteen infantry divisions. Two states, Ohio and Texas, attempted to find qualified officers, organize new units, and recruit volunteers sufficient to make up a division. Their efforts resembled the traditional volunteer practice in that they commissioned officers and gave them the responsibility to organize units and recruit men. Ohio nearly made its minimum manpower quota, but Texas fell short of the mark.[48]

Other states undertook less ambitious organizational efforts. Some succeeded and others did not. Washington state had husbanded its military budget carefully since the early 1900s by supporting one infantry regiment. Following the declaration of war, the state successfully organized a field artillery
battalion, a cavalry squadron, and a signal battalion to serve along with the
Second Washington Infantry Regiment. In North Dakota, efforts to revive a
moribund infantry regiment did not fare so well. Former Spanish-American
War officers spearheaded the effort to create the Second North Dakota Infantry. However, they encountered the resentment of National Guard officers in
the First Infantry and the challenges of recruiting in the state's small towns.
The Second North Dakota barely won federal recognition and entered federal
service woefully under strength. Belated state efforts to organize new units
again brought to mind volunteer practices of yesteryear as aspiring captains,
majors, and colonels scrambled to win commissions and enlist recruits.[49]

States vigorously recruited volunteers from mid-April to mid-July, while
the War Department struggled to build training camps and purchase supplies
and equipment. Recalling the embarrassment of June 1916, when thousands
of Organized Militia failed to answer the president's call, state officials emphasized to their men that they were legally bound to report. Captain Fred E.
Ellis of Company D, Second Kansas Infantry, urged his men to "not lose
sight of the fact that you are *ordered* out, and this means business" (emphasis
in original). Those failing to report would be tried for desertion.[50] President
Wilson "called" the Guard to federal service on 15 July. State forces were to
remain at their home stations until 5 August, when the president would
"draft" the Guard into United States military service. Divisional training
camps were still under construction on 5 August, however, forcing Guard
units to spend additional weeks at their armories or on furlough. Only in late
September and early October did the state soldiers head south for training.[51]

When Guardsmen reported to the Southern camps, the War Department
immediately reorganized their units to meet the requirements for a newly
adopted and greatly enlarged divisional arrangement, called the square division. Revised tables of organization reduced the number of infantry regiments, added an artillery regiment, dropped the cavalry regiment, and created organizations not included in the old divisions. The latter included
machine gun and trench mortar battalions, supply trains, and military police.
In addition, the new system eliminated state names and adopted numerical
unit identifications that were to prevail throughout the Army. Finally, the new
tables doubled manpower in infantry regiments and increased total divisional

strength. Guardsmen were unaware of the pending changes when they left their states and reacted to them with incredulity and a sense of betrayal.

Many field grade infantry officers lost their commands while others were placed in charge of units for which they had no training. Surplus infantry regiments were either merged to create larger units or converted to new specialties. Reorganization took place rapidly, implemented by Army officers who rarely conferred with Guardsmen or displayed much sympathy for state officers stripped of their commands. Reorganization caused the most resentment and protest when smaller states saw their units disappear in mergers that favored larger states. In the Thirty-sixth Division, for example, Oklahoma's First Infantry was broken up, and no single unit in the division could be identified as deriving directly from the Oklahoma Guard. Two hundred enlisted men from the Sooner State went absent without leave in protest. Historically notable units lost their old identities. New York's famous Seventh Regiment became the One hundred seventh U.S. Infantry, for example, and also absorbed all of the First New York Infantry and other elements from the state's Guard. "To be broken up and transferred to a strange regiment was very discouraging," a historian of the Seventh wrote, "and the men of the 1st came to us with very bitter feelings."[52]

Reactions to the changes, particularly because of their unexpectedness, were understandable, but resistance and resentment also reflected the provincial perspective of the National Guard. Regimental consolidations, complained Missouri's adjutant general, Harvey C. Clark, "threw organizations from different localities and states together in the same company." The end result, he lamented, "was to greatly discourage and dishearten" Guardsmen.[53] If state soldiers objected to serving in the same unit with men from another part of their state or a neighboring state, they resented even more the assignment of reserve officers from a different part of the country. J. D. Lawrence of the Second South Carolina Infantry recalled the response of his outfit to the arrival of two Jewish second lieutenants from the North. Because of their religion, the two men were viewed suspiciously, Lawrence noted, but "the fact that they were not 'invited,' as was customary among state troops, also made them unwelcome members of the company."[54] Eli Helmick of the inspector general's office, now a brigadier general, found that in most older regiments "a prejudice had quickly developed against" junior reserve officers assigned to the National Guard.[55]

State military and political leaders vigorously protested the reorganization. Congressional delegations inundated the War Department with queries about the fate of disbanded Guard regiments. The volume of protests prompted Secretary of War Baker to advise Army officers commanding Guard divisions to make every effort to preserve the identity of the oldest state regiments in the reorganization process. Chief of Staff Tasker H. Bliss directed the War College Division to prepare a public statement fully explaining "the necessity of reorganizing the old N.G. divisions."[56] Press releases dampened public concern about state units but did not assuage what Missouri Adjutant General Clark described as the "heartburnings and humiliation" suffered by officers who lost their commands.[57] A Sixth Massachusetts veteran later wrote of the "sadness" and "bitterness" that swept his unit when it learned it was to be broken up.[58] A Pennsylvania Guardsman used similar terms to describe the dissolution of the Thirteenth Infantry from the Keystone State. Following the "mutilation" of the regiment, its chaplain met a major who "confessed that he had to go to his quarters and blubber."[59]

Many combat units were changed abruptly from one branch to another. Utah's fate from May 1916 through August 1917 illustrated graphically how War Department indecision on unit organization affected state forces. At the urging of the Militia Bureau, Utah changed its five infantry companies and two artillery batteries to cavalry in May 1916. The new cavalry squadron received extensive training for four months while on the border. From April through May 1917, the state worked to recruit a full cavalry regiment. Then, in June, without warning, the Militia Bureau ordered Utah to convert its force back to artillery. The unexpected directive left Utah's Guard in disarray for the rest of the summer. Ohio's squadron, also at work raising a regiment, learned in May 1917 that the new divisional arrangement did not call for cavalry. In this instance, the Buckeye troopers requested they be converted to artillery. Units that lost their combat designations particularly resented the changes. J. D. Lawrence described the Guardsmen's reactions when the Second South Carolina Infantry and infantry regiments from North Carolina and Tennessee were converted to the Fifty-fifth Depot Brigade of the Thirtieth Division. Depot brigades served as training units. The conversion "was quite a blow to the pride of the Second South Carolina," Lawrence remembered, "as there was no glory to be gained from a Depot Brigade."[60]

The War Department's imposition of the square division on the state forces without consultation symbolized the Guard's World War I experience. The abrupt change disregarded state interests and concerns, while a powerless National Guard failed to influence its destiny or protect its cherished organizations. The unexpected reorganization after the Guardsmen had entered federal service destroyed the nascent sense of identity they had developed on the Mexican border for the divisions and brigades the DMA had so long extolled. Mergers and conversions then placed Guard officers and men in units whose military functions they did not understand. Six of the new divisions created in September and October were broken up once they reached France, with their men dispersed as replacements for understrength divisions. Finally, when the war ended, the War Department demobilized Guardsmen as individuals and sent them home one by one. Divisions and other units formed from National Guard organizations ceased to exist. So too did the state soldiery, for the War Department inadvertently discharged Guardsmen from all military service, state as well as national.[61]

World War I permanently altered the state soldiery's place in manpower policy. The demands of mass war and the Army's long quest to assert national control over all military activities coincided with broader centralizing trends in America to ensure congressional approval of conscription. Selective service laws and the 1916 NDA secured the Guard a role in the war, but it was a restricted one. The May law permitted the Army and Guard to enlist volunteers from draft-eligible men through December 1917, but the states failed to recruit enough men to bring their units to war strength before going overseas. Nearly 450,000 men, approximately 12 percent of the war army, entered service through the Guard. Their contribution to the American Expeditionary Force, about 20 percent, was more significant. But when compared with the part volunteer state soldiers played in war armies from 1775 through 1898, the World War I contribution appeared modest indeed.[62]

The National Guard reconstituted itself after World War I, but never again would the state soldiery dominate the nation's war armies. Ironically, the victory Guardsmen purportedly won when Congress approved the 1916 NDA proved a false one. Over the preceding five decades, political and military leaders had neglected to devise a public policy that would incorporate the developing state soldiery into military policy. That neglect allowed the National Guard to evolve largely according to its own dictates and encouraged Guardsmen to believe they shared an equal place with the Army in national defense. Despite efforts at reform after the Spanish-American War, the Guard's place in military policy and the extent to which Guardsmen could shape that policy remained undecided. The 1916 NDA resolved those issues.

However, mobilization in 1916, and again in 1917, left many state soldiers believing they had been deceived, even cheated. Guardsmen failed to appreciate that while the 1916 law guaranteed their service a place in military policy it was to be a circumscribed one. From 1916 on, as established by law, state volunteers entering the war army would be limited to the number of National Guardsmen authorized by Congress and the general staff would determine how the Guard was organized and commanded. State soldiers could no longer use their political connections or their state's manpower contributions to win general officer commissions for their important leaders. Volunteers recruited by the states from the general population would no longer form the war army, and National Guard regiments would no longer provide the skeleton of an expansible army as they had in 1898.

Epilogue

The National Guard struggled to rebuild itself in the four years after World War I. State soldiers had entered federal service according to the Selective Service Act of 18 May 1917, which had allowed President Wilson to draft Guardsmen as individuals rather than call up their units as the 1916 NDA allowed. State soldiers were discharged from state military service when drafted and released as individuals when their wartime federal service ended. Consequently, the states were left with no military force in the autumn of 1917. Although some states organized home guards for the war's duration, these forces were small and ineffective. From mid-1919 through 1922, the states reconstituted their organized militias only with difficulty, finding it particularly hard to convince war veterans to enlist in the Guard.

In the meantime, Congress casually reconsidered military policy before approving legislation in June 1920. The War Department called for a half-million-man army and universal military training for nineteen-year-olds. Although the proposal left untouched sections of the 1916 NDA that pertained to the National Guard, the general staff clearly intended to relegate the state soldiery to a minor role in military affairs. After much debate and intense lobbying, Congress at last simply amended the 1916 NDA. The Guard fared well under these changes. It retained its status as the Army's major reserve component and won inclusion of a section that provided that Guardsmen would not be discharged from state service when called to national duty. Above all, following NGA pressure, Congress separated the Militia Bureau from the general staff and stipulated that a National Guard officer serve as chief of the bureau.

The 1920 National Defense Act outlined a scheme that shapes military policy to this day. It stipulated that the Army, National Guard, and Organized Reserve Corps would comprise the peace establishment, with one Army division, two National Guard divisions, and three Reserve divisions in each of nine corps areas. Theoretically, the Army's chief peacetime occupation was to instruct and train the reserve components. The statute set the Army's peace strength at 275,000 and the Guard's at 435,000. Unfortunately, from 1921 through 1935, Congress appropriated only enough money to maintain the Army at half its authorized strength and restricted National Guard enrollment to under 200,000. A shortage of funds also prevented the Army from fulfilling its instructional role and limited the Organized Reserve to a mere list of officers available for duty.[1]

Most treatments of interwar military affairs understandably lament the sorry state of the nation's armed forces. For all the difficulties engendered by a lack of money, however, the 1920s and 1930s seem retrospectively to be a golden age for the National Guard. The interwar years appear serene when compared with the turbulent squabbles between the Guard and the War Department during the 1903–16 period. With military policy fixed by the 1920 legislation and no substantive change in unit tables of organization for nearly twenty years, the Guard-Army wrangles so common in the years before World War I disappeared. In 1933, the Guard even won an uncontested legislative victory by convincing Congress to amend the 1920 law by creating the National Guard of the United States under the Constitution's army clause. The Guard became, and still remains, simultaneously the constitutional state militia and a reserve component of the Army governed by federal law and regulations. In addition, the act permitted the president to order rather than draft the state soldiery into federal service once war began. "Ordering" the Guard meant individual soldiers were not discharged from state service as they had been in 1917. Moreover, the change ostensibly preserved the integrity of state units.[2]

As noted in chapter 7, the 1916 NDA as amended in 1920 circumscribed state and local control of the Guard. The War Department established requirements for officers' commissions, assigned specific tactical and support units to states according to general staff plans, and set efficiency standards for training. Yet during the interwar years, Washington seldom intruded on state military affairs and then only when states failed to meet minimum federal requirements. With basic military policy firmly established, the general staff made no effort to alter reserve policy or change the Guard's organization. Lack of funds prevented the War Department from supporting joint Army-Guard maneuvers until 1936, leaving the states to conduct their annual summer training camps according to their own dictates.[3]

In its yearly operations, the Guard functioned much as it had before the war. Despite federal strictures governing the commissioning of officers, some states continued to elect their leaders. Athletics and social affairs returned to center stage in the annual cycle of local unit life. Armory training resumed its unchallenging and boring weekly routine of calisthenics and close order drill. In the early 1920s, and again in the mid to late 1930s, substantial numbers of Guardsmen mobilized to quell civil disorder, most of it connected with labor-management conflict. Governors now frequently called on state soldiers to help civil authorities cope with natural or man-made disasters. The latter function assumed greater import during the interwar years in large part because federal aid left state units better equipped than they had been before 1917.[4]

Federal dollars in the interwar years, however, provided the National Guard with a prosperity it had never known. States did not benefit from the expanded funding authorized by the 1916 NDA until after 1920, but from 1921 through 1940 federal aid averaged $32 million annually, more than five times the amount allotted just before the war. Washington paid for all state military costs except administrative expenses and armory and camp construction, and after 1935 the Works Progress Administration, a New Deal relief agency, built armories and summer camp facilities in many states. Moreover, the Guard's permanent place in military policy compelled states to spend more money than they had before 1917, if for no other reason than to qualify for their federal allotments. Texas, for example, rarely gave its soldiers even $40,000 in the prewar years but appropriated nearly $120,000 in 1921, before the state had reorganized fully. Its annual federal allotment through the 1930s ranged between $250,000 and $300,000. Remarkably, few states cut their military budgets substantially during the Depression, and the Guard fared well in those years.[5]

Federal support also assured a stability in the Guard unlike anything it had ever experienced. The steady flow of money from Washington ensured unit continuity and allowed most companies, troops, and batteries to establish permanent places in their communities. Most importantly, armory and camp pay solved the recruiting problem. Although privates only earned a dollar per drill, the twelve dollars paid quarterly proved attractive to the largely teenage boys who filled the ranks. Depending on their rank and years in service, officers and NCOs could garner two to five hundred dollars a year simply for armory service. The onset of the Depression in the early 1930s made recruiting even easier, and many units established waiting lists for men eager to earn even a dollar a week.

As had been true since its post–Civil War revival, the organized state soldiery fared best in towns and cities. Although rural dwellers comprised 65 percent of the population of Kansas, for example, sixteen of the state's fifty-three units were located in just four cities, with another five organizations in Lawrence, the home of the University of Kansas. Nonetheless, rural states had little difficulty filling their ranks, partly because more and more farm boys had access to automobiles and trucks or lived in town while attending high school. The lure of drill pay, social or athletic activities at the armory, and town life proved attractive to rural residents in the modernizing 1920s. World War I veterans and young second lieutenants produced by the Reserve Officer Training Corps, a provision of the 1916 NDA, gave the Guard officers who were more qualified for command than had been available before 1917.[6]

Although the interwar National Guard was not an unqualified success, the state soldiery was more stable, better equipped, more fully manned, and better commanded during these years than at any time since its revival in the 1870s. A guaranteed role in national defense gave the Guard the resources and prestige needed to win community support and willing recruits. The Guard's retention of the divisional and subordinate organizational identifications it was assigned during World War I enhanced its standing by giving it Army unit designations. Although national defense laws constrained it in significant ways, state soldiers would never again experience a two-decade period during which they would be permitted so much leeway in governing themselves while receiving substantial federal funding.

The illusion of the Guard's semi-independence would last only as long as military policy remained unchanged and the nation at peace. A major disturbance of the status quo would again highlight the fact that the federal government held the authority to determine when, where, and for how long the National Guard might be called to serve the nation. Military practice underwent modest change in the mid-1930s, but these alterations benefited rather than threatened the Guard. As military funding increased slowly from 1932 on, Chief of Staff Douglas MacArthur and his successor General Malin Craig worked to make mobilization planning more realistic. MacArthur and Craig insisted that staff planners base initial mobilization schemes on existing Army and National Guard forces rather than assume the existence of forces not likely to be formed for years. Planning efforts led the general staff to seek a modest increase in the National Guard so that units originally authorized in 1921 could be organized. Congress responded in 1935 by approving an expansion of the Guard from 190,000 to 210,000 in five-thousand-man increments over the next four years. To improve National Guard training, MacArthur initiated combined field maneuvers at the corps and army level in 1935, the first since 1915, and maneuvers and war games continued through the summer of 1940.

Following the German invasion of Poland in September 1939, President Franklin D. Roosevelt declared a limited national emergency and directed that the Army be increased to 227,000 men. Roosevelt also ordered that Guard strength be raised to 235,000, that Guardsmen conduct sixty armory drills rather than forty-eight, and that they perform an additional seven days of summer camp training during the coming year. Some Guardsmen, especially adjutants general, objected to the new training schedule, arguing that the added time in armory and camp demanded too much of citizen soldiers. Key leaders of the NGA argued, however, that if the Guard did not accept the new requirements, the Army might seek to establish active training units in the Organized Reserve.[7]

The Guard faced a greater challenge in the autumn of 1940. After much debate within the general staff and the White House, the Roosevelt administration asked for and received congressional approval in late August 1940 to order the National Guard to active duty for extended training. In light of German victories in Western Europe during the summer, Chief of Staff George C. Marshall wanted the Guard mobilized in order to leave part of the Army free to act as an expeditionary force in the event of an emergency. More importantly, with a peacetime selective service bill pending, Marshall argued that the Army needed the Guard to train selectees. The first Guard units reported for duty on 16 September 1940, just as Congress approved selective service. With conscription in the offing, the Guard was permitted to accept volunteers only until the draft actually began. All told, some three hundred thousand state volunteers served in World War II, one hundred thousand fewer than in the Great War.[8]

The mobilization of 1940 destroyed the interwar illusion that the National Guard had partial control over its own affairs. From September 1940 through the Japanese attack on Pearl Harbor on 7 December 1941, state soldiers dis-

covered, as they had in the 1916 border call-up and the World War I mobilization, that once in federal service the National Guard was wholly under the
sway of the War Department. Despite promises to respect Guard unit integrity, the Army totally reorganized the state forces, breaking up the World War
I–style divisions the states had maintained through the interwar years. As in
1917, the reorganization in 1941 generated resentment among state soldiers
because established units were broken up or separated from the parent organizations with which they had been affiliated for two decades. Many Guardsmen either did not understand or appreciate the geopolitical necessity that
mandated a peacetime mobilization. When Congress extended the time of active duty in September 1941, grumblings similar to those heard along the
Mexican border swept the Guard training camps.[9]

Other War Department policies, all justified as necessary components of
an effective national defense, also offended Guardsmen. General Marshall,
fearful that overage, physically unfit Army officers hindered preparedness,
instituted an age-in-grade policy in mid-1941. The policy established maximum ages for each officer grade. Men exceeding the upper-age limit were removed from combat command or honorably retired. As the Guard was in federal service, the age-in-grade regulation affected state officers and fell most
heavily on company grade officers. Many state soldiers unjustifiably saw the
policy as deliberately aimed at eliminating National Guard combat officers.
The influx of drafted soldiers and reserve officers raised again the World War I
question of posting "strangers" to Guard units. Transfers of Guardsmen also
altered the local character of state organizations. Particularly from the autumn of 1941 on, the Army turned to Guard units to find men to attend officer
candidate and technical schools. By the time National Guard divisions were
deployed overseas, few resembled the organizations called to duty in 1940.
Reorganization, the age-in-grade policy, transfers of Guardsmen, and the addition of draftees and reservists had effectively destroyed the state composition of many Guard divisions from the company or battery level on up.

The treatment of the National Guard during the mobilization period animated the NGA. Martha Derthick sees the wartime years as the period when
the NGA established itself as a "vigorous " and permanent lobby.[10] As Derthick's study shows, the NGA of the early 1940s pursued goals that would protect the basic organizational interests of those in the National Guard. Major
General Ellard A. Walsh, a long-time Minnesota Guardsman and president of
the NGA during World War II, later recalled that the association's major concern had been "the preservation" of the "integrity" of the Guard's "organi-

zation and units."[11] Maryland's Major General Milton A. Reckord, Walsh's close collaborator, included in the association's list of major concerns superintending the interests of Guard officers while they were in federal service.[12]

The call to action that Generals Walsh and Reckord issued to their brother officers during World War II was far less ambitious than that urged by Guardsmen at the turn of the century. National Guardsmen asserted then that they represented the traditional American volunteer soldier in organized form. They maintained that while they were willing to serve the nation in war, and so deserved national financial aid, in peacetime they would train and administer themselves according to militia tradition. Guardsmen also claimed that they bore the major responsibility for raising the nation's war army and therefore deserved a place in the counsels that set military policy. The vagaries of modern war, the growing power of the general staff, and the expanding authority of the federal government virtually eliminated the state role in the conduct of war. If Generals Walsh and Reckord set NGA goals that echoed institutional self-interest rather than broad claims for the traditional rights of state citizen soldiers, they merely accepted a reality that had existed since 1916. The aspiration of a state soldiery that would claim an equality with the Regular Army in fighting the nation's wars and shaping its military policy had expired more than two decades before along the Mexican border and on the Western Front.

Appendix 1

Federal and State Spending on the National Guard by State, 1903

	Federal	State	Combined
Northeast			
Connecticut	$13,963	$153,000	$166,963
Delaware*	5,984	5,000	10,984
Maine	11,963	32,000	43,963
Maryland	15,958	50,000	65,958
Massachusetts	31,916	327,825	359,741
New Hampshire	7,979	35,000	42,979
New Jersey	23,937	160,000	183,937
New York	77,796	450,000	527,796
Pennsylvania	67,822	407,000	474,822
Rhode Island	7,979	51,550	59,529
Vermont	7,979	18,000	25,979
South			
Alabama*	21,942	15,000	36,942
Arkansas*	17,952	0	17,952
Florida*	9,973	10,000	19,973
Georgia*	25,932	20,000	45,932
Kentucky*	25,932	20,000	45,932
Louisiana	17,952	27,500	45,452
Mississippi*	19,947	4,000	23,947
North Carolina*	23,937	6,000	29,937
South Carolina*	17,952	8,000	25,952
Tennessee*	23,937	12,500	36,439
Texas*	35,905	5,000	40,905
Virginia*	23,937	20,000	43,937
West Virginia	13,963	35,000	48,963
Midwest			
Illinois	53,858	150,000	203,858
Indiana	29,921	75,000	104,921
Iowa	25,932	57,350	83,282
Michigan	27,926	121,000	148,926
Minnesota	21,942	65,000	86,942
Missouri*	35,905	23,500	59,405
Ohio	45,879	175,000	220,879

Wisconsin	25,932	130,000	155,932
Plains			
Colorado	9,973	37,000	46,973
Kansas	19,947	25,000	44,947
Montana	5,984	10,000	15,984
Nebraska	15,958	33,250	49,208
North Dakota	7,979	11,000	18,979
Oklahoma*	10,817	800	11,617
South Dakota	7,979	15,000	22,979
Wyoming*	5,984	5,000	10,984
West			
Arizona	4,760	5,000	9,760
California	19,947	160,000	179,947
Idaho*	5,984	1,000	6,984
Nevada*	5,984	0	5,984
New Mexico*	4,321	1,500	5,821
Oregon	7,979	30,000	37,979
Utah	5,984	13,500	19,484
Washington	9,973	31,500	41,473

Note: States marked by an asterisk received half or more of their combined budgets from the federal government.

Appendix 2

Federal and State Spending on the National Guard by State, 1913

	Federal	State	Combined
Northeast			
Connecticut	$76,435	$193,855	$270,290
Delaware*	16,695	15,100	31,795
Maine*	56,467	55,000	111,467
Maryland	57,007	75,000	132,007
Massachusetts	166,830	603,575	770,405
New Hampshire	31,920	67,325	99,245
New Jersey	103,948	399,395	503,343
New York	375,269	922,594	1,297,863
Pennsylvania	316,044	392,500	708,544
Rhode Island	40,792	85,439	126,231
Vermont*	41,785	40,000	81,785
South			
Alabama*	101,722	25,000	126,722
Arkansas*	69,149	0	69,149
Florida	53,249	69,117	122,366
Georgia*	106,609	25,000	131,609
Kentucky*	93,845	20,000	113,845
Louisiana*	69,311	30,000	99,311
Mississippi*	66,471	10,000	76,471
North Carolina*	94,280	76,725	171,005
South Carolina*	53,124	15,000	62,124
Tennessee*	83,986	23,700	107,686
Texas*	133,269	37,000	170,269
Virginia*	101,940	72,000	173,940
West Virginia*	70,071	65,419	135,490
Midwest			
Illinois	207,188	401,917	609,105
Indiana*	104,302	85,000	189,302
Iowa	108,351	151,000	259,351
Michigan	108,834	168,610	277,444
Minnesota*	112,702	102,460	215,162
Missouri*	113,055	66,000	179,055
Ohio	162,932	476,712	639,644

Wisconsin	107,185	158,000	265,185
Plains			
Colorado	44,704	72,944	117,648
Kansas*	79,168	67,100	146,268
Montana*	37,465	10,000	47,465
Nebraska*	63,700	38,500	102,200
North Dakota*	43,594	30,000	73,594
Oklahoma*	71,356	33,060	104,416
South Dakota*	49,081	18,200	67,281
Wyoming*	20,477	20,250	40,727
West			
Arizona*	34,002	30,000	64,002
California	95,492	237,100	332,592
Idaho*	44,067	25,000	69,067
New Mexico*	42,098	15,630	57,728
Oregon	55,049	70,000	125,049
Utah	28,383	43,540	71,923
Washington	59,840	108,425	168,265

Note: States marked by an asterisk received half or more of their combined budgets from the federal government.

Notes

I. THE MILITIA IN AMERICAN MILITARY PRACTICE AND POLICY

1. Generalizations in this and subsequent chapters are drawn from studies annotated in Jerry M. Cooper, *The Militia and the National Guard in America since Colonial Times: A Research Guide* (Westport CT: Greenwood Press, 1993).

2. The terms *compulsory militia, obligated militia*, and *regular militia* are used interchangeably.

3. John Ferling, *Struggle for a Continent: The Wars of Early America* (Arlington Heights IL: Harlan Davidson, 1993), 105–8, 133–35.

4. Lawrence Cress provides the clearest analysis of the role of Radical Whig thought. See his excellent book, *Citizens in Arms: The Army and Militia in American Society to the War of 1812* (Chapel Hill: University of North Carolina Press, 1982).

5. Royster, *A Revolutionary People at War: The Continental Army and American Character, 1775–1783* (Chapel Hill: University of North Carolina Press, 1979), 25–26.

6. See Richard Buel Jr., *Dear Liberty: Connecticut's Mobilization for the Revolutionary War* (Middleton CT: Wesleyan University Press, 1980) for a rare look at how a state mobilized its Continental regiments and state militia forces.

7. On the role of the militia during the Revolution, see Don Higginbotham, "The American Militia: A Traditional Institution with Revolutionary

Responsibilities," in Higginbotham, ed., *Reconsiderations on the Revolutionary War: Selected Essays* (Westport CT: Greenwood Press, 1983), 83–103; John Shy, "The Military Conflict Considered As a Revolutionary War," in Shy, ed., *A People Numerous and Armed: Reflections on the Military Struggle for American Independence* (New York: Oxford University Press, 1976), 193–224.

8. Richard Kohn examines the era in detail in *Eagle and Sword: The Federalists and the Creation of the Military Establishment, 1783–1802* (New York: Free Press, 1975).

9. See William Skelton, *An American Profession of Arms: The Army Officer Corps, 1784–1861* (Lawrence: University Press of Kansas, 1992); and Theodore Crackel, *Mr. Jefferson's Army: Political and Social Reform of the Military Establishment, 1801–1809* (New York: New York University Press, 1987).

10. In his *Eagle and Sword*, 109–11 and chap. 11, respectively, Kohn discusses the volunteer levies raised in 1791 and authorized in 1798–99.

11. Emory Upton, *The Military Policy of the United States* (Washington DC: Government Printing Office, 1904; repr., New York: Greenwood Press, 1968), xiii; see also 90–95.

12. In his *Eagle and Sword*, Kohn describes Federalist efforts to establish a viable Army and War Department. They achieved much, but Skelton, in *An American Profession of Arms*, shows that the Army did not gain institutional stability until the mid-1820s. For the District of Columbia Militia, see Martin K. Gordon, "The Militia of the District of Columbia, 1790–1815" (Ph.D. diss., George Washington University, 1975).

13. Shy, "Force, Order, and Democracy in the American Revolution," in Jack P. Greene, ed., *The American Revolution: Its Character and Limits* (New York: New York University Press, 1987), 75–79.

14. Skelton, *An American Profession of Arms*, 129.

15. Skelton's *An American Profession of Arms* is enlightening on the internal development of the antebellum Army but neglects its weaknesses, particularly the lack of any means for planning and coordinating not only its own operations but its mobilization for war. Russell F. Weigley's *History of the United States Army*, enlarged ed., pt. 2 (Bloomington: Indiana University Press, 1984) remains the best general treatment of the Army's limitations in these areas.

16. Paludan, "The American Civil War Considered as a Crisis in Law and Order," *American Historical Review* 77 (Oct. 1972): 1015, 1031, respec-

tively. See also Robert Wiebe, *The Segmented Society: An Introduction to the Meaning of America* (New York: Oxford University Press, 1976), 33–39, 42–48.

17. For attempts to reform the militia, see Marcus Cunliffe, *Soldiers and Civilians: The Martial Spirit in America, 1775–1865*, 2d ed. (New York: Free Press, 1973), 192–203; and John K. Mahon, "A Board of Officers Considers the Condition of the Militia in 1826," *Military Affairs* 15 (summer 1951): 85–94.

18. Mary Ellen Rowe, "The Sure Bulwark of the Republic: The Militia Tradition and the Yakima War Volunteers" (Ph.D. diss., University of Washington, 1988), 14 and passim.

19. On politics and commissions, see Lyle D. Brundage, "The Organization, Administration, and Training of the United States Ordinary and Volunteer Militia, 1792–1861" (Ph.D. diss., University of Michigan, 1958), chap. 8.

20. On South Carolina, see Kenneth Otis McCreedy, "Palladium of Liberty: The American Militia System, 1815–1861" (Ph.D. diss., University of California, Berkeley, 1991), chap. 8. See also Allan Robert Purcell, "The History of the Texas Militia, 1835–1903" (Ph.D. diss., University of Texas, Austin, 1981), 94–98; and Tom D. Dillard, "An Arduous Task to Perform: Organizing the Territorial Arkansas Militia," *Arkansas Historical Quarterly* 41 (summer 1982): 174–90.

21. In her "The Militia Fine, 1830–1860," *Military Affairs* 15 (fall 1951): 133–44, Lena London reviews political efforts to abolish fines and compulsory training.

22. McCreedy, "Palladium of Liberty," 53.

23. Steven Watts, *The Republic Reborn: War and the Making of Liberal America* (Baltimore: Johns Hopkins University Press, 1987), 10–14, 74, passim.

24. Howland to Barbour, 12 Oct. 1826, box 4, Miscellaneous Papers, adj. gen. document file, miscellaneous, RG94.

25. To avoid confusion between those volunteer units that states mobilized to meet federal requests and volunteer militia organizations that were maintained by the states in peacetime, I will refer to the latter as *uniformed militia*.

26. In his "The Citizen Soldier in National Defense, 1789–1815" (Ph.D. diss., University of California, Los Angeles, 1950), 191–226, John K. Mahon provides background on early uniformed companies.

27. *An Unsettled People: Social Order and Disorder in American History* (New York: Harper and Row, 1971), 254.

28. Stewart Lewis Gates, "Disorder and Social Organization: The Militia in Connecticut Public Life, 1660–1860" (Ph.D. diss., University of Connecticut, 1975), chap. 6; and Robert Reinders, "Militia and Public Order in Nineteenth Century America," *Journal of American Studies* 2 (1977): 81–90, are the most explicit exponents of this view.

29. Scholars seldom comment on militia finances or note the relationship between the lack of state support and the many social events carried on by the uniformed militia that centered on fund-raising. A notable exception is Dello G. Dayton, "The California Militia, 1850–1866" (Ph.D. diss., University of California, Berkeley, 1951), chap. 8.

30. For New York, see McCreedy, "Palladium of Liberty," 240–50; and Fred L. Israel, "New York's Citizen Soldiers: The Militia and Their Armories," *New York History* 42 (Apr. 1961): 146–48, 154. See also Gates, "Disorder and Social Organization," chap. 5; and Robert F. McGraw, "Minutemen of '61: The Precivil War Massachusetts Militia," *Civil War History* 15 (June 1969): 101–15.

31. In his *To the Halls of the Montezumas: The Mexican War in the American Imagination* (New York: Oxford University Press, 1974), chap. 1, Robert W. Johannson looks at the Mexican War mobilization.

32. See Benjamin F. Cooling, ed., *The New American State Papers: Military Affairs* (Wilmington DE: Scholarly Resources, 1979), vol. 6, 99–198, for the correspondence between Brig. Gen. John E. Wool, U.S. Army, and Secretary of War William Marcy concerning Wool's efforts to muster in troops. The exchange dramatically reveals the administrative weaknesses of both the states and the nation.

33. See, e.g., Walter S. Glazer, "Wisconsin Goes to War: April 1861," *Wisconsin Magazine of History* (winter 1967): 147–64. In his *History of the United States Army*, 198–200, 216, Weigley comments on the militia's inherent flexibility when responding to a crisis, as in 1861.

34. For the increased central control of manpower policy in North and South, see Richard Franklin Bensel, *Yankee Leviathan: The Origins of Central State Authority in America, 1859–1977* (New York: Cambridge University Press, 1990). For the strong preference for volunteering in mid-nineteenth-century America and for a sound analysis of Northern conscription, see James W. Geary, *We Need Men: The Union Draft in the Civil War* (DeKalb: Northern Illinois Press, 1991).

35. See Robert S. Chamberlain, "The Northern State Militia," *Civil War History* 4 (June 1958): 105–9. See Richard E. Beringer, Herman Hattaway, and Archer Jones, *Why the South Lost the Civil War* (Athens: University of Georgia Press, 1986), passim, on the Confederacy.

36. See Jerry M. Cooper, "The Wisconsin Militia, 1832–1900," Master's thesis, University of Wisconsin, Madison, 1968, 191–94; for Ohio, see Lowell D. Black, *The Negro Volunteer Militia of the Ohio National Guard, 1870–1954: The Struggle for Military Recognition and Equality in the State of Ohio* (Manhattan KS: Military Affairs/Aerospace Historian, 1976), 34–36. On California, see Dayton, "California Militia," 327–47 and chap. 9. For New York, see Emmons Clark, *History of the Seventh Regiment of New York, 1806–1889* (New York: Seventh Regiment, 1890), 2: 81; and Chamberlain, "Northern State Militia," 106, 109, respectively, on total strength and New York's strength.

37. Cited in Cooper, "Wisconsin Militia," 230.

2. THE RISE OF THE NATIONAL GUARD

1. 5 (13 June 1868): 677.

2. In Annual Returns, 1875–76, box 7, entry 1, RG168. See the list of abbreviations in the front of the book for the full titles of all abbreviated sources.

3. See Annual Returns for yearly militia returns. See also Kenneth R. Bailey, *Mountaineers Are Free: A History of the West Virginia National Guard* (St. Albans WV: Harless Press, 1978), 34–41.

4. On the militia in the South during Reconstruction, see three works by Otis Singletary: *Negro Militia and Reconstruction* (2d printing, Austin: University of Texas Press, 1971); "Militia Disturbances in Arkansas during Reconstruction," *Arkansas Historical Quarterly* 15 (summer 1956): 140–50; and "The Negro Militia during Radical Reconstruction," *Military Affairs* 10 (winter 1955): 177–86. See also James M. McPherson, *Ordeal by Fire: The Civil War and Reconstruction*, 2d ed. (New York: McGraw-Hill, 1992), 558–59, 581–89.

5. "The National Guard of Pennsylvania: Policeman of Industry, 1865–1905" (Ph.D. diss., University of Connecticut, 1971), 54.

6. *History of the Twenty-second Regiment*, 435.

7. See Adj. Gen. Alexander L. Russell to the War Department, 31 Dec. 1869, submitting Pennsylvania's annual militia returns, box 4, Annual

Returns, 1860–69, entry 1, RG168; Fred L. Israel, "New York's Citizen Soldiers: Their Militia and Their Armories," *New York History* 42 (Apr. 1961): 149–50; Wingate, *History of the Twenty-second Regiment*, 231–32; Holmes, "The National Guard of Pennsylvania," 51–54.

8. See U.S. Congress, Senate, *Militia Force of the United States*, 43d Cong., 1st sess., 1873, S. Exec. Doc. 41.

9. See *Militia Force of the United States*. The regions as used here are defined as follows: The *Northeast* includes eleven states: Connecticut, Delaware, Maine, Maryland, Massachusetts, New Hampshire, New Jersey, New York, Pennsylvania, Rhode Island, and Vermont. The *South* includes thirteen states: Alabama, Arkansas, Florida, Georgia, Kentucky, Louisiana, Mississippi, North Carolina, South Carolina, Tennessee, Texas, Virginia, and West Virginia. The *Midwest* includes eight states: Illinois, Indiana, Iowa, Michigan, Minnesota, Missouri, Ohio, and Wisconsin. The *Plains* region includes eight states and territories: Colorado, Kansas, Montana, Nebraska, North Dakota, Oklahoma, South Dakota, and Wyoming. The *West* includes eight states and territories: Arizona, California, Idaho, New Mexico, Nevada, Oregon, Utah, and Washington.

10. The information on Connecticut, Massachusetts, and New York is contained in a pamphlet entitled "The National Guard of the United States. Provisions for its Support, etc." The pamphlet is attached to the manuscript version of the 1871 annual report of the adj. gen., Colorado Territory, folder C714, in Colorado Military–Colorado National Guard, entry 142, Colorado State Historical Society, Denver CO. See also Holmes, "National Guard of Pennsylvania," 53–54, 74; Dayton, "California Militia", 346–47; Robert Laudino, "Riot in Cincinnati: A Look at the Ohio National Guard in 1884" (seminar paper, Ohio State University, 1974), 1–2; Martin K. Gordon, "The Milwaukee Infantry Militia, 1865–1892," *Historical Messenger* (Milwaukee County Historical Society) 24 (Mar. 1968): 5–8; and Cooper, "Wisconsin Militia," 235–37.

11. See Peter H. Haraty, *Put the Vermonters Ahead: A History of the Vermont National Guard, 1764–1978* (Burlington VT: Queen City Printers, 1978), 121–25; Holmes, "National Guard of Pennsylvania," 74–75; and Cooper, "Wisconsin Militia," 237.

12. U.S. Department of Commerce, Bureau of the Census, *Historical Statistics of the United States: Colonial Times to 1970*, pt. 1 (Washington DC: Government Printing Office, 1975), 24–37.

13. Data for 1875, 1880, 1885, and 1890 are taken from *Militia Force of the United States*, annual returns to the Secretary of War, found in Senate, 44th Cong., 1st sess., 1875, S. Exec. Doc. 45; House, 46th Cong., 3d sess., 1880, H. Exec. Doc. 74; Senate, 49th Cong., 1st sess., 1885, S. Exec. Doc. 52; Senate, 52d Cong., 2d sess., 1890, S. Exec. Doc. 48. For the 1895 data, see MID 1895.

14. For the preceding paragraphs and table 5, see *Militia Force*, 1875 and 1880.

15. *Militia Force*, 1885.

16. On the reorganizations, see Massachusetts militia returns to the Secretary of War for 1875 and 1885, boxes 7 and 13, respectively, entry 1, RG168. See also AGR Massachusetts, 1876, 3–5; AGR Massachusetts, 1877, 3–5; AGR Massachusetts, 1882, 5; and Charles Winslow Hall, ed., *Regiments and Armories of Massachusetts: An Historical Narrative of the Massachusetts Volunteer Militia* (Boston: W. W. Potter, 1899), 1: 196, 200–201, 209–10.

17. See Pennsylvania militia returns to Secretary of War, 1875 and 1885, in boxes 7 and 13, respectively, entry 1, RG168; Uzal W. Ent, *The First Century: A History of the 28th Infantry Division* (Harrisburg PA: Twenty-eighth Infantry Division, 1979), 66–67, 75–77; *Our State Army and Navy* 1 (Feb. 1898): 4–6. The latter is a newspaper, published in Harrisburg, Pennsylvania, in the late nineteenth and early twentieth centuries to serve Pennsylvania Guardsmen.

18. Israel, "New York's Citizen Soldiers," 149–53.

19. John H. Nankivell, *History of the Military Organizations of the State of Colorado, 1860–1935* (Denver: W. H. Kistler Stationery, 1935), 44–50, 65–70, 90–91; State of Washington, Office of the Adj. Gen., *The Official History of the Washington National Guard* (Tacoma WA: Office of the Adj. Gen., 1961), 1: 384, 399–401.

20. See U.S. Army, Office of the Adj. Gen., *Special Return of the . . . Uniformed Active Militia of the United States* (Washington DC: Government Printing Office, 1887); and U.S. Congress, Senate, *Militia Force of the United States*, 52d Cong., 2d sess., 1892, S. Exec. Doc. 51.

21. The annual militia returns in *Militia Force*, 1885 through 1892, and MID reports, 1893 through 1897, provide the statistical details for the ensuing overview.

22. See Richard G. Stone Jr., *A Brittle Sword: The Kentucky Militia, 1776–1912* (Lexington: University Press of Kentucky, 1977), 75–88; Christian

G. Nelson, "Rebirth, Growth and Expansion of the Texas Militia, 1868–1898," *Texas Military History* 2 (Feb. 1962): 9–14; and Purcell, "The History of the Texas Militia," 257–81.

23. Charles Johnson Jr., *African American Soldiers in the National Guard: Recruitment and Deployment during Peacetime and War* (Westport CT: Greenwood Press, 1992), 40–41; MID 1895, 4–5 and MID 1896, 4–5.

24. See Cyril B. Upham, "Historical Survey of the Militia in Iowa, 1865–1898," *Iowa Journal of History and Politics* 18 (Jan. 1920): 24–30, 34–40, 46–49; Hiram D. Frankel, ed., *Company "C," First Infantry Minnesota National Guard: Its History and Development* (St. Paul: no publisher, 1905), 7–15; Cooper, "Wisconsin Militia," chap. 5.

25. See Jerry M. Cooper, with Glenn Smith, *Citizens as Soldiers: A History of the North Dakota National Guard* (Fargo: North Dakota Institute for Regional Studies, 1986), chap. 1; Richard Campbell Roberts, "History of the Utah National Guard, 1894–1954" (Ph.D. diss., University of Utah, 1973), 28–29, 167–69; and Patrick Henry McLatchy, "The Development of the National Guard of Washington as an Instrument of Social Control, 1954–1916" (Ph.D. diss., University of Washington, 1973), chaps. 7 and 11.

26. Larry D. Ball, "Militia Posses: The Territorial Militia in Civil Law Enforcement in New Mexico Territory, 1877–1883," *New Mexico Historical Review* 55 (Jan. 1980): 47–64; Nankivell, *History of the Military Organizations*, 49–50 and chap. 4; Brian Dexter Fowles, *A Guard in Peace and War: The History of the Kansas National Guard, 1854–1987* (Lawrence KS: Sunflower University Press, 1989), 75–76, 79.

27. SWR 1890, 1: 278.

28. Fogelson, *America's Armories: Architecture, Society, and Public Order* (Cambridge: Harvard University Press, 1989).

29. See AGR Delaware, 1885–86, 8. See MID 1893, 156, on New York.

30. Figures for 1891 come from U.S. House Committee on the Militia, *Efficiency of the Militia*, 52d Cong., 1st sess., 1891, H. Rept. 754, 25–26; for 1895 and 1897, see MID 1895 and MID 1897, 4–5 (both reports).

31. In addition to the five Northeastern states, California, Illinois, Ohio, and Wisconsin exceeded $100,000 in 1895. Two states, Arkansas and Nevada, and one territory, Oklahoma, failed to support their soldiery in that same year. See House Committee, *Efficiency of the Militia*, H. Rept. 754, 25–26, for 1891; and MID Reports, 1895 through 1897.

32. Data for the preceding two paragraphs are taken from MID 1895.

33. AGR Virginia, 1892, 6–7.
34. See MID 1895, 4–5.
35. AGR Tennessee, 1888, 7; and AGR Tennessee, 1889, 3.
36. See MID 1897, 4–5. For general information on the preceding two paragraphs, see MID reports for the 1890s.
37. AGR Colorado, 1880, 5–6.
38. AGR Colorado, 1881, 5–7, and MID 1893, 21. Virginia committed one-half of 1 percent of general revenue, excluding school funds, to support its soldiery. Calls from adjutants general to increase the military fund got nowhere, as noted in AGR Virginia, 1892, 6–7. Also see AGR Alabama, 1894, 35; and Cooper, *Citizens as Soldiers*, 13–14.
39. *Affairs of State: Public Life in Late Nineteenth Century America* (Cambridge: Belknap Press of Harvard University Press, 1977), 328, 114, respectively.

3. THE NATIONAL GUARD AND CIVIL DISORDER

1. William H. Riker, *Soldiers of the States: The Role of the National Guard in American Democracy* (Washington DC: Public Affairs Press, 1957; repr., New York: Arno Press, 1979), 46–64. See AGR New York, 1921, 53, on the Seventh Regiment; Ent, *The First Century*, 67–69, 82–86, 90–91; and William H. Zierdt, *Narrative History of the 109th Field Artillery, Pennsylvania National Guard, 1775–1930* (Wilkes-Barre PA: E. B. Yordy, 1932), 89–90; AGR Massachusetts, 1875, 16–19.
2. House Committee, *Efficiency of the Militia*, H. Rept. 754, 16–20, covers 1868 through 1885; Maj. Winthrop Alexander, District of Columbia National Guard, "Ten Years of Riot Duty," *JMSI* 19 (July 1896): 1–26, for 1886 through 1895; Report AWC 9744-C, "Duty Performed by the Organized Militia in Connection with Domestic Disturbances from 1894 to 1908, Inclusive," in RG165 for 1896 through 1899.
3. See House Committee, *Efficiency of the Militia*, H. Rept. 754, 16–20; "Ten Years of Riot Duty," 1–26; and Report AWC 9744-C, for details.
4. Alexander, "Ten Years of Riot Duty," 26 and passim.
5. Stone, *A Brittle Sword*, 82–87; Ball, "Militia Posses," 47–69; McLatchy, "Development of the National Guard of Washington" (Ph.D. diss., University of Washington, 1973), 312–15; and folder 1, correspondence for May and June 1896, Charles F. Beebe Papers, MSS

1378, Oregon Historical Society, Portland, Oregon. Gen. Beebe commanded the Oregon National Guard brigade and supervised the operation.

6. Alexander, "Ten Years of Riot Duty," passim. In his *Lynching in the New South: Georgia and Virginia, 1880–1930* (Urbana: University of Illinois Press, 1993), app. A, W. Fitzhugh Brundage makes clear how frequently "aiding civil authorities" meant stopping a lynching. See also Bruce Olson, "The Houston Light Guards: Elite Cohesion and Social Order in the New South, 1873–1940" (Ph.D. diss., University of Houston, 1989), chap. 5 and app. H. As two examples, see AGR Virginia, 1886, 42–43, and AGR Virginia, 1890, 4–5.

7. See George C. Wright, *Racial Violence in Kentucky, 1865–1940: Lynchings, Mob Rule, and "Legal Lynchings"* (Baton Rouge: Louisiana State University Press, 1990), 156–60, 180–83; Brundage, Lynching in the New South, 161–62, 169–73, 181–87; and Olson, "Houston Light Guards," chap. 5. Appendix I in the National Association for the Advancement of Colored People's (NAACP) *Thirty Years of Lynchings in the United States, 1889–1918* (New York: NAACP, 1919, repr., New York: Arno Press, 1969) provides the necessary statistics.

8. AGR Virginia, 1890, 5.

9. AGR Florida, 1890, 24, and AGR Texas, 1892, 14. Brundage, *Lynching in the New South*, passim, and Wright, *Racial Violence in Kentucky*, passim, discuss the late arrival of troops to halt lynchings.

10. AGR Virginia, 1893, 10–11; Brundage, *Lynching in the New South*, 166–68, 173.

11. Steven J. Ross, *Workers on the Edge: Work, Leisure, and Politics in Industrializing Cincinnati, 1788–1890* (New York: Columbia University Press, 1985), 264–71; Mark V. Kwasny, "A Test for the Ohio National Guard: The Cincinnati Riot of 1884," *Ohio History* 98 (winter/spring 1989): 23–51; Laudino, "Riot in Cincinnati" (seminar paper, Ohio State University, 1974), 8–24.

12. Brundage, *Lynching in the New South*, esp. 161–62, 171–73, 181–82, 187.

13. Strike duty numbers are taken from the sources listed in note 2 of this chapter. Eleanor Hannah provided information on Illinois.

14. H. M. Boies, "Our National Guard," *Harper's New Monthly Magazine* 60 (May 1880): 915.

15. Robert V. Bruce, *1877: Year of Violence* (Indianapolis: Bobbs-Merrill, 1959); and Jerry M. Cooper, *The Army and Civil Disorder: Federal Military Intervention in Labor Disputes, 1877–1900* (Westport CT: Greenwood Press, 1980), chap. 3. For a sampling of opinion on the impact of 1877 on the Guard, see T. F. Rodenbough, "The Militia of the United States," *United Service* 1 (1879): 284; Boies, "Our National Guard," 917; and Francis V. Greene, "The New National Guard," *Century Magazine*, n.s. 21 (Feb. 1892): 486. AGR Pennsylvania, 1877, 3–20, gives unvarnished assessments of Adj. Gen. James Latta on the Pennsylvania Guard's woeful performance in 1877.

16. See Holmes, "National Guard of Pennsylvania," 167–72, 183–95; Ent, *The First Century*, 70–80; Zierdt, *Narrative History of the 109th Field Artillery*, 90–91; and *Our State Army and Navy* 1 (Feb. 1898): 4–6.

17. MID 1896, 210.

18. Holmes, "National Guard of Pennsylvania" and MID 1894, 174. AGR Pennsylvania, 1887, 2, outlines the distribution of companies.

19. Frederick L. Hitchcock, *History of the 13th Regiment, National Guard of Pennsylvania and 109th Inf.; 108th MG BN, USAEF; and 109th Pennsylvania National Guard* (Scranton PA: International Textbook Press, 1924), iv.

20. Hitchcock, *History of 13th Regiment*, 3–12; Holmes, "National Guard of Pennsylvania," 111–15, 195–217, and chap. 6.

21. Roy Turnbaugh, "Ethnicity, Civic Pride, and Commitment: The Evolution of the Chicago Militia," *Journal of the Illinois State Historical Society* 72 (May 1979): 120–22; AGR Illinois, 1877–78, 3–4.

22. AGR New York, 1877, 7–11; Israel, "New York's Citizen Soldiers," 149–53; MID 1895, 166, 168, 172.

23. Horatio C. King, "The National Guard of the United States," *United Service* 14 (Jan. 1886): 52–63, provides an overview. See also Stone, *Brittle Sword*, 80–81, 88; Upham, "Historical Survey of the Militia in Iowa," 34–40, 46–49.

24. Frank B. Culver, comp., *Historical Sketches of the Militia of Maryland with Brief Biographies of the Adjutants General of the State* (Baltimore: no publisher, 1907), 274–77; William J. Watt and James R. H. Spears, *Indiana's Citizen Soldiers: The Militia and National Guard in Indiana History* (Indianapolis: Indiana State Army Board, 1980), 80–84; John Glendower Westover, "The Evolution of the Missouri Militia, 1804–1919" (Ph.D. diss., University of Missouri, 1948), 191–206; Bailey,

Mountaineers Are Free, 45–46 and chap. 5; Brian M. Linn, "'Pretty Scaly Times': The Ohio National Guard and the Railroad Strike of 1877," *Ohio History* 94 (summer/autumn 1985): 174–75; and Kwasny, "A Test for the Ohio National Guard," 23–25.

25. See Gephardt's "Politicians, Soldiers and Strikers: The Reorganization of the Nebraska Militia and the Omaha Strike of 1882," *Nebraska History* 46 (June 1965): 103–4, 120, respectively.

26. Cooper, "Wisconsin Militia," 342–53.

27. AGR Massachusetts, 1877, 25, 27.

28. AGR Delaware, 1885–86, 5.

29. AGR Virginia, 1892, 8–9.

30. Cited in Cooper, "Wisconsin Militia," 244.

31. AGR Alabama, 1894, 4.

32. MID 1893, 159. In his "The Literature of Riot Duty: Managing Class Conflict in the Streets, 1877–1927," *Radical History Review* 56 (spring 1993): 26–34, Eugene E. Leach examines riot manuals of the late nineteenth century and erroneously assumes that the Guard regularly conducted riot training. State adjutants general reports and Army inspection commentary rarely mention that kind of training.

33. Cooper, "Wisconsin Militia," 353.

34. Cited in Christian G. Nelson, "Organization and Training of the Texas Militia, 1870–1897," *Texas Military History* 2 (May 1962): 102. See also AGR Texas, 1891, 33, 51–52, and 66–71.

35. MID 1893, 156.

36. MID 1895, 168 on New York; 184 on Ohio.

37. 1 Sept. 1877, 24.

38. 11 (Aug. 1894), 689.

39. Coffee to Col. O. Summers, 6 July 1896, in Beebe Papers. Emphasis in original. Also see Col. Summers to Brig. Gen. Charles F. Beebe, 8 July 1896, on other problems with employers of men from the First Regiment.

40. SWR 1883, 1: 376.

41. Cooper, "Wisconsin Militia," 308.

42. Cooper, "Wisconsin Militia," 309. The problem regularly received critical comment in state adjutants general reports and military service journals.

43. See, e.g., AGR Massachusetts, 1875, 17–20, and AGR Massachusetts, 1889, 11–12; and Charles Peckham, "The Ohio National Guard and Its

Police Duties, 1894," *Ohio History* 83 (winter 1974): 51. AGR Florida, 1890, 24; AGR Texas, 1891, 10; AGR Virginia, 1893, 10–11, recount Southern examples.

44. McLatchy, "Development of the National Guard of Washington," 206–23, 237–55; and Kent D. Richards, "The Police Power and Washington Statehood: Insurrection, Agitation, and Riots," *Montana* 37 (1987): 10–21. I am indebted to Eleanor Hannah, through her dissertation in progress, for information on the Illinois Guard's problems.

45. McLatchy, "Development of the National Guard of Washington," 256–59.

46. Beebe to adj. gen., 31 May 1896, in Beebe Papers. See also Linn, "'Pretty Scaly Times,'" 174–80; Andrew Birtle, "Governor George Hoadly's Use of the Ohio National Guard in the Hocking Valley Coal Strike of 1884," *Ohio History* 91 (1982), passim; and Peckham, "Ohio National Guard," passim.

47. Gerda Ray, "'We Can Stay until Hell Freezes Over': Strike Control and the State Police in New York, 1919–1913," *Labor History* 36 (summer 1995): 405–7. On Governor Pattison, see Paul Krause, *The Battle for Homestead, 1880–1892: Politics, Culture, and Steel* (Pittsburgh: University of Pittsburgh Press, 1992), 25–30, 332–34.

48. Pennsylvania, Executive, "Governor's Message," in *Governor's Message and Reports* (Harrisburg PA: no publisher, 1878), 23. Hartranft preferred that Pennsylvania create a state police to oversee strike disorders and allow the Guard to concentrate on training as reserve soldiers.

49. *History of the Twenty-second Regiment*, 606; On the California troops, see MID 1894, 269–70; AGR California, 1894, 211–22; and *Army and Navy Journal*, 14 July 1894, 812–13. For the Washington incident, see McLatchy, "Development of the National Guard of Washington," 277–94; and *Army and Navy Journal*, 14 July 1894, 812.

50. 1 Sept. 1877, 30.

51. Cited in Fowles, *A Guard in Peace and War* (Manhattan KS: Military Affairs/Aerospace Historian, 1989), 37.

52. "The National Guard," *Harper's Weekly*, 3 Sept. 1892, 858.

53. *The National Guard in Service: A Course of Lectures* (Washington DC: 1891), 307.

54. See Cooper, *Army and Civil Disorder*, chaps. 8–9; Leach, "The Literature of Riot Duty," 23–34; and Robert Fogelson, *America's Armories:*

Architecture, Society and Public Order (Cambridge: Harvard University Press, 1989), chap. 1.

55. *Cigar Maker's Official Journal* 16 (Aug. 1892): 6.
56. 1 (Apr. 1894) 28. See also Cooper, *Army and Civil Disorder*, 14–15; Fogelson, *America's Armories*, 43–44.
57. 10 Sept. 1892, 2.
58. 19 July 1894, 7.
59. In his *America's Armories*, 43, Fogelson, along with other historians, contends that the Guard's rank and file were largely middle class. State studies and labor journals make it clear that large numbers of workers enlisted.
60. For example, in his "Literature of Riot Duty," 25, Leach states that strike duty accounted for half or more of all National Guard mobilizations. At most, 35 percent of mobilizations in the late nineteenth century dealt with labor-related disorders. See table 13 in this book.
61. See Harring's *Policing a Class Society: The Experience of American Cities, 1865–1915* (New Brunswick NJ: Rutgers University Press, 1983), chap. 6. See also David Montgomery, "Strikes in Nineteenth Century America," *Social Science History* 4 (1980): 97.
62. See Cooper, *Army and Civil Disorder*, 8–10; Harring, Policing a Class Society, 147; and Morton Keller, *Affairs of State: Public Life in Late Nineteenth Century America* (Cambridge: Belknap Press of Harvard University Press, 1977), 398.
63. Montgomery, "Strikes in Nineteenth Century America," 87–98.
64. See Philip Taft and Philip Ross, "American Labor Violence: Its Cause, Character, and Outcome," in Hugh Davis Graham and Ted Robert Gurr, eds., *Violence in America: Historical and Comparative Perspectives* (New York: F. A. Praeger, 1969), 291–92; Cooper, "The Wisconsin National Guard in the Milwaukee Riots of 1886," *Wisconsin Magazine of History* (autumn 1971): 36–37. See also Alexander, "Ten Years of Riot Duty," passim, on the number of Guardsmen on active duty in 1886.
65. In his *The Battle for Homestead*, Krause provides a thorough account of the crucial struggle at Homestead. See Alexander, "Ten Years of Riot Duty," passim, for Guard mobilizations during 1892.
66. Quoted in Krause, *The Battle for Homestead*, 336.
67. Krause, *The Battle for Homestead*, passim.
68. See Alexander, "Ten Years of Riot Duty," passim; and Cooper, *Army and Civil Disorder*, passim.

69. Robert D. Ward and William W. Rogers, *Labor Revolt in Alabama: The Great Strike of 1894* (University: University of Alabama Press, 1965).

70. Sarah M. Henry, "The Strikers and Their Sympathizers: Brooklyn in the Trolley Strike of 1895," *Labor History* 32 (summer 1991): 329–52. On the Hazelton intervention, see Michael Novak, *The Guns of Lattimer: The True Story of a Massacre and a Trial, August 1897–March 1898* (New York: Basic Books, 1978), 151–55, 174–78, 189–90.

71. In Cooper, "Wisconsin Militia," 307.

72. See Harring, *Policing a Class Society*, 103, and Clarence C. Clendenen, "Super Police: The National Guard as a Law-Enforcement Agency in the Twentieth Century," in Robin Higham, ed., *Bayonets in the Street: The Use of Troops in Civil Disturbances* (Lawrence: University Press of Kansas, 1969), 85–87. Examples of strikebreaking in which troops were committed under the rubric of riot duty are given in Kenneth R. Bailey, "Hawk's Nest Coal Company Strike, January, 1880," *West Virginia History* 30 (1969): 625–34; and Henry J. Brinks, "Marquette Iron Range Strike, 1895," *Michigan History* 50 (1966): 293–305.

73. "Strikes in Nineteenth Century America," 97.

74. *Battle for Homestead*, 10. See also Montgomery, "Strikes in Nineteenth Century America," 88–99; and his *Citizen Workers: The Experience of Workers in the United States with Democracy and the Free Market during the Nineteenth Century* (New York: Cambridge University Press, 1993); Richard Hofstadter, "Reflections on Violence in the United States," in Hofstadter and Michael Wallace, eds., *American Violence: A Documentary History* (New York: Vintage Books, 1971), 18–20.

75. In his *Affairs of State*, 404–6, Keller summarizes the legal provisions constraining strike activity.

76. See Sidney Lens, *The Labor Wars: From the Molly Maguires to the Sitdowns* (Garden City NY: Doubleday, 1973), 117–21; Nankivell, *History of the Military Organizations*, 64, 99–109; and Allan M. Osur, "The Role of the Colorado National Guard in Civil Disturbances," *Military Affairs* 46 (Feb. 1982): 19–22.

77. "Captain Fred, Co. I, and the Workers of Homestead," *Pennsylvania History* 46 (Oct. 1979): 311.

78. On the state police idea, see *Twentieth Century*, 18 Aug. 1892, 1; and Novak, *Guns of Lattimer*, 181.

79. "National Guard of Illinois," *United Service* 13 (1885): 702.

4. THE NATIONAL GUARD PARADOX

1. Cited in Cooper, "Wisconsin Militia," 290.

2. See DMA 1906, 113–21; DMA 1908, 341–46; and Hall, *Regiments and Armories of Massachusetts*, 1: 400, 726–58; 2: 471–72, 486, 492.

3. Speech by Gen. C. F. Beebe, a founding member, given some time in 1911, in MSS 1378, folder 9, Charles F. Beebe Papers, Oregon Historical Society, Portland, Oregon; Cooper, "Wisconsin Militia," 295; no author, "A Brief History of the Oldest Minnesota National Guard Company," *National Guardsman* 7 (May 1901): 6–7.

4. In Cooper, "Wisconsin Militia," 291.

5. *History of the Military Organizations of the State of Colorado, 1860–1935* (Denver: W. H. Kistler Stationery, 1935), 75; minutes of meetings, 1882–85, Emmett Light Artillery, St. Paul, Minnesota, box 2, Minnesota National Guard Papers, 1880–1940, BG8/M665n, Minnesota Historical Society, St. Paul, Minnesota.

6. *History of the Seventh Regiment of New York* (New York: Seventh Regiment, 1890), 2: 419; Cooper with Smith, *Citizens as Soldiers*, 22–23.

7. *Seventh Regiment*, 2: 419.

8. MID 1895, 264.

9. Lloyd S. Bryce, "A Service of Love," *North American Review* 145 (Sept. 1887): 281.

10. Hall, *Regiments and Armories of Massachusetts*, 2: 315.

11. Survey of Military Information Division (hereafter MID reports, 1893–97.

12. "The Army Organization Best Adapted to a Republican Form of Government Which Will Ensure an Effective Force," *JMSI* 14 (Nov. 1893): 1167.

13. Cited in Donald M. Douglas, "Social Soldiers: The Winona Company and the Beginnings of the Minnesota National Guard," *Minnesota History* (winter 1976): 131.

14. AGR Virginia, 1893, 6.

15. Cited in T. F. Rodenbough, "Militia Reform without Legislation," *JMSI* 2 (Aug. 1882): 419.

16. "Reasons for Increasing the Army," *North American Review* 166 (Apr. 1898): 458.

17. Cited in Cooper, "Wisconsin Militia," 287.

18. See Stuart McConnell, *Glorious Contentment: The Grand Army of the Republic, 1865–1900* (Chapel Hill: University of North Carolina Press,

1992), chap. 4; and Mary Ann Clawson, *Constructing Brotherhood: Class, Gender, and Fraternalism* (Princeton: Princeton University Press, 1989), 123–35.

19. *American Manhood: Transformation in Masculinity from the Revolution to the Modern Era* (New York: Basic Books, 1993), 203.

20. *American Manhood*, 222, and chap. 10; Clawson, *Constructing Brotherhood*, 172–79; Donald J. Mrozek, "The Habit of Victory: The American Military and the Cult of Manliness," in J. A. Mangan and James Walvin, eds., *Manliness and Morality: Middle-Class Masculinity in Britain and America, 1800–1940* (New York: St. Martin's Press, 1987), 220–41.

21. See Cooper, "Wisconsin Militia," 314–19, and *Citizens as Soldiers*, 21–22; State of Washington, *Official History of the Washington National Guard*, 392; Martha Derthick, *The National Guard in Politics* (Cambridge: Harvard University Press, 1965), 19; MID 1894, 160.

22. See Barr, "The Black Militia of the New South: Texas as a Case Study," *Journal of Negro History* 43 (July 1878): 209–19; Charles Johnson Jr., *African American Soldiers in the National Guard*; Lowell D. Black, *The Negro Volunteer Militia of the Ohio National Guard*, chaps. 8 and 9.

23. Johnson, *African American Soldiers in the National Guard*, chaps. 1–2; and Black, *Negro Volunteers of Ohio*, chaps. 8–9, are particularly valuable. In addition, see Barr, "Black Militia of the New South," 210–16; B. I. Diamond and J. O. Baylen, "The Demise of the Georgia Guard, Colored, 1868–1914," *Phylon* 45 (Dec. 1984): 311–13; Martin K. Gordon, "The Black Militia in the District of Columbia, 1867–1898," in Francis C. Rosenberger, ed., *Records of the Columbia Historical Society . . . , 1971–1972* (Washington DC: 1973), 411–20; Beth T. Muskat, "The Last March: The Demise of the Black Militia in Alabama," *Alabama Review* 43 (Jan. 1990): 18–25; and Willard B. Gatewood Jr., "An Experiment in Color: The Eighth Illinois Volunteers, 1898–1899," *Journal of the Illinois State Historical Society* 65 (autumn 1972): 293–312.

24. Cited in Cooper, "Wisconsin Militia," 287.

25. On old and new middle classes, see Robert Wiebe, *The Search for Order, 1877–1920* (New York: Hill and Wang, 1967), 112–25; Olivier Zunz, *Making America Corporate, 1870–1920* (Chicago: University of Chicago Press, 1990), 1–10, chaps. 1–2; Burton J. Bledstein, *The Culture of Professionalism: The Middle Class and the Development of Higher Education* (New York: W. W. Norton, 1976), chaps. 1–3.

26. *Seventh Regiment*, 2: 418. Virtually any general periodical piece that assessed the National Guard invariably mentioned the Seventh Regiment. This reflected more a triumph of the regiment's self-publicity, however, than its military efficiency.

27. Clark, *History of the Seventh Regiment*, 2: passim; Wingate, *History of the Twenty-second Regiment*, passim.

28. Alfred Mewett, *A Brief History of Troop A, 107th Regiment of Cavalry, Ohio National Guard: The Black Horse Troop* (Cleveland: no publisher, 1923), 8 and 7–29.

29. "Biennial Report, 1895–1896," 1, in F. L. Carroll Papers, Arizona Historical Society, Tucson; Cooper, "Wisconsin Militia," 318–19; Derthick, *National Guard in Politics*, 19; Cooper, *Citizens as Soldiers*, 21.

30. MID 1895, 190.

31. Cited in Fowles, *A Guard in Peace and War*, 79–80. A policy shop operated numbers games—illegal lotteries.

32. MID 1895, 20; MID 1897, 189.

33. MID 1897, 234 and 304, respectively; Richard C. Roberts, "History of the Utah National Guard, 1894–1954" (Ph.D. diss., University of Utah, 1973), 187–88.

34. Nelson, "Organization and Training of the Texas Militia," *Texas Military History* 2 (May 1962): 85–87.

35. "Memoirs of Frederick Pfisterer," 137, typescript in possession of the author. Fogelson, *America's Armories*, 52–65; Olson, "Houston Light Guards," 108–10; Mewett, *A Brief History of Troop A*, 7–15. In his "The Ohio National Guard and Its Police Duties, 1894," *Ohio History* 83 (winter 1974), 52 n. 8, Charles A. Peckham explains Ohio's law on contributing members.

36. In Cooper, "Wisconsin Militia," 292.

37. MID 1897, 191.

38. AGR Texas, 1891, 29.

39. In *SWR* 1887, 1: 255.

40. Baem to the adj. gen., U.S. Army, 17 July 1886, in no. 4012, Adj. Gen.'s Office, 1886, entry 2, box 21, RG168, NARA.

41. Cited in Richard Cropp, *The Coyotes: A History of the South Dakota National Guard* (Mitchell SD: Education Supply Company, 1962), 90; McLatchy, "Development of the National Guard of Washington," 320–25.

42. AGR Texas, 1891, 91.

43. Peckham, "Ohio National Guard, 1894," 54; MID 1897, 191; 1894 report of adj. gen., Arizona Territory, 3, in F. L. Carroll Papers.

44. Cited in Nelson, "Rebirth, Growth and Expansion," 12.

45. Nelson, "Rebirth, Growth and Expansion," 11–12; Purcell, "The History of the Texas Militia," chap. 5.

46. MID 1896, 115.

47. *SWR* 1888, 1: 224.

48. MID 1896, 206.

49. *SWR* 1890, 1: 318.

50. MID 1893, 78.

51. Cited in Cooper, "Wisconsin Militia," 360.

52. MID 1894, 266.

53. Lt. A. C. Sharpe, "The National Guard of Iowa, 1893," *United Service*, n.s. 5(1893): 7.

54. Lodor to adj. gen., U.S. Army, 10 Aug. 1886, in box 22, entry 2, RG168.

55. "Organization and Training," 92.

56. MID 1893, 111.

57. In report of Maj. S. B. M. Young, U.S. Army, *SWR* 1889, 1: 279.

58. MID 1897, 187.

59. *SWR* 1890, 1: 338. See also Nelson, "Organization and Training," 89–104; and Olson, "Houston Light Guards," 135–39 and 416, table 38, on the meets.

60. To adj. gen., U.S. Army, no day, 1885, in box 21, entry 2, RG168.

61. To adj. gen., Mississippi, 15 Apr. 1886, in box 21, entry 2, RG168; Olson, "Houston Light Guards," 137–38.

62. Louis Cantor, "The Creation of the Modern National Guard: The Dick Act of 1903" (Ph.D. diss., Duke University, 1963, 66–75); and Frederick P. Todd, "Our National Guard: An Introduction to Its History," *Military Affairs* 5 (summer 1941): 156–58.

63. MID reports for the 1890s.

64. In National Guard Association (NGA), *Proceedings, Third Annual Convention* (n.p.: 1881), 15; Cooper, "Wisconsin Militia," 304–5, 310–11.

65. MID 1895, 207.

66. Telfer to Beebe, 31 Mar. 1895, folder 7, Beebe Papers.

67. Telfer to Beebe, 31 Mar. 1895.

68. *Affairs of State: Public Life in Late Nineteenth Century America* (Cambridge: Belknap Press of Harvard University Press, 114.

69. Cited in Cooper, "Wisconsin Militia," 287.

70. MID 1895, 204. Beebe's military service record appears in folder 4, Beebe Papers; Cooper, "Wisconsin Militia," 319–20.
71. Cantor, "The Modern National Guard," chaps. 2–3. See NGA, Ohio, *Proceedings, Second Annual Convention, 1885* (Columbus, 1885), 5–7, 21–22. The NGA represents one of many state associations.
72. NGA, New York, *Sixth Annual Convention*, 1884 (Buffalo: 1884), 16.
73. Cooper, "Wisconsin Militia," 252–53.
74. MID 1897, 160.
75. "Instruction in Armories," *United Service*, n.s. 1 (May 1889): 454.
76. Russell S. Gilmore, "Crackshots and Patriots: The National Rifle Association and America's Military-Sporting Tradition, 1871–1929" (Ph.D. diss., University of Wisconsin, 1974), 40–46, 53–54, 70–78, 84–86.

5. TO SERVE THE NATION

1. *SWR* 1880, 1: 245.
2. *SWR* vii, 245, viii, respectively.
3. C. Joseph Bernardo and Eugene H. Bacon, *American Military Policy: Its Development since 1875* (Harrisburg PA: Stackpole, 1955; repr., Westport CT: Greenwood Press, 1977), 248–49; Gilmore, "Crackshots and Patriots," 52–57, 70–75, 128–33.
4. NGA, *Proceedings of the Convention of National Guards . . . Oct. 1, 1879* (St. Louis, 1879), title page, 2.
5. NGA, *Proceedings . . . 1879*, 10–11. See Louis Cantor, "The Modern National Guard" (Ph.D. diss., Duke University, 1963), 55–62, 74–75; Derthick, *National Guard in Politics*, 20–21. In his "Crackshots and Patriots," 84–86, Gilmore discusses the NGA's early years.
6. AGR Massachusetts, 1882, 3.
7. In NGA, *Proceedings of the Third Annual Convention . . . NGA of the United States* (n.p.: 1881), 17.
8. Cited in Cooper, "Wisconsin Militia," 355. See also Riker, *Soldiers of the States*, 55–62; Derthick, *National Guard in Politics*, 15–21; Cantor, "Modern National Guard," 88–90, provides background.
9. Lloyd S. Bryce, "A Service of Love," *North American Review* 145 (Sept. 1887): 285.
10. "The Defense of Our Frontier," *JMSI* 18 (Mar. 1896): 304.
11. Cited in Cooper, "Wisconsin Militia," 354.

12. J. C. Kelton, asst. adj. gen., to Lt. Robert Stevens, 6 May 1886, no. 2137, Adj. Gen.'s Office, 1886 in entry 2, box 21, RGI68.

13. Capt. D. M. Taylor to Kelton, 14 June 1889, and accompanying reports; and Kelton to the adj. gen. of Maine, 30 Mar. 1889, no. 2137, Adj. Gen.'s Office, in entry 2, box 23. William T. Sherman, "The Militia," *JMSI* 6 (Mar. 1885): 1–14; Sheridan's remarks in SWR 1887, 1: 80.

14. 8 (Mar. 1889), 317.

15. "Inspector General's Report," in *SWR* 1890, 1: 275. Also see 271–72.

16. MID 1895, 307, and a survey of MID reports for 1893 through 1897.

17. For example, MID 1897, 4; Edward M. Coffman, *The Old Army: A Portrait of the American Army in Peacetime, 1784–1898* (New York: Oxford University Press, 1986), 250–51.

18. *SWR* 1885, 1: 307, 308, respectively.

19. Report of Capt. John Egan to adj. gen., U.S. Army, 20 Aug. 1885, on his inspection of the Rhode Island National Guard, in no. 7835, Adj. Gen.'s Office, 1885, entry 2, box 22, RGI68. The observations made by Totten, Lacey, and Egan were repeated numerous times in inspection reports throughout the 1880s and 1890s.

20. "The Militia," 9.

21. "Instruction in Armories," *United Service* 1, n.s. (May 1889): 460; James L. Abrahamson, *America Arms for a New Century: The Making of a Great Military Power* (New York: Free Press, 1981), chap. 2.

22. "Militia Reform without Legislation," *JMSI* 2 (1882): 403.

23. "Discussion," *JMSI* 7 (1886): 110. See also Cantor, "Modern National Guard," 88–100, 105–8; Gilmore, "The NRA," 128–33.

24. House Committee on the Militia, *Reorganization of the Militia*, 46th Cong., 1st and 2d sess., 1880, H. Rept. 763, 10.

25. NGA bills appear in House Committee, *Reorganization of the Militia*, H. Rept. 763 (1880); Senate, *Report on Reorganizing the Militia*, S. Rept. 742 (1881); House, *Reorganization of the Militia*, H. Rept. 590 (1882); Senate, *Report on Senate Bill 1596*, S. Rept. 345 (1882); House, *Efficiency of the Militia*, H. Rept. 805 (1890); and House, *Efficiency of the Militia*, H. Rept. 754 (1892).

26. Cantor, "Modern National Guard," 109–10, and Derthick, *National Guard in Politics*, 20–22, on militia reform. Abrahamson, *America Arms for a New Century*, chaps. 2 and 3, on doubts within the Army on the Guard's viability as a reserve.

27. "Reasons for Increasing the Regular Army," *North American Review* 166 (Apr. 1898): 456. Russell F. Weigley's *Towards an American Army: Military Thought from Washington to Marshall* (New York: Columbia University Press, 1962), chaps. 7 and 9; and *History of the United States Army*, enlarged ed. (Bloomington: Indiana University Press, 1984), chap. 12, examine Army reform ideas, as does Abrahamson's *America Arms for a New Century*, chaps. 1–3.

28. "The Military Necessities of the United States, and the Best Provisions for Meeting Them," *JMSI* 5 (Sept. 1884): 255.

29. "Based on Present Conditions and Past Experiences, How Should Our Volunteer Armies Be Raised, Organized, Trained, and Mobilized for Future Wars?" *JMSI* 21 (Jan. 1898): 41. See also Upton, *The Military Policy of the United States*, introduction; Weigley, *Towards an American Army*, chaps. 7 and 9; Abrahamson, *America Arms for a New Century*, 32–44; Graham A. Cosmas, *An Army for Empire: The United States Army in the Spanish-American War* (Columbia: University of Missouri Press, 1971), 46–50.

30. "Organization and Training of a National Reserve for Military Service," *JMSI* 10 (Mar. 1889): 12, 14, respectively.

31. "The Army Organization, Best Adapted to a Republican Form of Government, Which Will Ensure An Effective Force," *JMSI* 14 (Mar. 1893): 253–54.

32. "A National Militia," North American Review 135 (Apr. 1882): 399.

33. Commentary on Lt. Col. James Rice, "Our National Military System: Military Education and the Volunteer Militia," *Century Magazine* 36 (Oct. 1888): 945.

34. "The National Guard: National in Name Only," *JMSI* 20 (May 1897): 521.

35. NGA, *Proceedings . . . 1879*, 8–15; Cantor, "Modern National Guard," 64–69. On Molineux's objections, see his letter to the Senate Committee on Military Affairs, 28 Feb. 1880, in *Report on Reorganizing the Militia*, S. Rept. 742, 1.

36. NGA, *Proceedings of the Third Annual Convention*, 53, 54, 2–6.

37. Records for the NGA's early years are scanty. The Edward Martin Library at the headquarters of the National Guard Association of the United States, Washington DC, holds letters, newspaper clippings, and convention reports compiled by George Wingate. It is evident that for most of

these years Wingate and the NGA were virtually synonymous. Riker, *Soldiers of the States*, 59–61, is wont to show the NGA as powerful.

38. "National Guard National in Name Only," 522.

39. "Militia Reform without Legislation," 388.

40. "Comment and Criticism," *JMSI* 14 (May 1893): 583.

41. Cited in Cooper, "Wisconsin Militia," 249–50.

42. *Army and Navy Journal*, 23 Aug. 1890, 971.

43. *The Volunteer Soldier of America* (Chicago: R. S. Peale, 1887), 578.

44. "Comment and Criticism," *JMSI* 13 (May 1892): 540.

45. "The Age of Progress in the National Guard," *Report of the Sixth Annual Convention of the National Guard Association of Illinois, 1888* (Rockford IL, 1888), 80.

46. "The National Guard and Its Relation to the General Government," NGA Ohio, *Ninth Annual Convention* (Columbus OH, 1892), 22.

47. Lieber to Kelton, 13 Jan. 1892, in no. 21765 AGO PRD 1891, entry 25, RG94.

48. "The Present Congress and the National Guard," *JMSI* 19 (Nov. 1896): 453, 470, respectively.

49. MID 1895, passim, and MID reports, 1893–97, generally; Maj. H. P. Ward, "The National Guard: The Importance to the Government of the Citizen Soldiery," *National Guard Gazette* 1 (Jan. 1897): 13–15.

50. "Political Staff Officers in the National Guard," *National Guard Gazette* 1 (Sept. 1897): 302–4.

51. 3 Sept. 1892, 24.

52. 3 Sept. 1892, 24; 16 Aug. 1890, 951.

53. "Comment and Criticism," *JMSI* 22 (Feb. 1898): 437.

54. "The Militia," 2.

55. *SWR* 1889, 1: 282.

56. Two works by Graham A. Cosmas, "From Order to Chaos: The War Department, the National Guard, and Military Policy," *Military Affairs* 29 (fall 1965): 105–21; and *An Army for Empire* are the most useful overviews of the war. Also see Lewis L. Gould, *The Spanish-American War and President McKinley* (Lawrence: University Press of Kansas, 1982); Marvin A. Kreidberg and Merton G. Henry, *History of Military Mobilization in the United States Army* (Washington DC: Department of the Army, 1955), chap. 5; Gerald F. Linderman, *The Mirror of War: American Society and the Spanish-American War* (Ann Arbor: University of Michigan Press, 1974), chap. 4; David F. Trask, *The War with Spain in*

1898 (New York: Macmillan, 1981); Weigley, *History of the United States Army*, chap. 13; Jim Dan Hill, *The Minute Man in Peace and War: A History of the National Guard* (Harrisburg PA: Stackpole, 1964), chap. 6.

57. See Cosmas, *Army for Empire*, 89–110; and Stephen Skowronek, *Building a New American State: The Expansion of National Administrative Capacities, 1877–1920* (New York: Cambridge University Press, 1982), chap. 4.

58. AGR New York, 1898, 13.

59. See Walter L. Prichard, ed., "Louisiana in the Spanish-American War, 1898–1899, As Recorded by Colonel Elmer Ellsworth Wood, Commander of the Second Regiment of Louisiana Volunteer Infantry," *Louisiana Historical Quarterly* 26 (July 1943): 792–93; Ruby W. Waldeck, "Missouri in the Spanish-American War, Part I," *Missouri Historical Review* 30 (July 1936): 380–92; and James E. Payne, *History of the Fifth Missouri Volunteer Infantry* (Kansas City: no publisher, 1899).

60. File of Jones Palm, Company M, Fourteenth Minnesota Volunteer Infantry, Spanish-American War Survey, U.S. Army Military History Institute, Carlisle, Pennsylvania.

61. Cited in Jerry Cooper, with Glenn Smith, *Citizens as Soldiers: A History of the North Dakota National Guard* (Fargo: North Dakota Institute for Regional Studies, 1986), 38.

62. Funston, *Memories of Two Wars: Cuban and Philippine Experiences* (New York: no publisher, 1911), 150–62. Also, see Fowles, *A Guard in Peace and War*, 94–95; MID 1898, 93–95; Willard B. Gatewood Jr., "Kansas Negroes and the Spanish-American War," *Kansas Historical Quarterly* 37 (autumn 1971): 300–313.

63. *Story of the 15th Minnesota Volunteer Infantry* (Minneapolis: Lessard Printing, 1899), 10, 53, respectively, for quotations; 10–13 for the regiment's organization.

64. *History of the 5th Missouri*, 34.

65. *History of the 5th Missouri*, 34–35.

66. *Story of the 15th Minnesota*, 10.

67. AGR Pennsylvania, 1898, 219. Linderman, *The Mirror of War*, 62–85; William Schellings, "Florida Volunteers in the War with Spain," *Florida Historical Quarterly* 41 (July 1962): 50–51.

68. AGR Massachusetts, 1898, 11.

69. Cited in Cooper, "Wisconsin Militia," 368. Also, see AGR Pennsylvania, 1898, 209; AGR Massachusetts, 1898, 11–12, 22–23; Walter W.

Ward, *Springfield in the Spanish-American War* (Easthampton MA: Enterprise Printing, 1899), 11–12; and Harry E. Webber, *Twelve Months
with the Eighth Massachusetts in the Service of the United States* (Salem:
Newcomb and Gauss Printers, 1908), 37–39.

70. Cited in Jerry M. Cooper, "National Guard Reform, the Army, and the
Spanish-American War: The View from Wisconsin," *Military Affairs* 42
(Feb. 1978): 22.

71. Cooper, "National Guard Reform," 21. On Massachusetts and Pennsylvania, see Hall, *Regiments and Armories of Massachusetts*, 2: 217; AGR
Pennsylvania, 1898, 19.

72. On Pennsylvania, see AGR Pennsylvania, 1898, passim; and Ent, *The
First Century*, 91–98 and app. A; Alexander L. Hawkins, *Official His-
tory of the Operations of the 10th Pennsylvania Infantry, U.S.V. in the
Campaign in the Philippine Islands* (n.p., n.d.), 1–2, 30–72. For Mas-
sachusetts, see AGR Massachusetts, 1898, passim; Ward, *Springfield in
the Spanish-American War*, 2–13; and Webber, *Twelve Months*, 37–39.
On Wisconsin, see Cooper, "Wisconsin Militia," 373–77. J. A. Tilley,
"The Mobilization of the Ohio National Guard, 1898" (seminar paper,
Ohio State University, 1974), 6–16, covers the Buckeye State. For North
Dakota, see Cooper and Smith, *Citizens as Soldiers*, 38–47.

73. See Purcell, "The History of the Texas Militia," 282–83 and app. E; and
Christian G. Nelson, "Texas Militia in the Spanish-American War,"
Texas Military History 2 (Aug. 1962): 194, 200–201. On Missouri, see
Waldeck, "Missouri in the Spanish-American War," 377–92; and
Payne, *History of the Fifth Missouri*, 3–7. For Florida, see George C.
Bittle, "In Defense of Florida: The Organized Florida Militia from 1821
to 1920" (Ph.d. diss., Florida State University, 1965), 355–63; and
Schellings, "Florida Volunteers in the Spanish-American War," 48–51.
For Louisiana, see Prichard, "Louisiana in the Spanish-American
War," 791–96.

74. Prichard, "Louisiana in the Spanish-American War," 807, 809, 811, respectively.

75. AGR Missouri, 1897–98, 126; Payne, *History of the Fifth Missouri*, 6;
Nelson, "Texas Militia in the Spanish-American War," 202–6; Bittle,
"In Defense of Florida," 355–60.

76. See AGR New York, 1898, 6–7, 13–14; Kenneth R. Bailey, "A Search for
Identity: The West Virginia National Guard, 1877–1921" (Ph.D. diss.,
Ohio State University, 1976), 90–91; AGR Oregon, 1897–98, 4–7; W. D.

B. Dodson, *Official History of the Operations of the Second Oregon Infantry, U.S.V. in the Campaign in the Philippine Islands* (n.p., n.d.), 2–4; Nankivell, *History of the Military Organizations*, 112–15; McLatchy, "Development of the National Guard of Washington," 326–29; and Roberts, "History of the Utah National Guard," 76–83.

77. A series of articles by Willard B. Gatewood Jr. discuss the formation of many black units, as annotated in Cooper, *The Militia and the National Guard in America*, 150–51. See also Johnson, *African American Soldiers in the National Guard*, 59–76; Marvin Fletcher, "The Black Volunteers in the Spanish-American War," *Military Affairs* 38 (Apr. 1974): 48–53; and Frank E. Edwards, *The '98 Campaign of the 6th Massachusetts, U.S.V.* (Boston: Little, Brown, 1898), 112–19, 124–25.

78. For example, John J. Leffler, "The Paradox of Patriotism: Texans in the Spanish-American War," *Hayes Historical Journal* 8 (spring 1989): 36–42; and Jeff L. Patrick, "Nothing But Slaves: The Second Kentucky Volunteer Infantry and the Spanish-American War," *Register of the Kentucky Historical Society* 89 (summer 1991): 287–99.

79. Hill, *Minute Man in Peace and War*, 162, 167–69; Weigley, *History of the United States Army*, 307–8; Frank Harper, "Fighting Far from Home: The First Colorado Regiment in the Spanish-American War," *Colorado Heritage* 1 (1988): 2–11; and Thomas D. Thiessen, "The Fighting First Nebraska: Nebraska's Imperial Adventure in the Philippines, 1898–1899," *Nebraska History* 70 (fall 1989): 210–72.

80. AGR Pennsylvania, 1898, 253.

81. *Official History, 2nd Oregon*, 1.

82. *The '98 Campaign*, v and 3–4, respectively.

83. AGR New York, 1898, 7; George P. Nichols, *The First Hundred Years: Records and Reminiscences of a Century of Company I, Seventh Regiment, N.G.N.Y., 1838–1938* (New York: no publisher, 1938), 203–5; and Walter Millis, *The Martial Spirit: A Study of Our War with Spain* (Boston: Houghton-Mifflin, 1931), 155–58. See also Olson, "Houston Light Guards" 265–70; Nelson, "Texas Militia in the Spanish-American War," 194–97; and Leffler, "The Paradox of Patriotism," 34–36.

84. AGR Pennsylvania, 1898, 20.

85. Bitting file in Spanish-American War Survey, U.S. Army Military History Institute, Carlisle, Pennsylvania.

86. Ward, *Springfield in the Spanish-American War*, 12–13 for quotation; AGR Massachusetts, 1898, 130–31; and Frederick E. Pierce, *Reminis-*

cences of the Experiences of Company L, Second Regiment Massa-chusetts Infantry, U.S.V., in the Spanish-American War (Greenfield MA: E. A. Holland, 1900), 7–8.

87. Ward, *Springfield in the Spanish-American War*, 13.

6. NATIONAL GUARD REFORM

1. See Elihu Root, *The Military and Colonial Policy of the United States: Addresses and Reports* (Cambridge: Harvard University Press, 1916; repr., New York: Arno Press, 1970); Skowronek, *Building A New American State*, chap. 7; Weigley, *History of the United States Army*, chap. 14, and "The Elihu Root Reforms and the Progressive Era," in William Geffen, ed., *Command and Commanders in Modern Warfare*, 2d ed. (Washington DC: Government Printing Office, 1971), 28–34; and Barrie E. Zais, "The Struggle for a 20th Century Army: Investigation and Reform of the U.S. Army after the Spanish-American War" (Ph.D. diss., Duke University, 1981), chaps. 6–7, 9.

2. To W. A. Simpson, U.S. Army, Office of the Adj. Gen., 22 Sept. 1899, box 23, entry 2, RGI68.

3. "In What Way Can the National Guard Be Modified So as to Make It an Effective Reserve to the Regular Army in Both War and Peace?" *JMSI* 27 (Mar. 1900): 155–88.

4. Britton's pamphlet, published in New York in 1901, has a lengthy title that begins "A Commission to Compile and Prepare a Bill"; it can be found in box 24, entry 2, RGI68. See Ordway, District of Columbia, "A National Militia," *North American Review* 135 (Apr. 1882): 395–400.

5. Memorandum of Board of Officers, 24 Oct. 1900, in AGO document file, no. 311224, entry 25, RG94. See also Sanger, "The Army Organization Best Adapted to a Republican Form of Government Which Will Ensure an Effective Force," *JMSI* 14 (Nov. 1893): 1145–81; and Zais, "Struggle for a 20th Century Army," 250.

6. In Richard Kohn, ed., *Military Laws of the United States from the Civil War through the War Powers Act of 1973* (New York: Arno Press, 1979). Formally titled "An act to promote the efficiency of the militia, and for other purposes," historians frequently refer to the statute as the Dick Act after the congressman. The law will be referred to here as the Militia Act of 1903. See Cantor's "Modern National Guard," chap. 5; and "Elihu Root and the National Guard: Friend or Foe?" *Military Affairs* 33 (Dec.

1969): 361–73. See also Elbridge Colby, "Elihu Root and the National Guard," *Military Affairs* 23 (spring 1959): 28–34.

7. See swr 1903, 150–55, for the 1903 law and DMA 1908, 10–14, for the law as amended in 1908.

8. Information for the preceding paragraphs comes from swr, for 1900 through 1907; thereafter, from DMA reports for 1908 through 1915. Total federal spending on the Organized Militia can only be estimated insofar as even the DMA itself was unsure of the amount, as seen in a 20 Feb. 1915 memo in wcd no. 7520, rgi65, and *mbr* 1917, 12. Charles D. McKenna, "The Forgotten Reforms: Field Maneuvers in the Development of the United States Army" (Ph.D. diss., Duke University, 1981), passim, provides the costs of joint maneuvers.

9. The 1903 law uses the term *National Guard* only once. All other references to state troops in the law and federal reports use the term *Organized Militia*. The two phrases will be used here interchangeably.

10. To Maj. Gen. S. B. M. Young, 3 Mar. 1903, no. 470905, box 26, entry 4, rgi68.

11. Comments of the Army adj. gen. in swr 1903, 162–63, 168–70, 170–71. See also Lt. Col. James Parker, "The New Militia Act of 1903," *North American Review* 77 (Aug. 1903): 278–87.

12. *swr* 1908, 146.

13. *swr* 1908, 146–56; Oliver to Sen. Francis E. Warren, 27 Feb. 1908, in no. 44830, DMA, rgi68; *mbr* 1917, 5–12; A. L. Mills, chief of DMA, to Army chief of staff, 6 Jan. 1916, report no. 12165, entry 5, rgi65.

14. DMA 1909, 4, 7, respectively.

15. DMA 1910, 125, 8, respectively.

16. The other divisions in the reformed general staff were Mobile Army, Coast Artillery, and War College. See DMA 1910, 283; A. L. Mills memo, 6 Jan. 1916, cited in note 13 of this chapter; and Weigley, *History of the United States Army*, 328–40.

17. DMA 1913, 333.

18. DMA 1913, 8.

19. DMA 1915, 5; *National Guard Magazine* 10 (Nov. 1913): 335.

20. DMA 1915, 9.

21. Memo to chief of DMA, 25 Aug. 1910, no. 18818, DMA, box 113, entry 7, rgi68. Kerth added, "this is a question for the General Staff of the Army—not for the National Guard Assn." Also see DMA 1910, 88.

22. DMA 1915, 58. On Arkansas, see DMA 1912, 42–44; and *Army-Navy Register*, 12 July 1913, 51.

23. Reprinted in DMA 1912, 23. Crowder's opinion, 29 Dec. 1911, is in no. 1878466, entry 25, RG94; memoranda in report no. 8399, Dec. 1911, entry 5, RG165.

24. 9 (June 1912), 235.

25. 9 (June 1912), 235; 13 (Mar. 1916), 71.

26. *SWR* 1912, 125–27. On Capt. John McAuley Palmer, principal author of the 1912 plan, see his *America in Arms* (New Haven: Yale University Press, 1941; repr. 1979), 124–57; and I. B. Holley Jr., *General John M. Palmer, Citizen Soldiers, and the Army of a Democracy* (Westport CT: Greenwood Press, 1982), 202–11, 230–38. See also McKenna, "Forgotten Reforms," 111, 128, 150–51; and John B. Wilson, "Army Readiness Planning, 1899–1917," *Military Review* 64 (July 1984): 61–72. See consolidated file no. 11254, DMA, entry 7, boxes 95, RG168, on the First Field Army and the divisional innovation.

27. Cover letter to all governors, no date, 1912, in WCD no. 7409, RG165; DMA 1913, passim; DMA 1914, 201–4.

28. DMA 1912, 28.

29. See DMA 1913, 199–210.

30. Mills's speech to the 1913 NGA convention, in NGA, *Proceedings: Fifteenth Annual Convention of the National Guard Association of the United States* (Columbus OH, 1913), 336.

31. NGA, *Proceedings: Fifteenth Annual Convention*, 336; DMA 1912, 27–32, 95–96; DMA 1913, 197–210; DMA 1914, 207–10.

32. Cited by Gen. Mills, chief of DMA, in memo of 20 Feb. 1915, WCD no. 7520-7, RG165.

33. *National Guard Magazine* 6 (June 1910), 522.

34. *National Guard Magazine* 6 (Dec. 1910), 520.

35. In letter to Adj. Gen. Charles C. Weybright, Ohio, 19 Apr. 1912, in no. 21925, DMA, entry 7, box 126, RG168.

36. See Consolidated files no. 21925, DMA, entry 7, box 126, RG168, and report no. 6786, entry 5, RG165. See also *SWR* 1912, 24–26 and 269; and *National Guard Magazine*, for all of 1912. On Congress, see George C. Herring Jr., "James Hay and the Preparedness Controversy, 1915–1916," *Journal of Southern History* 30 (Nov. 1964): 384–85.

37. Cited in Gen. Mills's memo, 20 Feb. 1915, 12.

38. *Statement of Proper Military Policy* (Washington DC: Government Printing Office, 1916), passim.; *SWR* 1915, 21–36; consolidated studies WCD no. 8222 and WCD no. 7835 1915, RG165; and *National Guard Magazine*, for all of 1913 and 1914. For background on the preparedness movement and its impact on War Department planning, see John Whiteclay Chambers II, *To Raise an Army: The Draft Comes to Modern America* (New York: Free Press, 1987), chaps. 3 and 4; John G. Clifford, *The Citizen Soldiers: The Plattsburg Training Camp Movement, 1913–1920* (Lexington: University of Kentucky Press, 1972); and John P. Finnegan, *Against the Specter of a Dragon: The Campaign for American Military Preparedness* (Westport CT: Greenwood Press, 4).

39. Elbridge Colby, *The National Guard of the United States: A Half Century of Progress* (Manhattan KS: Military Affairs/Aerospace Historian, 1977), chaps. 3–4; Riker, *Soldiers of the States*, 70–77; Derthick, *National Guard in Politics*, 27–32; and Hill, *Minute Man in Peace and War*, chaps. 8–9.

40. AWC no. 13, "Study of the Laws Relating to the Organization of the Militia and Volunteers . . . ," pt. 4: 48, AWC Studies, 1905–6, entry 299, RG165.

41. AWC no. 168, "The Military Policy of the United States and a Comprehensive Scheme for the Organization of the Armed Forces on Land," (1908), 27, AWC Studies, entry 299, RG165.

42. See *SWR* 1912, 122; Brig. Gen. Robert K. Evans, chief, DMA, "A Proposed Solution," *Infantry Journal* 8 (Mar.–Apr. 1912): 713–15; and his remarks in DMA 1910, 11–12, and DMA 1911, 155–57. See also Abrahamson, *America Arms for a New Century*, chaps. 5–6; McKenna, "Forgotten Reforms," passim; Zais, "Struggle for a 20th Century Army," chap. 10; and Marvin A. Kriedberg and Merton G. Henry, *History of Military Mobilization in the United States Army, 1775–1945* (Washington DC: Department of the Army, 1955), 179–87.

43. In no. 30485, DMA, 5 Jan. 1912, box 156, entry 7, RG168.

44. WCD no. 8222, "Study of Army, Militia, Reserves, etc.," July 1913, War College Division correspondence, 1903–19, RG165.

45. To Secretary of War Lindley Garrison, Aug. 1915, WCD no. 7520-6, enclosure to WCD no. 7520. See also Capt. William Mitchell, "The Militia as Organized under the Constitution and Its Value to the Nation as a Military Asset," WCD no. 7835-9; unsigned study, WCD no. 8160, Nov. 1915;

Gen. Mills, "Federal Employment of the Organized Militia," 22 Dec. 1915, report no. 12332; all in RGI65.

46. In memo to chief of staff, 28 Dec. 1915, file 370.01, folder 2, box 429, entry 12, RGI68. For mobilization regulations, see U.S. War Department pamphlet, "United States Mustering Regulations . . ." (Washington DC: Government Printing Office, 1912); Secretary of War Lindley M. Garrison to governor of Pennsylvania, 20 May 1914, WCD no. 8160, RGI65; "Organization, Training, and Mobilization of Volunteers under the Act of April 25, 1914," a supplement to *Statement of a Proper Military Policy*.

47. Mills to chief of staff, 4 May 1914, in file 325.451/North Dakota, box 323, entry 12, RGI68; supplement WCD 9053-40, *Statement of a Proper Military Policy*, 8.

48. *Statement of a Proper Military Policy*, 8.

49. *Military and Colonial Policy of the U.S.*, 141.

50. AWC no. 20 (1906), "Resources of the United States—Men," 37, AWC Studies, entry 299, RGI65.

51. See AWC study no. 13, 52. See also AWC no. 20; AWC no. 13; AWC no. 168; and WCD no. 8222 (1913), all in RGI65. See also published work by Army officers: Capt. William Mitchell, "Military Organizations of the United States," *Infantry Journal* 10 (Nov.–Dec. 1913): 350–92; Maj. John McAuley Palmer, "The Militia Pay Bill," *Infantry Journal* 11 (Nov.–Dec. 1914): 336–45; and Col. E. E. Hatch, "The Swiss and Australian Militia Systems," *Infantry Journal* 12 (May–Apr. 1915): 613–40.

52. AWC no. 168, 51.

53. WCD no. 8222-1, "Study of Army, Militia, Reserves, etc.," July 1913, in War College correspondence, 1903–19, RGI65. See also Gen. A. L. Mills, "The Organized Militia," *Infantry Journal* 11 (Sept.–Oct. 1914): 153–68.

54. To William Hutchinson, 30 Mar. 1912, in no. 21925, DMA, RGI68.

55. To Matthew Forney Steele, 8 Sept. 1912, in Steele Papers, United States Army Military History Institute, Carlisle Barracks, Pennsylvania.

56. WCD no. 7835-8, RGI65. Also see Col. R. L. Bullard, "From a Summer with the National Guard," *National Guard Magazine* 10 (Apr. 1913): 99–100.

57. *SWR* 1912, 76.

58. *Statement of a Proper Military Policy*, 3–5.

59. To M. F. Steele, 8 Sept. 1912, Steele Papers.

60. See "The New National Guard," *jmsi* 34 (May–June 1904): 474; and Charles S. Clark, "The Future of the National Guard," *North American Review* 170 (May 1900): 731–44.

61. *National Guard Magazine* 5 (Jan. 1910): 16–17.

62. *"Tin Soldiers": The Organized Militia and What It Really Is* (Boston: no publisher, 1912), 166, 163, respectively.

63. To William Cary Sanger, 24 Mar. 1903, in awc no. 335, entry 288, rg165.

64. Letter to Wood, 28 Dec. 1910, in awc no. 6786, entry 5, rg165.

65. 10 (Nov. 1913), 331.

66. *National Guard Magazine* 10 (Dec. 1913): 371.

67. nga, *Proceedings: Fifteenth Annual Convention*, 40.

68. *National Guard Magazine* 10 (Nov. 1913): 334.

69. 10 (Nov. 1913): 332. On the Army's inability to keep up units according to regulations, see *Army and Navy Journal*, 1 Nov. 1913, 264, and 29 Nov., 393–94.

70. 6 (Jan. 1900), 13.

71. 9 (June 1912), 241.

72. Letter to *Army and Navy Journal*, 10 Jan. 1914, 588.

73. 10 (Nov. 1913), 331.

74. nga, *Proceedings: Fifteenth Annual Convention*, 44.

75. *National Guard Magazine* 10 (Nov. 1913), 333. On the National Militia Board, see nga, *Proceedings: Fifteenth Annual Convention*, passim.

76. nga, *Proceedings: Fifteenth Annual Convention*, 56. Also see Harris's comments, 74–75.

77. Quoted in *Army and Navy Journal*, 18 Oct. 1913, 204.

78. nga, *Proceedings: Fifteenth Annual Convention*, 72. Hill's *Minute Man in Peace and War*, chap. 9, reflects the Guard's intense suspicions of the War Department.

79. nga, *Proceedings: Fifteenth Annual Convention*, 77.

80. *National Guard Magazine* 11 (Mar. 1914), 70.

81. On the nga's condition in the early twentieth century, see "History of the ngaus Chronology," Edward Martin Library, headquarters, National Guard Association of the United States, Washington dc; and Derthick, *National Guard in Politics*, 27–38.

82. "What the Guard Wants," *Infantry Journal*, 10 (Jan.–Feb. 1914): 507, 508, respectively.

83. AGR Massachusetts, 1914, 8. See also Maj. Gen. John F. O'Ryan, tactical commander of the New York National Guard, in "The Role of the National Guard," *North American Review* 202 (Sept. 1915): 364–72. Divisions at the 1913 convention are in NGA, *Proceedings: Fifteenth Annual Convention*, 74–85; *Army and Navy Journal*, 18 Oct. 1913, 208; and *Infantry Journal* 10 (Jan.–Feb. 1914): 574–77.

84. *National Guard Magazine* 11 (Feb. 1914): 37–38; and (Sept. 1914): 177; 12 (Mar. 1915): 56; and (Apr. 1915): 69–70.

85. To Woodrow Wilson, 30 Oct. 1915, in Arthur S. Link, ed., *The Papers of Woodrow Wilson* (Princeton: Princeton University Press, 1980), 35: 138.

86. 12 (Dec. 1915), 221.

87. 23 Oct. 1915, Link, *Papers of Woodrow Wilson*, 35: 105–6.

88. The content and consequences of the 1916 NDA will be discussed in chap. 7. Herring, "James Hay and the Preparedness Controversy," 383–404, provides the legislative background. The *Papers of Woodrow Wilson*, vols. 34–36, passim, covering mid-1915 through March 1916, are essential.

89. 13 (May 1916), 104.

7. THE NATIONAL GUARD DILEMMA

1. AGR Missouri, 1903–4, 15.

2. *SWR* 1903, passim, and DMA 1915, passim.

3. AGR Massachusetts, 1914, 21.

4. AGR Missouri, 1913–14, 5.

5. McLatchy, "Development of the National Guard of Washington," 342–63; Truss, "Alabama National Guard," 149–79.

6. Cited in Watt and Spears, *Indiana's Citizen Soldiers*, 99.

7. See *SWR* 1903 and 1904, passim, for table 14, and DMA 1914, 302–6, for table 15.

8. *SWR* 1903 and 1904 and DMA 1914.

9. Ketchum to chief, War College Division, no date, 1912, in WCD no. 6786, entry 5, RG165. See also DMA 1909, 232–33; DMA 1912, 229; and DMA 1913, 304–5.

10. AGR Massachusetts, 1914, 4, 86–88, 91, and AGR Massachusetts, 1915, 98–99. On New York, see *National Guard Magazine* 6 (Nov. 1910): 463. For Connecticut, see *National Guard Magazine* (Feb. 1910): 113–16; for California, see *National Guard Magazine* 5 (Mar. 1910): 247; on Wash-

ington, see *National Guard Magazine* 12 (Mar. 1915): 45; and Holmes, "National Guard of Pennsylvania," 192–93. Fogelson, *America's Armories*, passim, discusses armory building generally.

11. See *National Guard Magazine* 9 (Aug. 1912): 334, on Pennsylvania; Upham, "Historical Survey of the Militia in Iowa," 425, 430, 436; AGR Virginia, 1913, 13; Truss, "Alabama National Guard from 1900," 77–78; Elmer Ray Milner, "An Agonizing Evolution: A History of the Texas National Guard, 1900–1945" (Ph.D. diss., North Texas State University, 1979), 34; and AGR Georgia, 1914, 106.

12. SWR 1905, 277; DMA 1910, 113–14.

13. AGR West Virginia, 1907–8, 7.

14. States bore the responsibility for providing armories until 1950, when Congress approved federal armory support to pay 75 percent of the costs, with the states contributing the remainder.

15. Roberts, "History of the Utah National Guard," 175, n. 14; AGR Massachusetts, 1914, 36; Bailey, "A Search for Identity," 98; and Upham, "Historical Survey of the Militia in Iowa," 416.

16. Roberts, "History of the Utah National Guard," 173–80.

17. AGR Missouri, 1903–4, 55.

18. AGR California, 1909–10, 15.

19. AGR Georgia, 1914, 106–7.

20. DMA 1914, 303.

21. For Arkansas's troubles, see *National Guard Magazine* 10 (May 1913): 148–49; and (July 1913), 208; see also 11 (Feb. 1914), 55. *National Guard Magazine* 12 (May 1915), 99, notes West Virginia's difficulties.

22. 8 (July 1911), 66.

23. AGR Missouri, 1909–10, 42. See *National Guard Magazine* 7 (May 1910): 561, on the Frankfort company.

24. MBR, 1916, 59–60.

25. MBR, 1916, 59–60.

26. Johnson, *African American Soldiers in the National Guard*, 76–96; Muskat, "The Last March," 18–34; Olson, "Houston Light Guards," 201–3.

27. MBR 1916, 59–60.

28. AGR New Jersey, 1913, 7; and Lt. W. W. Wright, California, "What the National Guard Needs," *National Guard Magazine* 12 (Aug. 1915): 139.

29. Letter to editor, *National Guard Magazine* 6 (July 1910): 54.

30. Letter to editor, *National Guard Magazine* 6 (Jan. 1910): 33.

31. AGR Minnesota, 1905–6, 71.
32. *National Guard Magazine* 6 (Jan. 1910): 32.
33. AGR Oregon, 1907–8, 30.
34. 6 (Mar. 1910), 209.
35. Letter of 1 July 1912, in WCD 6786, entry 5, RG165.
36. Letter of 1 July 1912, in WCD 6786, entry 5, RG165.
37. McKenna, "Forgotten Reforms." On officer instruction camps, see Col. Byron L. Bargar, Ohio, "National Guard Officers at School," *National Guard Magazine* 6 (Aug. 1910): 111–18.
38. DMA 1912, 68.
39. Colby, *National Guard of the United States*, pp. 22–23 of chap. 3.
40. To Michigan Adj. Gen. Roy C. Vandercook, 22 Dec. 1913, Vandercook Papers, University Archives and Historical Collections, Michigan State University, East Lansing, Michigan.
41. "Observations of an Inspector-Instructor," *Infantry Journal* 11 (Jan.-Feb. 1915): 497. See also DMA 1914, 216, for inspector-instructors serving with the states. The number rose to 105 in 1915; see DMA 1915, 6.
42. 6 Feb. 1914, "Scrapbook, 1911–1917," Moseley Papers, Library of Congress.
43. J. C. Wilson to Moseley, 12 Sept. 1914, "Scrapbook."
44. 10 July 1914, Vandercook Papers.
45. AGR Oregon, 1913–14, 38–45.
46. AGR Washington 1903–4, 5–7, and *National Guard Magazine* 12 (Mar. 1915): 44; Lt. John F. O'Ryan, New York, "The Selection of National Guard Officers," *JMSI* 32 (1903): 259–60; AGR Texas, 1903–4, 79; Brian D. Fowles, "A History of the Kansas National Guard, 1854–1975" (Ph.D. diss., Kansas State University, 1982), 122–23.
47. Maj. Walter M. Lindsay, Massachusetts, "Reserve Officers and Their Instruction," *Infantry Journal* 3 (July 1906): 71–79; AGR Massachusetts, 1908, 8, 99–100; AGR Massachusetts, 1913, 11–12, 91–92, and AGR Massachusetts, 1914, 22, 91–94. For New York, see *National Guard Magazine* 10 (June 1913): 167; on Wisconsin, see Adj. Gen. Charles R. Boardman, letter to editor, *Infantry Journal* 3 (Oct. 1906): 169–71.
48. Paul Pruitt, "New South Soldier: The Pre-War Military Career of Walter E. Bare, 1902–1917," *The Alabama Review* 36 (Jan. 1983): 18–36. On O'Ryan, see *National Guard Magazine* 10 (Sept. 1913): 240.
49. Interview, untitled newspaper clipping, June 1915, Vandercook Papers. See also Pratt, *"Tin Soldiers."*

50. *National Guard Magazine* 9 (June 1912): 265.

51. *National Guard Magazine* 9 (Feb. 1912): 57.

52. "Thirty Reasons Why You Should Enlist," *National Guard Magazine* 7 (May 1911): 421–23.

53. DMA 1912, 36–38, and AGR Virginia, 1913, 17–18, discuss the frequent turnover of enlisted men. The South Dakota example appears in *National Guard Magazine* 10 (Feb. 1913): 50, and the Michigan report in *National Guard Magazine* 10 (Apr. 1913): 102.

54. Absentee statistics taken from annual reports of the Secretary of War, 1903–7, and DMA reports thereafter.

55. For Chicago's Guard track team and meet, see *National Guard Magazine* 7 (Mar. 1911): 217–18. The *National Guard Magazine*, 1910–15, regularly featured discussions about encouraging drill attendance.

56. *National Guard Magazine* 8 (Dec. 1911): 453.

57. 27 Dec. 1914, clipping in Vandercook Papers.

58. *National Guard Magazine* 7 (June 1911): 522.

59. *National Guard Magazine* 9 (Dec. 1912): 435.

60. *National Guard Magazine* 10 (Aug. 1913): 241.

61. *National Guard Magazine* 9 (Dec. 1912): 443.

62. See AWC 9744-5, RG165. "Miscellaneous" covers a range of civil problems, including disorderly crowds at public events, illegal gambling, or prize fights.

63. On Minnesota, see that state's report to DMA in 1908, in no. 3135, DMA, box 57, RG168, and "Indian Campaign of Co. A-3, Duluth," *Northwestern Guardsman* 7 (Dec. 1900): 4–6. For duty in Ohio, see Mewett, *A Brief History of Troop A*, 79–82. On troops serving along the Mexican border, see AGR Arizona, 1911, 3; AGR Arizona, 1914, 6; AGR California, 1912–14, 46–47; and Olson, "Houston Light Guards," 466–77.

64. AWC 9744-5 provides general information. For Evansville, Indiana, see Watt and Spears, *Indiana's Citizen Soldiers*, 104–5. On Missouri, see Adj. Gen. James A. DeArmond, Missouri, to chief, DMA, 19 Dec. 1908, in no. 3134, DMA.

65. Brundage, *Lynching in the New South*, 178–82, 191–97, 202–6; and Wright, *Racial Violence in Kentucky*, chap. 6, provide background. Also see AGR Georgia, 1911–12, 17–21; Truss, "Alabama National Guard from 1900," chap. 2, and Ruth Smith Truss, "The Alabama National Guard and the Protection of Prisoners, 1900–1916," *Alabama Review* 49

(Jan. 1996): 3–28. See also Olson, "Houston Light Guards," 466–77; and adj. gen. reports of Virginia, 1901–15.

66. Graham Adams, *The Age of Industrial Violence: The Activities and Findings of the U.S. Commission on Industrial Violence* (New York: Columbia University Press, 1966); P. K. Edwards, *Strikes in the United States, 1881–1974* (Oxford: Blackwell, 1981); David Montgomery, *The Fall of the House of Labor: The Workplace, the State, and American Labor Activism, 1865–1925* (New York: Cambridge University Press, 1987); Taft and Ross, "American Labor Violence," 304–32.

67. Adams, *Age of Industrial Violence*, passim; Taft and Ross, "American Labor Violence," passim; Harring, *Policing a Class Society*, chap. 6.

68. See James J. Hudson, "The California National Guard, 1903–1940" (Ph.D. diss., University of California, Berkeley, 1952), 131–36, on the Wheatland incident. See Melvyn Dubofsky, *We Shall Be All: A History of the Industrial Workers of the World* (Chicago: Quadrangle Books, 1969), chap. 10, 306–7, on the Lawrence and Butte strikes, and AGR Massachusetts, 1912, 5–7, 123–29; and Theodore Wiprud, "Butte: A Troubled Labor Paradise," *Montana* 21 (1971): 31–38. See also Bailey, *Mountaineers Are Free*, chap. 8; and "'Grim Visaged Men' and the West Virginia National Guard in the 1912–13 Paint and Cabin Creek Strike," *West Virginia History* 41 (1980): 111–25, for West Virginia. William Beck, "Law and Order during the 1913 Copper Strike," *Michigan History* 54 (winter 1970): 275–92; and the correspondence between Governor Woodbridge N. Ferris and Adj. Gen. Roy C. Vandercook, Vandercook Papers cover Michigan. See Nankivell, *History of the Military Organizations*, chap. 12; Osur, "The Role of the Colorado National Guard," 19–24; and George S. McGovern and Leonard F. Guttridge, *The Great Coalfield War* (Boston: Houghton Mifflin, 1972) on Colorado.

69. AGR Massachusetts, 1912, 7.

70. On Lawrence, see AGR Massachusetts, 1912, 5–7, 123–29, and Dubofsky, *We Shall Be All*, chap. 12. Bailey, "'Grim Visaged Men,'" 118–25, treats West Virginia.

71. In his *Colorado's War on Militant Unionism: James H. Peabody and the Western Federation of Miners* (Detroit: Wayne State University Press, 1972), George G. Suggs Jr. examines the 1903–4 conflict. For 1913–14, see McGovern and Guttridge, *The Great Coalfield War*; Osur, "The Role of the Colorado National Guard," 22–23; and Nankivell, *History of the Military Organizations*, chap. 12. Condemnations of the Colorado troops

may be found in the *Army and Navy Journal* and *National Guard Magazine* for May, June, and July 1914.

72. Correspondence in Vandercook Papers, Jul.-Sept. 1913. See also Beck, "Law and Order," 291–92.

73. *SWR* 1906, 161.

74. Report of 11 May 1904, in no. 525711, DMA, box 28, entry 4, RG168.

75. AGR Washington, 1911–12, 31.

76. Circular no. 1, 1 Mar. 1907, adj. gen., Maryland, 33.

77. *National Guard Magazine* 7 (Sept. 1910): 239.

78. Letter to New York Times, 22 Mar. 1916, 1. See also Nankivell, *History of the Military Organizations*, 182–83, 198; and Osur, "The Role of the Colorado National Guard," 21–23.

79. *National Guard Magazine* 7 (Oct. 1910): 352.

80. *National Guard Magazine* 12 (Mar. 1915): 38. See also Palmer, "The Militia Pay Bill," 350; and Editor, "The State Militia and the State Police," *Outlook*, 5 Apr. 1912, 771.

81. "Comment and Criticism," *JMSI* 29 (1901): 427.

82. Speech to Minnesota NGA, reprinted in AGR Minnesota, 1905–6, 97.

83. 19 Nov. 1910, 327.

84. *National Guard Magazine* 7 (Oct. 1911): 232.

85. *The Coyotes* (Mitchell SD: 1962), 107.

86. Gerda Ray, "Contested Legitimacy: Creation of the State Police in New York, 1890–1930" (Ph.D. diss., University of California, Berkeley, 1990).

8. THE NATIONAL GUARD IN FEDERAL SERVICE

1. Herring, "James Hay and the Preparedness Controversy," 383–404; Riker, *Soldiers of the States*, 80–82; Finnegan, *Against the Specter of a Dragon*, chaps. 5 and 9; Weigley, *History of the United States Army*, 346–50.

2. "An Act for Making Further and More Effectual Provision for the National Defense and for Other Purposes, June 3, 1917," sections 57 through 119, in Kohn, *Military Laws of the United States*.

3. Kohn, *Military Laws of the United States*, section 67 on appropriations, 81 on the Militia Bureau, and 109 and 110 on the federal armory and camp pay. See also *MBR* 1916, 41–55.

4. *MBR* 1916, 8.

5. *MBR* 1916, 53. See also Finnegan, *Against the Specter of a Dragon*, chap. 9, and Kriedberg and Henry, *History of Military Mobilization*, 193–95.

6. *MBR* 1916, 39–41, 51–52. Scholars depicting the law as a Guard victory include Finnegan, *Against the Specter of a Dragon*, 138; Riker, *Soldiers of the States*, 84; Hill, *Minute Man in Peace and War*, 221–22; and Chambers, *To Raise an Army*, 116–17.

7. *MBR* 1916, 49.

8. Derthick, *National Guard in Politics*, 33–38; Todd, "Our National Guard," 165–66; Frederick B. Wiener, "The Militia Clause of the Constitution," *Harvard Law Review* 54 (Dec. 1940): 200–201; Colby, *National Guard of the United States*, pp. 22–23 of chap. 6.

9. The chief of the Militia Bureau's *Report on Mobilization of the Organized Militia and National Guard of the United States, 1916* (Washington DC: Government Printing Office, 1916) covers the mobilization in detail. See also Clarence C. Clendenen, *Blood on the Border: The U.S. Army and the Mexican Irregulars* (New York: Macmillan, 1969), passim, and chap. 10; John S. D. Eisenhower, *Intervention!: The United States and the Mexican Revolution, 1913–1917* (New York: W. W. Norton, 1993); Colby, *National Guard of the United States*, chap. 5; Finnegan, *Against the Specter of a Dragon*, chap. 10; Hill, Minute Man in Peace and War, chap. 10; Weigley, *History of the United States Army*, 350–52.

10. Militia Bureau, *Report on Mobilization . . . 1916*, 143–44, 153–55.

11. Militia Bureau, *Report on Mobilization*, 35–37, 94–97. See also AGR Massachusetts, 1916, 89; AGR Nebraska, 1915–16, 11–12, which document the unsanctioned discharge of married men and businessmen. See also Donald E. Houston, "Oklahoma National Guard on the Border, 1916," *Chronicles of Oklahoma* 53 (winter 1975–76): 454.

12. To Richard Olney, Massachusetts, 2 Aug. 1916, in no. 244942, entry 25, RG94.

13. Militia Bureau, *Report on Mobilization*, 4, 31–34; correspondence between Secretary of War Newton Baker; Gen. A. L. Mills, chief, Militia Bureau; and Army Judge Advocate General Enoch Crowder, in July 1916, folder 1, file 370.01, box 429, entry 12, RG168.

14. Bailey, *Mountaineers Are Free*, 120–22.

15. AGR Oregon, 1915–16, 57.

16. AGR Massachusetts, 1916, 9, and Militia Bureau, *Report on Mobilization*, 13–15, 97.

17. Reprinted in *JMSI* 60 (Jan.-Feb. 1917): 65–66.

18. Cited in Cooper and Smith, *Citizens as Soldiers*, 162.
19. See, for example, Margaret R. Wolfe, "The Border Service of the Tennessee National Guard, 1916–1917: A Study in Romantic Inclinations, Military Realities, and Predictable Disillusionments," *Tennessee Historical Quarterly* 32 (winter 1973): 374–88. Questionnaires and letters provided by Guardsmen for the World War I Survey, U.S. Army Military History Institute, Carlisle, Pennsylvania, often commented on the border mobilization as well. Insights from the survey inform this and preceding paragraphs.
20. AGR Nebraska, 1915–16, 12; Militia Bureau, *Report on Mobilization*, 40–41, 47.
21. See Militia Bureau, *Report on Mobilization*, 19–23, 43–44; Clendenen, *Blood on the Border*, 294–95; and AGR Oregon, 1915–16, 69.
22. AGR Nebraska, 1915–16, 11.
23. AGR Massachusetts, 1916, 9.
24. Militia Bureau, *Report on Mobilization*, 53–58, 106–14.
25. The Moses Thisted Papers, U.S. Army Military History Institute, Carlisle, Pennsylvania, contain material on every state that sent troops to the border. See particularly Thisted, *With the Wisconsin National Guard on the Mexican Border in 1916–1917* (Hemet CA: no publisher, n.d.); and Hobart M. Britton, Company E, Fifth Georgia Infantry, "The Mexican border Incident of 1916–1917," typescript. See also Houston, "Oklahoma National Guard," 448–50; Truss, "Alabama National Guard from 1900," chap. 6; and Nankivell, *History of the Military Organizations*, 201–6.
26. Ent, *The First Century*, 110–12; AGR Virginia, 1916, 8, 18, on the Light Infantry Blues.
27. McCain to Sen. Duncan U. Fletcher, 25 June 1916, in no. 2415227, entry 25, RG94.
28. To Army adj. gen., 28 June 1916, in no. 2423093, entry 25, RG94.
29. Entries for the end of August and 5 Oct. 1916, respectively, in "Diary of Service, 1899–1917," box 3, Charles and Horace Hobbs Papers, U.S. Army Military History Institute, Carlisle, Pennsylvania.
30. "Memoirs," 214, in Charles and Horace Hobbs Papers.
31. In his final report to the Army's adj. gen., 11 Nov. 1916, in folder—Reports, Inspector General, file 370.01, box 432, entry 12, RG168.
32. See Militia Bureau, *Report on Mobilization*, 151, 72–123, for extracts from the Southern Department's special inspection.

33. Mobilization planning and implementation can be followed in Militia Bureau, *Report on Mobilization*, 48–52; memos and letters from 1912 and 1914 in "Scrapbook, 1911–1917," George Van Horn Moseley Papers, Library of Congress; 1914 memos in folder 2, file 370.01, General, box 429, entry 12, RG168; and consolidated file on mustering the Organized Militia into federal service, no. 2160689, entry 25, RG94.

34. AGR Missouri, 1915–16, 11.

35. AGR Massachusetts, 1916, 81–83.

36. AGR Virginia, 1916, 8–11.

37. 4 Dec. 1916, in "Scrapbook, 1911–1917," Moseley Papers. See also Militia Bureau, *Report on Mobilization*, 25–30, 125–42, and Militia Bureau, *Report on Mobilization*, 25–30; Colby, *National Guard of United States*, chap. 5; Hill, *Minute Man in Peace and War*, 233–34; and Todd, "Our National Guard," 166–68.

38. Funston to Army adj. gen., 27 and 28 June 1916, respectively, in no. 2423093, entry 25, RG94; Mills to Army adj. gen., 19 July 1916, in folder—Provisional Divisions, 1916–17, file 322.13, box 251, entry 12, RG168; Undated memo, Militia Bureau (ca. Sept. 1916), folder—Provisional Divisions, file 322.13.

39. "War Diary," 11 Nov. 1916 entry, Moseley Papers.

40. To John T. Pratt, 20 Oct. 1917, "Scrapbook, 1911–1917," *Moseley Papers*.

41. Militia Bureau, *Report on Mobilization*, 146.

42. Parker to Commanding General, Southern Department, 24 Jan. 1917, in Thisted Papers.

43. Robert M. Johnston, "The Position of the National Guard," *Military Historian and Economist* 2 (Apr. 1917): 204–5.

44. Militia Bureau, *Report on Mobilization*, 131.

45. Chambers, *To Raise an Army*, 130–44, 153–61; Kreidberg and Henry, *Military Mobilization*, 236–46; Finnegan, *Against the Specter of a Dragon*, 176–88.

46. Chief of Militia Bureau, memo, 29 Mar. 1917, in folder—General 3, file 370.01, box 429, entry 12, RG168; Kreidberg and Henry, *Military Mobilization*, 224.

47. Abrahamson, *America Arms for a New Century*, chap. 6; Kreidberg and Henry, *Military Mobilization*, 294–95; Edward M. Coffman, *The War to End All Wars: The American Military Experience in World War I* (New York: Oxford University Press, 1968), chaps. 1–3.

48. Adj. gen., Army, to Commanding Gen., Eastern Department, 22 May 1917, and chief, Militia Bureau, to chief, War College Division, 4 July 1917, in folder—General 3, file 370.01, box 429, entry 12, RG168. On Ohio, see Joseph Gross, "Mobilization of 4th Ohio Infantry Regiment, 1917" (seminar paper, Ohio State University, 1974); and David G. Thompson, "Ohio's Best: The Mobilization of the Fourth Infantry, Ohio National Guard, in 1917," *Ohio History* 101 (winter-spring 1992): 37–53. For Texas, see Lonnie J. White, *Panthers to Arrowheads: The 36th (Texas-Oklahoma) Division in World War I* (Austin: Presidial Press, 1984), chap. 1; Charles Spurlin, "The Victoria Sammies," *Texana* 7 (1969): 56–76; and Emily T. Zillich, "History of the National Guard in El Paso, 1917–1919," *Texas Military History* 1 (Aug. 1961): 9–23.

49. Washington, Office of the Adj. Gen., *The Official History of the Washington National Guard* (Tacoma WA: Office of the Adj. Gen., 1961), 5: 507; and Cooper, *Citizens as Soldiers*, 179–98.

50. To Members of Company D, 29 July 1917, in Papers of Alexander H. Case, Thirty-fifth Division box, World War I Survey, MHI.

51. Wilson's July 3 proclamation and August 5 "draft" order in folder— General 5, file 370.01, box 429, entry 12, RG168.

52. Nichols, *The First Hundred Years*, 356; White, *Panthers to Arrowheads*, 18–19.

53. AGR Missouri, 1917–20, 7.

54. "Experiences of J. D. Lawrence in the American Expeditionary Forces in Europe, 1918–19," 4, in Thirtieth Division box, World War I Survey, MHI.

55. "Memoirs," Charles and Horace Hobbs Papers, 227.

56. Bliss to Col. Lochridge, no date (but early in Oct. 1917), in report no. 13361, entry 5, general staff correspondence, 1907–16, RG165.

57. AGR Missouri, 1917–20, 12.

58. William E. Eaton, *History of the Richardson Light Guard of Wakefield, Massachusetts, 1901–1926* (Wakefield MA: no publisher, 1926), 122. The Light Guard was Company A in the Sixth Massachusetts.

59. F. L. Hitchcock, *History of the 13th Regiment, Pennsylvania National Guard* (Scranton PA: International Textbook Press, 1929), 49.

60. "Experiences of J. D. Lawrence," 5. See also Roberts, "History of the Utah National," 136–45; Mewett, *A Brief History of Troop A*, 110–12.

61. Hill, *Minute Man in Peace and War*, 280–81, 298–300.

62. See Kreidberg and Henry, *Military Mobilization*, 222–24.

EPILOGUE

1. Edward M. Coffman, *The Hilt of the Sword: The Career of Peyton C. March* (Madison: University of Wisconsin Press, 1966), chaps. 14–15; Colby, *National Guard of the United States*, chap. 8; Hill, *Minute Man in Peace and War*, chap. 13; Holley, *General John M. Palmer*, 452–54, 478, 490–97, 513–24; and Weigley, *History of the United States Army*, 399–407.

2. Colby, *National Guard of the United States*, pp. 9–10 of chap. 9; Weigley, *History of the United States Army*, 401–2; and Wiener, "The Militia Clause of the Constitution," 208–9.

3. Derthick, *National Guard in Politics*, 45–52.

4. Generalizations are drawn from the relevant works annotated in Cooper, *The Militia and the National Guard in America*, chap. 8.

5. Harry Lynn Krenek, "A History of the Texas National Guard between World War I and World War II" (Ph.D. diss., Texas Tech University, 1979), 36–41; Robert L. Daugherty, *Weathering the Peace: The Ohio National Guard in the Interwar Years, 1919–1940* (Lanham MD: University Press of America, 1991), passim.

6. Fowles, "A History of the Kansas National Guard," 175.

7. Robert Bruce Sligh, *The National Guard and National Defense: The Mobilization of the Guard in World War II* (New York: Praeger, 1992), chap. 3.

8. Sligh, *National Guard and National Defense*, chap. 5.

9. Kenny A. Franks, "'Goodbye Dear, I'll Be Back in a Year': The Mobilization of the Oklahoma National Guard for World War II," *Chronicles of Oklahoma* 69 (winter 1991–92): 340–67; W. D. McGlasson, "Mobilization 1940: The Big One," *National Guard* (Sept. 1980): 10–23.

10. Derthick, *National Guard in Politics*, 69.

11. National Guard Association of the United States, *The Nation's National Guard* (Washington DC: 1954), 40.

12. Colby, *National Guard of the United States*, pp. 26–28 of chap. 9, chap. 10; Derthick, *National Guard in Politics*, chap. 3; Hill, *Minute Man in Peace and War*, chaps. 16–17; Sligh, *National Guard and National Defense*, passim.

Selected Bibliography

The footnotes detail many, although not all, of the sources used in the writing of this book. The generalizations and examples cited throughout the text are drawn from published works and dissertations annotated in Jerry Cooper, *The Militia and the National Guard in America since Colonial Times: A Research Guide* (Westport CT: Greenwood Press, 1993). *The Militia and the National Guard in America* discusses in general terms the archival and manuscript sources available for National Guard history and describes periodicals useful to the history of the state soldiery. In the descriptions that follow I note specific sources used in this study.

ARCHIVES AND MANUSCRIPTS

I. Three record groups at the National Archives and Records Administration, Washington DC, record the federal-state relationship, especially after 1900.

1. Record Group 94 [RG94], Adjutant General's Office, entry 25, document file, 1890–1917.
2. Record Group 165 [RG165], Records of the War Department General and Special Staffs. The entries of greatest value were the following:
   Entry 3, General Correspondence, Office of the Chief of Staff, 1903–6.
   Entry 5, General Correspondence and Reports, Office of the Chief of Staff, 1907–16.
   Entry 288, War College Board Correspondence.

Entry 299, Army War College Studies.

Entry 310, Army War College, Historical Section, 1900–41.

3. Record Group 168 [RGI68], Records of the National Guard Bureau, 1822–1954. RGI68 is most valuable for the period following the establishment of the Division of Militia Affairs in 1908.

II. Holdings of the United States Army Military History Institute (MHI). MHI's surveys of Spanish-American War and World War I veterans are invaluable for assessing the state role in the Spanish-American War, the Mexican border mobilization, and World War I. The Moses Thisted Papers also provide insight into the Mexican border incident. Finally, the papers of two Army officers who served as inspector-instructors, Eli A. Helmick and Horace Hobbs, provide the professional soldier's viewpoint.

III. Individual collections:

Frederick A. Aldrich Correspondence, Michigan Historical Collections, Bentley Historical Library, University of Michigan, Ann Arbor.

Charles F. Beebe Papers, MSS 1378, Oregon Historical Society, Portland.

F. L. Carroll Papers, Arizona Historical Society, Tucson, for reports of Arizona territory and state adjutants general, 1866–1914.

Colorado Military–Colorado National Guard, entry 142, Colorado State Historical Society, Denver.

Typescript of territorial adjutant general reports for the 1870s.

Minnesota National Guard Papers, 1880–1940

BG8/M665n, Minnesota State Historical Society, St. Paul, records of the Emmett Light Artillery of St. Paul.

George Van Horn Moseley Papers, Library of Congress.

Moseley's papers; "War Diary, 1916–1919"; typescript of an unpublished autobiography, "One Soldier's Journey"; "Scrapbook, 1911–1917."

Edward Martin Library, National Guard Association of the United States, headquarters, Washington DC. Early records of the National Guard Association, NGA convention proceedings, unit histories, and a limited collection of George Wingate's correspondence and published works.

Roy C. Vandercook Papers, University Archives and Historical Collections, Michigan State University, East Lansing. Correspondence, orders, and circulars.

Roy C. Vandercook Papers, Michigan Historical Collections, Bentley Historical Library, University of Michigan, Ann Arbor. Newspaper clippings.

PUBLISHED DOCUMENTS

Documents published by the states, particularly annual and biennial adjutants general reports, are a major source. I examined adjutants general reports from all regions randomly but searched reports from Colorado, Massachusetts, Minnesota, Missouri, Pennsylvania, Oregon, Texas, and Virginia at five-year intervals from 1870 through 1915. State adjutants general reports are cited in the endnotes without date or place of publication, for example, "AGR Massachusetts, 1875." Other published state documents include general and special orders, rosters, and proceedings of state National Guard Association meetings.

War Department reports document the general condition and status of the National Guard. The most valuable were the annual *The Organized Militia of the United States* issued by the Military Information Division, Adjutant General's Office, U.S. Army, for 1893 through 1898; yearly comments of the Army adjutant general on the condition of the organized militia, which appeared as part of the Secretary of War reports, issued annually in *Reports of the War Department*, 1900 through 1907; Division of Militia Affairs reports, 1908 through 1916; and Militia Bureau reports, 1917 through 1920.

Unit histories written by members, when used carefully, are informative sources. The most useful were the following:

Agate, C. C., ed. *History of the Essex Troop, 1890–1925*. Newark NJ: Essex Troop, 1925.

Clark, Emmons. *History of the Seventh Regiment of New York, 1806–1889*. Two volumes. New York: Seventh Regiment, 1890.

Eaton, William E. *History of the Richardson Light Guard of Wakefield, Mass., 1851–1901*. Wakefield MA: no publisher, 1901.

Frankel, Hiram D., ed. *Company "C," First Infantry Minnesota: Its History and Development*. St. Paul MN: no publisher, 1905.

Hall, Charles Winslow, ed. *Regiments and Armories of Massachusetts: An Historical Narrative of the Massachusetts Volunteer Militia*. Two volumes. Boston: W. W. Potter, 1899, 1901.

Hitchcock, Frederick L. *History of the 13th Regiment, National Guard of Pennsylvania and 109th Inf.; 108th MG BN, USAEF; and 109th Pennsylvania National Guard*. Scranton PA: International Textbook Press, 1924.

Meekins, George A. *Fifth Regiment, Infantry, Maryland National Guard, U.S. Volunteers*, rev. ed. Baltimore: no publisher, 1899.

Mewett, Alfred. *A Brief History of Troop A, 107th Regiment of Cavalry, Ohio National Guard: The Black Horse Troop*. Cleveland: no publisher, 1923.

Nichols, George P. *The First Hundred Years: Records and Reminiscences of a Century of Company I, Seventh Regiment, N.G.N.Y., 1838–1938*. New York: no publisher, 1938.

Porter, Valentine M. "A History of Battery 'A' of St. Louis, with an Account of the Early Artillery Companies from Which It Descended," *Missouri Historical Society Collections* 2 (March 1905), 1–48.

Pratt, Walter M. *"Tin Soldiers:" The Organized Militia and What It Really Is*. Boston: no publisher, 1912.

Swanner, Charles D. *The Story of Company L—"Santa Ana's Own."* Claremont CA: Fraser Press, 1958.

Thayer, George B., compiler. *History of Company K, First Connecticut Volunteer Infantry during the Spanish-American War*. Hartford: no publisher, 1899.

Ward, Walter W. *Springfield in the Spanish-American War*. Easthampton MA: Enterprise Printing, 1899.

Whipple, George M. *History of the Salem Light Infantry from 1805 to 1890*. Salem MA: 1890.

Wingate, George W. *History of the Twenty-second Regiment of the National Guard of the State of New York from Its Organization to 1895*. New York: Edwin W. Dayton, 1896.

Zierdt, William H. *Narrative History of the 109th Field Artillery, Pennsylvania National Guard, 1775–1930*. Wilkes-Barre PA: E. B. Yordy, 1932.

SECONDARY SOURCES

Secondary studies not annotated in *The Militia and National Guard in America* or appearing after 1993:

Adams, Graham. *The Age of Industrial Violence: The Activities and Findings of the U.S. Commission on Industrial Violence*. New York: Columbia University Press, 1966.

Brundage, W. Fitzhugh. *Lynching in the New South: Georgia and Virginia, 1880–1930*. Urbana: University of Illinois Press, 1993.

Edwards, P. K. *Strikes in the United States, 1881–1974*. Oxford: Blackwell, 1981.

Ferling, John. *Struggle for a Continent: The Wars of Early America*. Arlington Heights IL: Harlan Davidson, 1993.

Harring, Sidney L. *Policing a Class Society: The Experience of American Cities, 1865–1915*. New Brunswick NJ: Rutgers University Press, 1983.

Krause, Paul. *The Battle for Homestead, 1880–1892: Politics, Culture, and Steel*. Pittsburgh: University of Pittsburgh Press, 1992.

Leach, Eugene. "The Literature of Riot Duty: Managing Class Conflicts in the Streets, 1877–1927," *Radical History Review* 56 (spring 1993): 23–50.

McCreedy, Kenneth Otis. "Palladium of Liberty: The American Militia System, 1815–1961." Ph.D. diss., University of California, Berkeley, 1991.

Montgomery, David. *The Fall of the House of Labor: The Workplace, the State and American Labor Activism, 1865–1925*. New York: Cambridge University Press, 1989.

———. "Strikes in Nineteenth Century America," *Social Science History* 4 (1980): 81–104.

Ray, Gerda. "'We Can Stay until Hell Freezes Over:' Strike Control and the State Police in New York, 1919–1923," *Labor History* 36 (summer 1995): 403–25.

Skelton, William. *An American Profession of Arms: The Army Officer Corps, 1784–1861*. Lawrence: University Press of Kansas, 1992.

Truss, Ruth Smith. "The Alabama National Guard from 1900 to 1920." Ph.D. diss., University of Alabama, 1992.

———. "The Alabama National Guard and the Protection of Prisoners, 1900–1916," *Alabama Review* 49 (Jan. 1996), 3–28.

Wright, George C. *Racial Violence in Kentucky, 1865–1940: Lynchings, Mob Rule, and "Legal Lynchings."* Baton Rouge: Louisiana State University, 1990.

Index